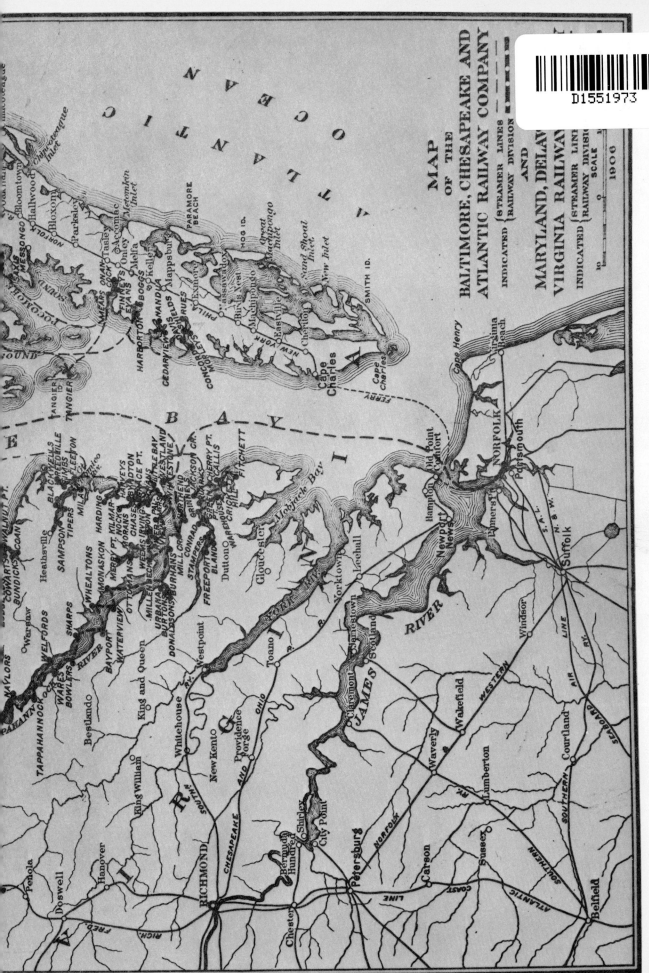

MAP
OF THE
BALTIMORE, CHESAPEAKE AND
ATLANTIC RAILWAY COMPANY
INDICATED { STEAMER LINES
{ RAILWAY DIVISION
AND
MARYLAND, DELAWARE
VIRGINIA RAILWAY
INDICATED { STEAMER LINE
{ RAILWAY DIVISION
SCALE
1906

This Was Chesapeake Bay

This
Was

The schooners *Sarah C. Conway* (left) and *Charles G. Joyce* load lumber at Hoskins Creek, Tappahannock, Virginia, April 23, 1941, for delivery to Baltimore. Photo: Author

Chesapeake Bay

By ROBERT H. BURGESS

CURATOR OF EXHIBITS, THE MARINERS MUSEUM, NEWPORT NEWS, VA.

CORNELL MARITIME PRESS, INC.

1963   *Cambridge, Maryland*

Library of Congress Catalog Card Number: 63-20545

Manufactured in the United States of America

To Bruce and Janet, son and daughter, who have accompanied me about the Chesapeake and in whom, it is hoped, I have instilled some love for this great Bay and its country.

Contents

Contents

(continued)

Preface

NO BODY OF WATER in this country has cast such a spell over those who have had the opportunity to spend some time in the area as has Chesapeake Bay. It has been that way since the time of the first settlers, who praised the waterways and surrounding shores, to the present-day boatmen who loudly proclaim it as the perfect boating region and rich in historical and scenic attractions.

To have been born along its shores, or those of its tributaries, is a distinctive claim to fame. Natives can be transported to other parts of the world, never to return to the Chesapeake, but they retain that sense of pride of having come from tidewater Maryland or Virginia.

I share that feeling for this great inland sea, being a Baltimorean by birth and now a resident of Virginia. Love for the Bay was inherited from my father who sailed its waters in pungies and schooners as a young man and ended his career as chief engineer of ocean-going steamships.

This love was kindled when I was a youngster traveling on the steamboats to my grandparents' farm in the Northern Neck of Virginia. Subjected to the sights and smells of the waterfront and steamboats and the colorful landings and sailing craft, I was so impressed with it all that I gradually initiated a one-man crusade to record some of that era. Even as a boy I could sense that those romantic days were nearing an end. So I started to make a photographic record of all phases of Chesapeake life. And this I have been doing faithfully for the past forty years, resulting in thousands of negatives of Bay steamboats and their landings, commercial sailing craft, shipyard activities, lighthouses, and other local maritime subjects.

Through the years I sailed the Chesapeake on various types of craft: a four-masted schooner, bugeyes, skipjacks, trawlers, steamboats, freighters, log canoes, and sail and power yachts. My camera was with me at all times to record the scene. On shore I scoured the waterfronts of the major Bay ports and the little tidewater towns, photographing scenes that are no more. At the same time I made an attempt to salvage objects of maritime history of the Bay to help keep alive the memory of the craft. Through the decades this has developed into an extensive collection of Chesapeake memorabilia made up of carved decorations from the steam and sailing craft, steam whistles that once echoed around the Bay, half-models, fittings, tools, logbooks, and ships' papers. The vessels from which they originated have long disappeared but their names will live on through this medium.

While delving into the historical background of the ships and the area, I came across numerous facts that served as the basis for articles I later prepared for newspapers and magazines. Such accounts were of a temporary nature and it was suggested that a selection of these be compiled into a more permanent form. And so this book came into being.

Presented herein are true tales of the Chesapeake gathered from the lips and memories of the men who experienced them and from countless sources in newspapers, books, annual reports, ship registers and clipping files in museums, libraries, and my personal collection. Numerous subjects and wide periods are covered. They can be read for enjoyment or enlightenment, and it is hoped the volume may serve as a reference work. Many readers will learn of the exploits and adventures of their ancestors. Others will have their nostalgia aroused when they read of the steamboats and their little voyages, the sailing vessels and their trades, lighthouses they may have seen, and many other memory-stirring subjects.

The Chesapeake seemed to cling to the old maritime ways longer than other bodies of water. Passenger steamboats and commercial sailing craft plied these waters long after they had been displaced elsewhere. This may have been due to the remoteness of the region within itself. Long peninsulas separated by deep, wide rivers were connected by bridges only within fairly recent years. Paved highways were long in coming to this area serviced by country roads and waterways ever since the first settlers arrived. These facts contributed to the continued use of steam and sail where they would have been outmoded if the area had been more accessible.

One who may have known the older Bay and lost contact through the years, may ask, "Where are the little white steamboats that once frequented the Chesapeake and its tributaries?" These vessels, with their distinctive steam whistles, have disappeared along with the country landings they serviced.

Loading lumber, cordwood, grain, or canned goods in some little out-of-the-way creek would be the rams, schooners, pungies, or bugeyes. Or these picturesque craft could be seen in great numbers under sail or anchored awaiting a fair wind. Now, except for the few seasonal oyster dredging craft, commercial sail has disappeared from the Bay.

One may have expected the colorful square or hexagonal screw-pile lighthouses scattered about the Chesapeake to be with us always. But they are falling before the wrecker's hammer and are being replaced by the unsightly but more practical skeleton towers erected upon screw-pile foundations. Already dismantled are the Tue Marshes, York Spit, Tangier Sound, Holland Island, Old Plantation, Ragged Point, Mathias Point, Upper Cedar Point and Maryland Point lighthouses. Windmill Point, Stingray Point, and Choptank River lighthouses are scheduled for future dismantling.

In these times it is difficult to conceive of boarding a side-wheel steamboat for a long trip to a waterside amusement park for a picnic. The closest thing to that now is the Diesel *Port Welcome* that still operates between Baltimore and Betterton. How many readers recall the floating theatre that was towed about the Bay for week-long stands at country towns and featuring stage plays that smacked of antiquity even four decades ago? All of these subjects come alive in the following accounts.

In these pages a way of life that has passed from the Chesapeake is recorded in text and through photographs. Due to the variety of subject matter it has not been possible to arrange the material in any logical sequence. But each article is complete in itself and the reader can start and stop with any story without thought of continuity.

It is hoped that this volume will contribute in some degree to the documentation of Chesapeake activities of the past and that the reader will be able to absorb some of the atmosphere and flavor of the Bay of other days.

A second volume is in preparation and will be published in the Fall of 1964.

ROBERT H. BURGESS
Curator of Exhibits
The Mariners Museum
Newport News, Va.

Acknowledgments

THE CONTENTS of this book are made up of a selection of articles I have prepared during the past seventeen years for Sunday supplements, feature pages, historical and boating magazines. They originally appeared in the magazine section of *The Baltimore Sunday Sun*; in the feature sections of the *Newport News Daily Press* and *Norfolk Virginian-Pilot*; in *The Chesapeake Skipper* magazine; and in *The Commonwealth*, the magazine of the Virginia Chamber of Commerce.

I wish to thank the editors of those publications for their original acceptance of the material over these many years and for their kind permission to reproduce the articles in book form to make them available to a wider audience and to preserve them for future generations. Especial appreciation is extended to Harold A. Williams and M. Hamilton Whitman, editors of *The Baltimore Sunday Sun,* for their encouragement and interest in my efforts. Most of the articles in this volume originally appeared in *The Sun.*

To the scores of Bay watermen who took the time to talk about the Chesapeake, divulging little bits of history here and there—dockside aboard their vessels, out on the dredging grounds, and in the shipyards—goes my heartiest appreciation. Notable among them are steamboat captains, S. Boyd Chapman, P. L. Parker, Herbert A. Bohannon, and John D. Davis; that skipper of deep-water sail, Captain George H. Hopkins; sailmakers William L. Godfrey and Albert E. Brown; and J. Willis Smith, shipyard operator.

The research facilities of museums and libraries have been invaluable in compiling and checking facts presented in this book. The library of The Mariners Museum, Newport News, Virginia, with its ship registers and annual reports of the U. S. Lifesaving Service and Lighthouse Board, in addition to other source material, was of inestimable assistance. The Maryland Room of the Enoch Pratt Free Library, Baltimore, with its wealth of news clippings and microfilms of old Baltimore newspapers, contributed much to my research. The Maryland Historical Society, Baltimore, and the Library of Congress and National Archives, Washington, D.C., helped me track down some elusive facts.

Thanks are expressed to the photographers, credited herein, who have recorded various phases of the Chesapeake story on film and have kindly permitted the use of their pictures in this volume. Particular acknowledgment is accorded to William T. Radcliffe, that dedicated photographer of The Mariners Museum, for his assistance in preparation of some of the illustrations.

I am most grateful to A. Aubrey Bodine of Baltimore, that master of the Chesapeake pictorial scene who has been my companion on several picture-taking ventures about the Bay, for his encouragement to pursue the subject and for the use of several of his photographs. Raymond W. Mueller, of Baltimore, companion and means of getting to many remote regions of tidewater Maryland and Virginia, deserves thanks for his assistance in making it all possible.

To the scores of individuals who have responded to my queries, both verbal and written, I extend sincerest thanks.

ROBERT H. BURGESS

This Was Chesapeake Bay

The Chesapeake's Oldest Inhabitants

INCLUDED among the many attractions found in the Chesapeake Bay country are some of the finest fossil grounds in the United States. Some may find fossil hunting a far cry from their favorite pastime, even though the fossils are of a nautical nature and the beds border the Bay. The average cruising man is always set to do a little exploring and what is to follow may serve to open new fields to him.

To really appreciate this phase of fossil hunting, a brief glance into the geological background of this area is necessary. The region in which the deposits are found is part of the Coastal Plain that embraces the eastern part of Maryland, crossing the state from north to south in a broad belt with an average width of 75 miles. This Plain consists of a series of formations that were deposited in thin sheets, one above the other.

The towering Calvert Cliffs look foreboding to the boatman as he sails up the Bay.
Photo: Author

A number of geological periods are represented in the Coastal Plain but we are concerned with but one, the Miocene. The Miocene deposits have long been referred to as the Chesapeake group, due to the fine exposures of fossil beds found on Chesapeake Bay. These have been divided into three formations—the Calvert, Choptank, and St. Mary's —Maryland localities where the strata are well ex-

Scientists have proof that during the middle Miocene epoch, 3 to 10 million years ago, a considerable portion of the present tidewater country was submerged. The area was then tropical and coral, porpoises, sharks, whales, crocodiles, giant barnacles, and a multitude of shellfishes inhabited the waters. As the creatures died they settled to the bottom of the sea and their remains were grad-

Fossilized specimens of coral, clams, and scallop shells found in the Calvert Cliffs.
Photo: Wm. T. Radcliffe

posed. An outcropping of these deposits may also be found along the James and York Rivers in Virginia. The Miocene formations of Maryland and Virginia furnish data for the entire Atlantic Coast.

The best of these deposits are in the Calvert Cliffs, which form the eastern portion of Calvert County, Maryland, bordering Chesapeake Bay. Here for a distance of 35 miles, from Chesapeake Beach (Seaside Park) to Drum Point, there is an almost unbroken exposure of fossil-laden strata. In some places the cliffs rise to a height of more than 100 feet.

ually covered with silt. Ages passed and upheavals caused the floor of the sea to be thrust above the surface, forming new land. Through the millenniums many of the buried creatures and shells became fossilized and even more disintegrated.

The abundance of fossils early attracted the attention of geologists. The first illustration of an American fossil, drawn in 1685, was made from a specimen taken from the Miocene beds of Maryland. Since that time the grounds have been the source of collections of fossils destined to be exhibited in many museums.

The Calvert formations consist of clay, sand, and marl in which are embedded the fossils. Some strata are almost pure calcium due to the high percentage of shelly material found therein.

The best beds along this stretch present themselves at Chesapeake Beach and south of that point, Plum Point, and Governors Run. Specimens may be found almost anywhere along the shore where the high bluffs are prominent.

The accompanying illustrations bear evidence of some of the types of fossils to be found along the Calvert Cliffs. These specimens were picked up in a matter of a few hours. The best preserved are the teeth, those from sharks being in the majority. These range in length from one-quarter of an inch to five inches and may be found embedded in the cliffs or, more likely, mixed in with shells along the beach. It has been determined that the approximate size of the sharks from which the teeth originated was about thirty to thirty-five feet in length. The novice may find it difficult to differ-

The most artistic finds are the shells resembling those of scallops and which are known to paleontologists as Pecten (*Chlamys*) *madisonius Say*. This name refers to the more abundant scallop shells but there is no need to remember it unless one plans serious study on the subject. Some almost perfect specimens of these shells can be found, most still embedded in the cliffs. Care must be exercised in their removal as they are rather brittle.

Mass formations, in which are found the impressions of many fossil shellfish, are quite common. The shells disintegrated, leaving their delicate tracery in the soft ooze of the former sea bottom. Gradually the mass solidified and today huge pieces of this material lie at the base of the cliffs. The combined action of the elements and Chesapeake Bay have caused continual erosion of the cliffs, creating miniature landslides and revealing long-buried fossils.

Some rare specimens have been found here. In 1929, a whale skull 7 feet long was unearthed near

Examples of fossil shark's teeth found in and along the Calvert Cliffs.
Photo: Wm. T. Radcliffe

entiate between broken pieces of shell and the teeth. Eventually the eye becomes accustomed to the smooth, shiny surface of the teeth and they are easily segregated from the litter on the beach.

The Baltimore YMCA has a boy's summer camp along these cliffs and the boys attending the camp spend much of their free time combing the beach in search of shark's teeth. By the end of the season many of the boys have succeeded in picking up great quantities of the fossil teeth.

Fossil coral, as well as giant barnacles, are common. Fossil clams make an interesting find and they are easy to detect along the beach. They come in many sizes and look like fine cement castings of the original clams. On some, portions of the outer shell remain, revealing the solid interior.

Governors Run. Under the supervision of experts, it was carefully removed and taken to the U.S. National Museum for study and preservation.

A settlement known as Scientist's Cliffs has been established along this shoreline. As one can gather from its name, it is a favorite haunt for scientists who are ever on the alert to unearth a new and rare specimen from the cliffs.

Boatmen look upon the yellow Calvert Cliffs as an uninviting shoreline offering few harbors of refuge. These bluffs may take on another meaning if one walks along the beach at their base and discovers some of the specimens. The steep, rugged banks and the fossilized remains of marine life that were once part of a world too far in the past for most of us to visualize are an awesome sight.

The Early Chesapeake

THE EXISTENCE of the vast inland sea now known as Chesapeake Bay was known to the white man as early as the 16th century. Both the Dutch and the Spaniards had ventured into these waters but did not penetrate them very deeply. It remained for Captain John Smith and his little band of men to explore the Bay to any great extent; and they were the first of the English colonists to do so.

Records of Captain Smith's voyages up the Bay and descriptions of the surrounding country have been preserved and appear in various books. *Travels and Works of Captain John Smith,* edited by Edward Arber FSA, in 1884, has been used as a source of information in preparing this account. The following passages in quotation marks appear as they were originally written.

On June 2, 1608, Captain John Smith with 14 men sailed on his first exploration of the "Bay of Chisapeack." The boat he used on this mission has been described as ". . an open Barge neare three tuns burthen." They departed from the pinnace *Phoenix* at Cape Henry and ". . crossed the Bay to the Easterne shore, and fell with the Isles called Smiths Isles, after our Captaines name." These islands, even so called today, are situated in the Atlantic, just northeast of Cape Charles, Virginia.

At Cape Charles they met two ". . grim and stout Salvages . ." These Indians spoke the tongue of Powhatan, and, since Captain Smith was familiar with this language, he conversed with the natives who ". . made such descriptions of the Bay, Isles, and rivers, that often did us exceeding pleasure."

As they sailed up the Bay, "Seeing many Isles in the midst of the Bay we bore up for them, but ere we could obtaine them, such an extreame gust of wind, rayne, thunder, and lightening happened, that with great danger we escaped the unmercifull raging of that Ocean-like water." It seems as though our famed summer squalls made themselves known to the good captain rather early in his voyage.

The "Isles in the midst of the Bay" he named Russels Isles, after Walter Russell, the physician accompanying him. Today these are known as Tangier Island. "The next day searching them for fresh water, we could find none, the defect whereof forced us to follow the next Easterne Channell, which brought us to the river of Wighcocomoco." At first thought, one would take this to be the Wicomico River, in the Maryland county of the same name. But since the men were in dire need of water, it seems that they would enter the river nearest to the islands. Comparing a present-day map with the rather excellent map produced by Captain Smith, this river would be what is now known as the Pocomoke River.

The Indians in this locality were not too friendly at first but gradually changed their attitude. "Searching their habitations for water, we could fill but three barricoes, and that such puddle, that never till then we ever knew the want of good water. We digged and searched in many places, but before two daies were expired, we would have refused two barricoes of gold for one of that puddle water of Wighcocomoco."

A very good description of the shoreline of what is now Somerset County is given in this volume. From the mainland they crossed over to other islands in the Bay. No doubt these were the present Smith, South Marsh, and Bloodsworth Islands. During this passage they encountered another severe squall ". . that our mast and sayle blew overboard and such mighty waves overracked us in that small barge, that with great labor we kept her from sinking by freeing out the water."

They were forced to inhabit these islands for two days, calling them Limbo. Repairing the sail with their shirts, they set sail for the mainland

4

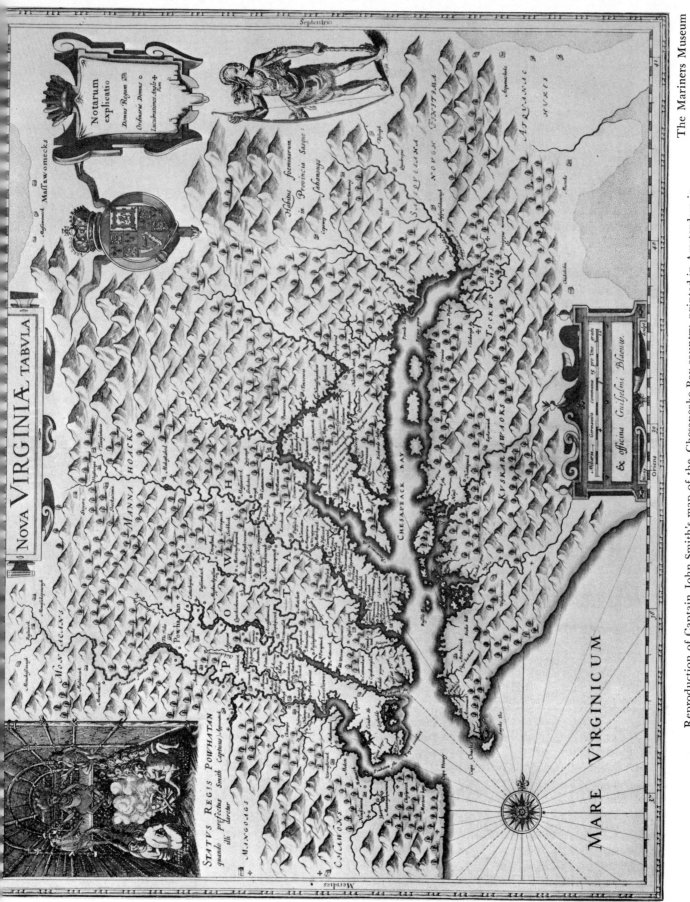

Reproduction of Captain John Smith's map of the Chesapeake Bay country, printed in Amsterdam in 1644. Contours of the Bay shoreline, as shown on the map, compare favorably with the present.

The Mariners Museum

again ". . and fell with a pretty convenient river on the East called Cuskarawaok;". Judging from what Captain Smith has marked "Limbo", this "convenient river" would be the present Nanticoke River. Here they encountered a number of Indians who at first were warlike, but a few shots in the air from the Englishmen's guns soon sent them scurrying. They eventually proved to be friendly.

"Finding this Easterne shore, (to be) shallow broken Isles, and for the most part without fresh water; we passed by the straites of Limbo for the Westerne shore:" Undoubtedly these are the present-day Hooper Straits. ". . so broad is the bay

If the "shallow creekes refer to the West, South, Severn, and Magothy Rivers, then the description is far from fitting. It has been determined that the Bolus is the Patapsco River.

At this point, after 12 days of exploring in the small boat, some of the men became discouraged, ". . oft tyred at the Oares, our bread spoyled with wet so much that it was rotten (yet so good were their stomacks that they could disgest it) they did with continuall complaints so importune him now to returne." Whereupon Captain Smith presented a noble speech to his followers admonishing their fears and worries. The speech revived their spirits but several of the men ". . fell sicke, whose pitti-

The reproduction of the Jamestown's settlers' ship *Susan Constant,* built for the Jamestown Festival of 1957, lies becalmed off Jamestown Island, Virginia. Photo: Author

here, we could scarce perceive the great high clifts on the other side: by them we Anchored that night and called them Riccards Cliftes." These cliffs, now known as the Calvert Cliffs, are the highest land on the western shore of the Chesapeake.

They continued up the Bay describing the wooded lowlands of the Eastern Shore and the "mountainous and barren" Western Shore. "We passed many shallow creekes, but the first we found Navigable for a ship, we called Bolus. . ."

full complaints caused us to returne, leaving the bay some nine miles broad, at nine and ten fadome water."

On the 16th of June they "fell with the River Patowomek: feare being gone, and our men recovered, we were all content to take some paines, to know the name of that seven mile broad river." As the Indian name implies, this was the Potomac River. They went as far as they could up this river with their boat where "we found mighty

Rocks, growing in some places above the grownd as high as the shrubby trees . ." They later ventured up a small river making off the Potomac, rowing as far as possible. Leaving the boat, they marched to a mine in search of valuable minerals finding only that which the Indians ". . put in little baggs and sell it all over the country to paint their bodyes, faces, or Idols . ."

They also obtained some furs and were impressed with the abundance of fish ". . lying so thicke with their heads above the water, as for want of nets (our barge driving amongst them) we attempted to catch them with a frying pan: but we found it a bad instrument to catch with . ."

Continuing down the Bay, they came to "the river of Rapahanock, by many called Toppahanock." Their boat ran aground "upon the many shoules lying in the entrances." Many fish were seen and Captain Smith passed the time by spearing them with his sword. As he was taking a stingray off the sword, its spike pierced his wrist, causing his hand, arm, and shoulder to swell. The men thought this was the end of him " . . and prepared his grave in an Island. . ." However, Doctor Russell soothed his pain to the extent that Captain Smith was able to eat some of the fish caught at the time of his injury. The "island" was named Stingray Isle after this incident. The name Stingray Point, that tip of Middlesex County, Virginia, jutting out into the Bay at the mouth of the Rappahannock River, identifies the "island" today.

As the barge continued down the Bay, the mouths of the "Payankatank River" (Piankatank) and the "Pamaunkee River" were passed. The latter is now known as the York River, which is made up by the confluence of the Pamunkey and Mattaponi Rivers. ". . the next day we arrived safely at Kecougtan" (Hampton). They then sailed up the Powhatan River to Jamestown, ". . . where we all, God be thanked, safely arrived the 21 of July." Powhatan River was the early name of the present James River.

On July 24, 1608, Captain Smith, with 12 men, departed for his second voyage of discovery in the Chesapeake. On this trip he sailed up the western shore to the head of the Bay. Most of this journal deals with his encountering, fighting, and dealing with the various Indian tribes.

Returning down the Bay they visited the Patuxent, Potomac, Rappahannock, and Piankatank Rivers. On September 7, 1608, after exploring the rivers and country in the vicinity of their colony, they arrived at Jamestown.

No description of the larger bodies of water on the Eastern Shore, from the present-named Chester River down to the Little Choptank River, appear in the records of Captain Smith's two voyages up Chesapeake Bay. However, on his map of the Virginia territory, originally published in 1612, a number of points within that area are named. There also appear "Winstons Iles." It is quite possible that these are the present Kent Island and that neck of land in Talbot County, Maryland, of which Tilghman Island is a part.

More than three centuries have passed since the redoubtable explorer first sailed these waters and prepared his map of the Chesapeake and the surrounding area. However, if one should compare Captain Smith's findings with a present-day map of the same area, he would find the old drawing remarkably accurate in contour. It is interesting to see how many of the names applied to the various islands, rivers, etc., in those early days have remained through all the years.

The White Rocks

STANDING like sentinels near the mouth of the Patapsco River, Maryland, are the White Rocks. They are the sole witnesses to the development of the port of Baltimore through the centuries. Other once prominent landmarks that overlooked these waters, such as large trees and outstanding bluffs, have succumbed to progress or have changed with the passing of the years. However, these huge stone formations have withstood the effect of the elements and will probably remain in position until the end of time.

When one considers how these rocks have witnessed the pageant of ships, from the time of the Indian dugout up to the present, they seem to deserve more recognition beyond their present classification as a menace to navigation. Perhaps their distinction can be measured in that they are the only representatives of such formations, except for several outcroppings of rocks from shore in the same general area, in the otherwise rock-free waters of the Chesapeake region. Some submerged rocks can be found in the vicinity of Havre de Grace and these obstructions are common on the Susquehanna. South of that area to the Virginia Capes, except for the aforementioned, they are virtually nonexistent.

The White Rocks mark the entrance to Rock Creek, in Anne Arundel County, and are situated about one-half mile NNW of Rock Point and a little more than two miles SW of the main ship channel leading to Baltimore. Few are those who have sailed down the Patapsco and have not observed these rocks. Yachtsmen, excursionists, and merchant seamen have been puzzled by their presence, looking upon them as misfits in this region of sand-fringed shores.

The White Rocks were first mentioned in the certificate of survey of a tract of land called "Radnage," that was laid out for George Yates, October 3, 1667, and are described as situated "on ye south side Patapsco *opposite ye rocks*." This survey is recorded at the Land Office of Maryland. Also recorded at the Land Office is a survey called "Stephen's Fishery," 5⅝ acres, dated August 7, 1733, whereby the Rocks were surveyed.

They are surrounded by legends. One is that in ages past the devil and a giant stood on the present site of Sparrows Point, each throwing a huge rock across the river. The rocks landed near each other but the one thrown by the giant is supposed to have had a slight edge over the other. Some records indicate that the Indians of this region referred to the rocks as The Devil's Works.

The best explanation for their existence lies in the geological field. The Maryland Geological Survey for Anne Arundel County explains that the White Rocks are products of the upper cretaceous beds of the Raritan formation. These beds extend from the Delaware border to the valley of the Potomac River. The formation receives its name from the Raritan River, New Jersey, along the shore of which the deposits are typically developed. In Anne Arundel County the formation is exposed in a belt 5 miles wide from the vicinity of the mouth of the Patapsco River to the Patuxent River above Priest Bridge.

The upper cretaceous strata consists of sands, clays, and marls. Geologists explain that the sands were first deposited by continental waters as shallow water deposits one hundred million years ago. Sometime later, water containing silica passed through the sands, depositing the cementing silica in the spaces to form the hard sandstone which makes up the White Rocks. During the repeated rise and fall of sea level since the cretaceous period, which falls within the Mesozoic era (the age of reptiles), the early eroded unconsolidated sands and clays were washed away. Left standing in relief above the surrounding surface were the cemented masses of sandstone.

The rocky ledges at Rocky Point, at the mouth of Back River in Baltimore County, and at Stony Point, at the mouth of Stony Creek in Anne Arundel County, are also assumed to be of the Raritan formation. Inland at Elvaton, 3 miles SE of Glen Burnie, there is a 60-foot hill that is also along the strike of this formation. There is no evidence when the transformation of the sands to the hard sandstone occurred but it is certain to have taken place more than one million years ago.

Another group of rocks appears off North Point, at the mouth of the Patapsco River, but according to available information these are said to have been deposited by man to prevent erosion of the point. Occasionally erosion of a shoreline bares a rock.

The White Rocks are situated in a highly traveled body of water and are actually a menace to navigation to smaller craft that do not remain in the marked channels. They played a major role by serving as a means of assisting ships into this port a century and more ago. Imprinted on the *Mapp of Bay of Chesepeack*, prepared in 1735 by Walter Hoxton for "the Merchants of London Trading to Virginia and Maryland," are sailing directions. Included are instructions for sailing from Love Point

employed to obtain bearings. On the *Survey of the Patapsco River and Part of the Chesapeake Bay,* dated 1819, is indicated: "Leading marks and ranges for entering and sailing up the River Patapsco observed on board the ship *Orozimbo* drawing 18 feet." Instructions for one course are to line up the center of the White Rocks with a yellowish bank in the mouth of Stony Creek.

Blunt's *American Coast Pilot,* a volume that contained the courses and distances of the principal harbors, capes, and headlands on the American east coast, relied upon the White Rocks as an important aid for seamen navigating the Patapsco River. In its field it was the most important work of that day. Virtually the same information which appeared on Hoxton's chart of 1735, employing the White Rocks as bearings, is repeated in Blunt's during the first half of the 19th century and perhaps later. In the 1833 issue, reference is made to

The White Rocks, near the mouth of the Patapsco River in Maryland, have witnessed the pageant of the Chesapeake. Photo: A. Aubrey Bodine

into the Patapsco River " . . . when abreast of North Point steer for the white rocks until you bring Leading Point which is pretty high bluff woods within 2 sails breadth of Hawkins Point and so keep it until you are almost abreast of the rocks then edge southward. . . ."

A New and Accurate Chart of the Bay of Chesapeake, 1776, carried the same directions for sailing up to Baltimore. Those were the days before the buoy system and outstanding landmarks, such as prominent trees, bluffs, rocks, and houses, were

spar and mast buoys that were making their appearance in marking channels. The White Rocks are still mentioned, however, for bearings. Even after lighthouses had been established at Bodkin Point, North Point, and Lazaretto, these rocks continued to be included in sailing directions in Blunt's, at least up to 1857.

The White Rocks are so prominent that they were once easily visible from Baltimore. Griffith, in his *Annals of Baltimore,* published in 1824, describes the view from the signal tower atop Federal Hill, "the vessels in the harbor, remarkable edifices in the city, and handsome villas adjacent to it." He continues, "How much more must the admiration be excited and the veneration extended on turning the sight towards those immense White Rocks which seem to have been carried many miles beyond this Eddy of a basin and their fellows of original formation by some tremendous eruption of Fire, Hurricane of Wind, or Deluge of Waters." Locust Point is barely visible today from Federal Hill because buildings and haze from industrial plants obstruct the view. From the heights of the Maryland National Bank Building, however, the rocks can be seen from the city on a clear day.

With the increase of pleasure boats in the lower Patapsco, these unlighted rocks proved to be the bane of yachtsmen frequenting the Rock Creek area at night. After receiving numerous complaints, the Coast Guard decided that a beacon on the rocks would be helpful. A small wooden house was erected on a concrete base on one of the rocks to support the light. Nineteen feet above mean high water, the 50 candlepower light, flashing white every 4 seconds, went into service in June 1938. It still warns unwary boatmen of the rocky mass.

The part the White Rocks once played in helping to direct ships into Baltimore has long ceased, but members of the Maryland Pilot's Association are still conscious of their presence. One pilot remarked that when their vessels are within the red sector of the light on Fort Carroll they are in that section known as the "rocky area." At least those whose chief business it is to conduct ships in and out of Baltimore with safety are not completely oblivious of these ancient obstructions, even though they are well beyond the limits of the channel.

A closeup of the White Rocks. Compare the size of the boat and occupant with this unusual rock formation. Photo: A. Aubrey Bodine

The Bay's First Steamboat

ON JUNE 13, 1813, Baltimoreans were offered their first excursion on the first steamboat built in Baltimore. To be sure, it was in decided contrast to the outings experienced by their fellow citizens a century later, but it at least afforded the local folks a means of enjoying Chesapeake Bay and they would be relatively sure of getting back to port the same day they embarked. This was more than the sailing packets, the best means of water travel up to that time, could guarantee.

Captain Edward Trippe, of Dorchester County, Maryland, was responsible for the introduction of the steamboat to local waters. Through his association with Robert Fulton, who in 1807 devised the *Clermont*, one of the first successful steamboats, Captain Trippe had become intrigued with this new method of water transportation.

Captain Edward Trippe, who was instrumental in introducing steam navigation on Chesapeake Bay. Photo: The Mariners Museum

Confident that a steamboat would be a paying proposition on Chesapeake Bay, he interested two of his shipping friends in the venture. They were Lieut. Colonel William McDonald, who commanded the Sixth Regiment of Maryland Infantry at North Point, and Mr. Andrew Fisher Henderson, who later became associated with the Baltimore Steam Packet Company.

All three of these men had maritime connections. Lieut. Colonel McDonald and Mr. Henderson are said to have started, in 1806, the first organized line of sailing packets from Baltimore to Philadelphia via Frenchtown, Maryland. Prior to that time the packets were operated by individuals.

At Frenchtown the freight and passengers would be transferred to wagons and stages to be transported to New Castle, Delaware. From that point they would continue to Philadelphia by water. Captain Trippe, with several other men, likewise operated packets. Their route was from Baltimore to Courthouse Point, on the Elk River, where freight and passengers were discharged and conveyed across to a point on the Delaware River and then on to Philadelphia by sailing vessel. Both of these lines were successful so consolidation was proposed, finally emerging as the Union Line.

McDonald and Henderson each agreed to put up one-third of the money necessary to build the steamer if Captain Trippe would furnish a like amount and supervise the vessel's construction. Trippe was in accord with this arrangement and the actual construction of the steamer was carried out by William Flannigan, who operated a yard at the end of McElderry's Wharf, Baltimore. After some delay, the vessel was completed in 1813 and given the name of the waters she was to traverse, the *Chesapeake*.

Among the present records of the Bureau of Marine Inspection and Navigation, in the National

Archives, Washington, D.C., is a copy of this vessel's second enrollment which was issued at Baltimore on August 14, 1815, because of a change of property in part. On this document appears the information as to when, where, and by whom she was built. Her specifications also are listed and she measured 137 feet in length, 21 feet in breadth, 6 feet 8 inches in depth, and 183 33/95 tons. She is described further as having one deck, one mast, a "full built square stern," a round tuck, and no figurehead.

An earlier writer stated, "The engine was a crosshead with 4½ foot stroke. It revolved a cog wheel that worked in teeth upon a castiron shaft. A flywheel was connected with the engine to enable it to pass its center. The smokestack was amidships behind the engine. The boiler was raised two feet above the deck and was about 20 feet long."

Her paddle wheels were 10 feet in diameter, her mast was forward, and the sail was used to take advantage of a fair wind. She was steered by a tiller, the helmsman relying upon steering instructions from a pilot stationed in the bow of the vessel who relayed orders by word of mouth to a man amidships. The latter, in turn, repeated them to the helmsman. There was no engine-room gong and signals were passed to the engineer either by voice or by stamping on the deck above the engine. On the quarter-deck, a bench extended parallel with the rail.

The interior of the steamboat has been described as follows: "The women's cabin, with berths, occupied the stern of the boat; and the men's cabin, with berths, was between that of the women's and the machinery. The men's cabin was also used as a dining saloon, while in front was the forward cabin. The gallery was amidships. Windows gave light and ventilation to these interior apartments. No provision was made for second class passengers, since all such travelled by sloops." The "gallery" referred to was probably meant to be "galley."

On June 12, 1813, the advertisement opposite appeared in the *Federal Gazette and Baltimore Daily Advertiser.*

Pier 1, Pratt Street, is now on the site of the original Bowley's Wharf. The signal for the steamboat's departure from the wharf was the firing of a swivel gun on the forward gangway.

Research does not reveal a description of this first trip. Such an item as the introduction of steam to Chesapeake Bay was overshadowed by the events that were taking place concerning another vessel named *Chesapeake,* this one the United States

frigate that had been captured by the British frigate *Shannon* off Boston Bay. Then, even as today, war news had priority.

The British had established a blockade of Chesapeake Bay, and, at the time of the *Chesapeake's* first excursion, there were between 35 and 40 hostile vessels reported in the Bay. In the Baltimore publication, *The Weekly Register,* June 12, 1813, the following note appeared "We have had some very handsome experimental firing from Fort McHenry this week. The defenses of Baltimore are daily increased, or rendered more perfect."

On June 19th, another notice appeared in the Baltimore papers stating that a trip to Rock Hall would be made, leaving Baltimore at 9 A.M. and returning in the evening. The fare was 75 cents each way and half fare for children. Soda water was to be served on board. An announcement was also made that the steamboat's regular run to Frenchtown was to start on Monday morning next. She was to leave the lower end of Bowley's Wharf every Monday, Wednesday, and Friday at 2 A.M. for Frenchtown. The steamboat at New Castle awaited the arrival of her passengers and then proceeded to Philadelphia. A footnote added that the *Chesapeake* had performed her first trip this day to Frenchtown and back in 24 hours, a distance of 140 miles.

All the while, the British were advancing up the Bay. In the July 10th issue of *The Weekly Register* appeared the information that, "The Marines and the troops of the enemy in the Bay are established to amount to at least 4000 men. The whole force may be about 8000."

STEAM BOAT.

The Steam Boat CHESAPEAKE, Edward Trippe, master, will leave the lower end of Bowley's wharf, on SUNDAY morning next, the 13th inst. at 8 o'clock precisely, for Annapolis, and return in the evening. Passage one dollar here and the same back. A cold dinner will be provided on board.

EDWARD TRIPPE, master.

June 12   1t‡

Announcement of first steamboat excursion on Chesapeake Bay. Photo: *The Baltimore Sunday Sun*

Several weeks later the *Chesapeake* was given a little space in the paper with the following item: "We understand that the steamboat running between this city and Frenchtown was yesterday turned back by the lookout squadron in consequence of the nearer approach of the enemy's ships. She had on board a number of Congressmen on their way to the Eastward." Another item in the same paper stated that, "A British brig was near the mouth of the Patapsco as seen from the observatory."

On August 8th, the *Chesapeake* left Bowley's Wharf at 9 A.M., stopped at Coffee House Wharf, Fells Point, and proceeded down the river to our squadron. The passage was one dollar and she was to return before dinner. A report at this time stated, "20 to 25 enemy sail of the blockading squadron were discernable from the dome of the State House, Annapolis. The enemy has taken Kent Island. An attack upon Annapolis is expected." As the British ships became more numerous and closer to Baltimore, the *Chesapeake's* excursion routes down the Patapsco River were shortened.

Excursionists were a daring lot in those days, judging from a brief notice inserted in the *Federal Gazette* of August 14th. It read, "The Steamboat has permission to pass the Fort and will proceed down as far as the Rocks, if safe." Dinner was to be served on board.

The following Sunday the steamboat barely went out of the boundaries of Baltimore harbor. It was advertised that she was to leave Bowley's Wharf at 9 A.M. and pass down the river as far as Hawkins Point, thence up Curtis Creek to Stansbury's Springs.

For two years the *Chesapeake* was the only steamboat in Baltimore. By 1815 competition loomed on the horizon when, in July, another vessel, the *Eagle,* came around the Virginia Capes from Delaware Bay in search of a charter. The Union Line's rival, Briscoe and Partridge, put this vessel on their run between Baltimore and Elkton and operated her for about four years, after which they went out of business. In 1816 the Union Line built two additional steamers and expanded their business. During their almost forty years of existence they added to their fleet until in the early 1850's the line was purchased by the Pennsylvania Railroad.

What of the *Chesapeake?* It has been recorded that she remained with the Union Line for about five years. Her movements after that are unknown. However, the National Archives reveals her fate, for in their files is the information that her enrollment was surrendered at Baltimore on June 6, 1820, and endorsed, "Vessel broken up."

The *Eagle,* first steamboat between Baltimore and Norfolk (see following article). The *Chesapeake,* though slightly smaller than the *Eagle,* must have been quite similar in design.
Photo: The Mariners Museum

The Weems Line

NO NAME connected with Chesapeake Bay steamboating stands out more prominently than that of Weems. One of the first companies to operate steam vessels on the Bay, the Weems Line served these waters for 87 years. Starting in 1817, it remained active until 1904, at which time it had about 600 employees and a fleet of propeller and side-wheel steamers. Some of their later-built steamers were to carry on into the 1930's when that style of steamboating came to an end on the Chesapeake.

It was only four years after the introduction of steam to the Bay that George Weems realized the possibilities of this means of ship propulsion. Weems was born at Marshall Seat, in southern Maryland, on May 23, 1784. He was the son of David Weems (or Wemyss, as was the Scotch spell-

ing), who had an inclination toward things maritime. George inherited this love of the sea and sailed deepwater before confining his activities to Chesapeake Bay.

Service of the Weems Line was inaugurated with the steamer *Surprise*. This vessel had been chartered to operate between Baltimore, Patuxent River, and landings on Maryland's western shore of the Bay. George Weems acted as captain of this steamer that served his line until 1821, when the *Eagle* was secured as a replacement.

The *Eagle* was the second steamboat on the Chesapeake. She was built in Philadelphia in 1813 and brought down to the Bay in 1815 seeking a charter. The *Eagle* met with misfortune on April 18, 1824, while off North Point bound from Annapolis to Baltimore. Her boiler exploded, severely

The *Wenonah,* built in Baltimore in 1864, shown as a transport during the Civil War.
This vessel later came under the Weems Line. Photo: The Mariners Museum

injuring Captain Weems and resulting in the loss of a passenger. That was the first fatal explosion on the Chesapeake and the only time a passenger met death on a Weems steamer.

Captain George Weems recovered and, in 1827, had the steamboat *Patuxent* built at Baltimore. That vessel has been described as superior to anything previously seen in Maryland waters. The following year she was placed on a run to Fredericksburg and landings on the Rappahannock River. She stopped en route at Herring Bay on the Chesapeake and at points on the lower part of the Patuxent River.

transports during the Civil War. The Weems Line made an effort to maintain their service with the *Matilda*, but it became necessary to charter her to the Quartermaster Corps until the end of the war.

Upon the cessation of hostilities, the company tried to pick up loose ends and resumed operations to the Patuxent and Rappahannock Rivers. In 1869, the *George Weems* was destroyed by fire. The *Theodore Weems* was built in 1872 and she, in turn, burned in 1889 and was rebuilt as the *St. Marys*, only to burn again in 1907.

In 1874, Henry Williams became manager of the Weems Line. Shortly thereafter, two lady heirs

The *Planter,* built for the Weems Line in 1851, is shown at an unknown Virginia site during her service as a transport in the Civil War. Photo: The Mariners Museum

The *Patuxent* served the Weems Line well and had a long career after she left their service. It is recorded that she was sold to the U.S. Quartermaster Department on July 1, 1864 and was redocumented the *Cumberland* on April 19, 1866. She was finally abandoned in 1868.

Weems had the *Planter* built in 1851 and, in 1854, the *Mary Washington* was purchased. The *George Weems* was built in Baltimore in 1858. Captain George Weems died in 1853 but he had turned over the management of the steamers earlier to his four sons who served in the capacities of captains or engineers on the vessels. In 1862, the U.S. Government seized the steamers to serve as

of Mason Locke Weems, last son of Captain George Weems to survive, purchased the interest of other heirs and became the sole owners of the line. Mr. Williams then was appointed President and he carried out a progressive program. The *Wenonah* came under the Weems flag during his tenure. He also had constructed the side-wheelers *Mason L. Weems, Westmoreland, Richmond, Lancaster,* and *Middlesex,* and the propeller-driven *Essex, Northumberland, Calvert,* and *Anne Arundel.* The *Essex* burned in 1887, was rebuilt, and burned again in 1911. The *Richmond* burned in 1902. The line bought out the Maryland and Virginia Steamboat Company in 1896 and acquired the *Potomac, Sue,* and *John E. Tygert* and operated to the Potomac River as well as the Patuxent and Rappahannock Rivers.

In October 1904, the Maryland, Delaware and Virginia Railway Company, a subsidiary of the Pennsylvania Railroad, bought out the Weems Line. They also acquired the Chester River Steamboat Company and the Queen Anne Railroad. Shortly thereafter the distinctive insignia of the Weems steamers, a red ball plaque with the letter W cut-out, was removed from vessels of that line. All of the newly acquired steamers then had the name of the new operator painted on their bows just below the deck line.

Thus a new era of steamboating was ushered in. The Baltimore, Chesapeake and Atlantic Railway Company, also controlled by the Pennsylvania Railroad, in 1894 had bought out the Eastern Shore Steamboat Company, Maryland Steamboat Company, Choptank Steamboat Company, Wheeler Line, and the Baltimore and Eastern Railroad. Along with the M. D. & V., the two companies controlled virtually all of the freight and passenger steamboats operating out of Baltimore to the Eastern and Western Shores of Maryland and Virginia. In the 1920's, these lines consolidated into the Baltimore and Virginia Steamboat Company, which lasted until March 1932.

Former Weems Line steamboat *Lancaster* at Wellfords, Virginia.
Photo: The Mariners Museum

Lightships Mark the Way

WHEN WE think of lightships, we usually picture a sturdy looking vessel wholly designed to withstand heavy weather while moored miles off the seacoast. Such craft serve as guides to shipping and mark the approach to a port or the outer limits of an off-lying shoal. That would be representative of the present-day lightship. The light vessel system in this country had its beginnings under less severe conditions. In fact, the so-called sheltered waters of Hampton Roads, Virginia, saw the inauguration of the lightship into our aids to navigation for it was there that the first lightship in this country was established.

Early in 1819, Congress made an appropriation for two light vessels, one to be stationed at Wolf Trap Shoal just south of the Rappahannock River, in Chesapeake Bay. The other was destined for Willoughby Spit, in Hampton Roads. The vessel for the latter station received first consideration.

Described as the "first object of its kind in the United States," great care was given preliminary studies of such a craft. Many persons were consulted and a strange variety of opinions was obtained. This ultimately resulted in the awarding of a contract on September 2, 1819, to John Pool, Hampton, Virginia, for the construction of a vessel to make the "first attempt to establish a Floating Light."

In accordance with the contract the ship was "to be of 70 tons burthen; copper fastened and coppered; to be provided with a cabin with at least four berths, an apartment for cooking, spars, a capstan belfry, a yawl and davids (sic), etc." Chain moorings were to be supplied and some thirty tons of ballast carried.

There were certain changes in design and delays in construction so that the vessel was not placed on her station until the summer of 1820. Then it was found she was too small for satisfactory service in the exposed waters off Willoughby Spit so was moved to a more protected station off Craney Island.

Lightships, or floating lights, as they were called then, proved to be popular. The following year four other light vessels were placed in Chesapeake waters, including one off Willoughby. Their number increased until, in 1825, there were ten in service on various stations in American waters.

An 1833 issue of Blunt's *American Coast Pilot* mentions those lightships in the Chesapeake area as being stationed off Craney Island, Willoughby, Rappahannock River, Smith's Point, Hooper's Straits, and Poplar Island. Others were later placed at Wolf Trap, Janes' Island in Tangier Sound, and York Spit.

In 1850 the screw-pile method of construction of lighthouses on sandy, shallow bottoms, was first tried out in this country. Proving successful, this method was adopted for many lighthouses in the sounds and bays and accounted for replacing many lightships. In 1858, there were 48 lightships in American waters but within twenty-five years the number had been reduced to 22, owing to replacement by lighthouses.

In one year, 1867, 8 lightships in the sounds of North Carolina and in Chesapeake Bay were replaced by screw-pile lighthouses. In 1872 there was only one lightship in the Fifth District, which included the Chesapeake area, and that was at Willoughby Spit. That same year the vessel was withdrawn from service, since the erection of the screw-pile lighthouse at Thimble Shoal had taken its place. For several years thereafter Chesapeake Bay was devoid of lightships.

Although lightships are expensive to maintain, the reason for their being replaced by lighthouses where practicable, they are versatile. They serve as a mark by day, identified by their form or signals displayed. At night they serve as a platform for a light. When visibility has been cut down by fog they issue fog signals. They may be moored on shifting shoals and banks where no foundation for a fixed structure could be placed. When the danger point of a shoal shifts, a corresponding change can be promptly made in the position of the lightship marking that shoal. They can be moored near a lighthouse under construction and used again when such a structure has been destroyed.

In January 1893, ice destroyed the screw-pile lighthouse at Wolf Trap. To mark this treacherous shoal, a lightship, *Number 46*, that had been serving on a station off Cape Charles, was brought to the site. There it remained until a new tower was completed in September 1894.

In February 1895, severe ice conditions carried away the lighthouse at Smith's Point. Again *Number 46* was ushered into service as a stand-by beacon until a new lighthouse was erected in 1897.

Old *Number 46,* a number assigned to the vessel by the Lighthouse Board and the one she retained throughout her career, although she served on various stations, was long associated with Chesapeake waters. She was a steel, wood-sheathed vessel built in 1887. This type of construction protected the interior of the hull from the effects of sudden changes and extreme temperatures. The plating was also stiffened by the bulk of the wood against sudden local shock or blows that might otherwise puncture the hull.

On February 18, 1899, Congress by act authorized the establishment of a light vessel at Tail of the Horseshoe, an extensive shoal making out from shore between Old Point Comfort and Back River entrance, Virginia. *Number 46* was assigned to the new station in 1901 and was a familiar sight there for almost a quarter of a century.

The Hampton Roads area clung to lightships longer than any other section of Chesapeake Bay. In 1908, a lightship was established at a point in the Chesapeake about midway between Back River and Cape Charles. This was designated as *Thirty Five Foot Channel* lightship. Assigned to this station was *Number 45,* which had previously served as the *Winter Quarter Shoal* lightship off the Virginia seacoast. This vessel was almost a duplicate of *Number 46,* having been built in the same year and being of the same tonnage. This station was discontinued in 1919 when it was replaced by a lighted whistle buoy.

One of the latter-day lightships to serve in these waters, and the last in Hampton Roads proper,

was that placed at Bush Bluff. This was a shoal making out from shore between Sewell's Point and Lambert Point. The station was first established in 1891 about one mile north of the old Craney Island lighthouse.

Lightship *Number 49* had been constructed especially for Bush Bluff but apparently she never served there, having been assigned the more rigorous and exposed post off Cape Charles. One of the first, if not the first, vessels posted at Bush Bluff was the old side-wheel, iron lighthouse tender *Holly.*

Thirty Five Foot Channel lightship that marked a shoal in lower Chesapeake Bay between Back River and Cape Charles. This vessel was *Number 45* and had previously served as the *Winter Quarter Shoal* lightship off the Virginia coast. Photo: The Mariners Museum

On February 14, 1895, the *Holly* was carried away by an ice floe and was replaced by the schooner *Drift* as a temporary measure. Several weeks later, the *Holly* again took the station. But apparently the 146-foot vessel was unwieldy and not suited for the purpose, so on December 9, 1895, the *Drift* again took over.

The *Drift* was a two-masted schooner that had been loaned to the Lighthouse Board by the Coast and Geodetic Survey. This 76-foot wooden vessel had been built in Baltimore in 1876 and had done yeoman duty for many years along the Atlantic and Gulf coasts for the Coast and Geodetic Survey. When she first took up her lightship duties she retained her rig of a two-masted schooner. Later she was rigged with just one mast atop of which was placed the light. On her sides, in huge white letters, appeared BUSH to identify her. This station was discontinued in 1918 and replaced by a lighted bell buoy. Today the shoal is marked with a flashing white light and gong.

Although the lightships stationed at these sheltered Bay points did not receive the brunt of heavy weather encountered by those vessels moored off the coast, they had their share of mishaps. On October 11, 1896, the *Drift*, while at Bush Bluff, parted her moorings in a gale and drifted about one hundred yards before being checked by her starboard anchor. On February 13, 1899, the *Drift* was dragged by running ice and was relieved temporarily by the old reliable tender *Holly*. The *Drift* returned to her post in Hampton Roads only to be rammed by the schooner *H. M. Sumner* on May 23, 1899.

Another case of a Bay lightship being rammed involved *Number 46* when she was serving at Tail of the Horseshoe. On March 27, 1914, she was struck by a scow being towed by the tug *Columbia*. Damages to the extent of $1700 were incurred by the lightship which necessitated her being relieved from her station and towed to a Baltimore shipyard for repairs. After repairs had been effected, *Number 46* returned to Tail of the Horseshoe and served there until November 3, 1922, when she was replaced by a lighted bell buoy.

On October 5, 1923, *Number 46* was sold to Norfolk shipping interests, renamed *W. T. Bell*, and that city became her home port. Fitted out with topmasts and bowsprit, and looking the part of a real sailing vessel, she started out on what proved to be a short but hectic venture.

In 1926 the *Bell* was libeled at Friendship, Maine, for an outstanding bill owed a Boston ship outfitter but was cleared of the libel. Five months later she was found in distress off Cape Sable, Nova Scotia, while bound from New York to Halifax and towed to her destination. On February 21, 1927, while bound from Halifax to New York, she stranded at Bayville, New York, and became a total loss. It is said that her cargo consisted of 25-gallon wooden kegs of blended whiskey.

Tail of the Horseshoe lightship in dry dock at Baltimore in 1914. Originally *Number 46*, this vessel marked a shoal in the lower Bay. In 1922 it was replaced by a lighted bell buoy and was the last lightship in the Chesapeake. Photo: C. C. Knobeloch

These last lightships in local waters were rather archaic for their day. *Numbers 45* and *46* were of a type of lightship design that carried no steam propulsion, but were rigged like two-masted schooners. They were towed between port and their stations and used sails only in emergency.

Number 46 found her sails rather useful when she parted her chains on October 23, 1889, while moored off the coast at her Cape Charles station. Finding herself adrift, sail was made and the vessel ran for shelter in the Chesapeake. Usually the bottoms of these vessels were so foul with marine growth that little actual sailing was accomplished.

At the tops of the masts of the lightship were perforated hoop-iron day marks. From a distance these appeared as huge balls. At night lights were displayed, the lighting apparatus set upon rings encircling the masts and the whole hoisted to the mastheads by winch. The lights, with eight reflectors, were enclosed in a lantern with large panes of glass to protect them from the weather. In the daytime the lanterns were lowered on deck into structures resembling small houses. A fog signal, operated by steam, was located amidships. On the forecastlehead was a huge bell to be sounded when the fog signal became disabled.

Lightships are still a very important factor in navigation along the coast and occasionally may be seen in harbors when they are relieved for overhaul and repairs. But, with their modern equipment, they are a far cry from the light vessels that served so faithfully in Chesapeake waters.

Bush Bluff lightship at her station in Hampton Roads, Virginia, in 1914. She was formerly the Coast and Geodetic Survey schooner *Drift*. Photo: The Mariners Museum

The *Mary Whitridge* Makes a Record

IN THE mid-eighteen hundreds, a sailing ship built, owned, and manned in Baltimore crossed the Atlantic Ocean, between Cape Henry, at the mouth of Chesapeake Bay, and the chops of the English Channel, in 13 days and 7 hours. There is no available record indicating that any commercial sailing ship has equaled this run between the two points, a distance of 2962 miles. Even after a century of maritime progress, many steamers today require almost as much time on this crossing.

The vessel that brought fame to Baltimore shipping for this remarkable sailing feat was the *Mary Whitridge*, a 978-ton full-rigged ship built by Hunt and Wagner at Fells Point, in 1855, and commanded by Captain Cheesebrough. If she had been built on the lines of the famed Baltimore Clippers, noted for their sailing qualities, fast passages would have been expected of her. Instead, she was termed a medium clipper, a type combining the beauty and speed of the extreme clipper with the stowage capacity of the early packet ships.

The maiden voyage of the new ship was from Baltimore to Liverpool. One day in June 1855, the *Whitridge* sailed down the Patapsco River to the Chesapeake, bound for the Virginia Capes. Off Cape Henry, on June 24, the ship took her departure for England. Little did those on board realize they were starting on a voyage that was to place the name of the *Mary Whitridge* on the roster of famous clippers.

If the logbook kept on that passage had been preserved, it would have been of historic importance. Notations of conditions of the sea and wind encountered across the Atlantic might have served as a clue to the record-making trip. A group of Baltimoreans, friends of Thomas Whitridge, the vessel's owner, were on the ship as passengers. Their observations appeared in contemporary local newspapers.

The *Morning Sun* of August 4, 1855, carried a description of the passengers and the record sailing, as follows:

". . . Among a number of passengers which she carried out were Miss Whitridge, daughter of Dr. Whitridge, and two Episcopalian clergymen of this city. Rev. Dr. Balch, Rector of Christ Church, who went with his family, chiefly on a visit to near relatives in England, was aboard."

"We learn," says the *Patriot*, "that letters were received this morning from some of the passengers which speak in the most glowing terms of the ship and her commander. A lady passenger, writing to her relatives, compares the entire voyage to a pleasant excursion, everything moving pleasantly and regularly as clock-work. The health of the entire party was remarkably good and all felt the invigorating influence of so pleasant a sea voyage. . . ."

In the *American and Commercial Advertiser*, Baltimore, of the same date, appeared a letter from a passenger on the *Whitridge*. It read, "We left Cape Henry on Sunday evening, June 24, and reached the mouth of the British Channel, in 13 days 7 hours, having sailed during that time 2962 miles. I doubt much whether any sailing vessel ever crossed the Atlantic in less time. This abundantly proves the admirable qualities of the noble ship and the skill, seamanship, and fidelity of Captain Cheesebrough who tested thoroughly her merits.

"I am sure few parties have ever crossed the Atlantic under such favorable conditions—a swift, staunch ship, a skillful captain, delightful weather, a quick passage, every comfort on board and a harmonious, good-tempered company—all combined to make the voyage long to be remembered."

Returning to this country, the *Mary Whitridge* took 30 days from Rotterdam to New York. Although owned in and closely linked with Baltimore during her career of thirty years as a sailing ship, this speedy clipper went far afield.

After returning to the States, she sailed around Cape Horn to San Francisco in 114 days. This run and a similar one of 138 days made in 1859 were her only Cape Horn passages. For a number of years she operated between San Francisco and Hong Kong, becoming a favorite on that route.

In 1866 the *Whitridge* was rebuilt and resumed trade between New York and China where she plied for over fifteen years. It is said that she was one of the best known ships in North China ports, particularly in Shanghai and Foochow.

About 1885, the *Mary Whitridge* was sold by her Baltimore owners to New York interests. Her new owners promptly cut her down to serve as a barge. For the rest of her life she was towed coastwise behind a tug, a lowly calling for a ship that has been termed "the peer of any of the famous clippers."

On February 22, 1902, while in tow from Nor-folk to New Bedford with a cargo of coal, the *Whitridge* foundered east of Ocean Grove, New Jersey, taking down her master and three men.

Now, a century after her record-breaking passage, the memory of the *Mary Whitridge* is kept alive in two Baltimore institutions. At The Merchants Club, 206 East Redwood Street, hangs a dramatic oil painting of the ship portrayed under reduced sail in heavy weather.

The Maryland Historical Society has a full model of her, and a half-model in its collection labeled as that of the *Mary Whitridge*. Her sailing abilities have been recorded in the outstanding histories of the clipper ships.

There may be Baltimore-built ships more prominent in shipping annals than the *Mary Whitridge*. These would include the privateer *Chasseur*, known as the "Pride of Baltimore," and the *Ann McKim*, the first extreme clipper ever built. When fast sailing records are discussed, however, the name of the *Whitridge* usually comes to the fore.

The *Mary Whitridge* depicted in heavy weather in a painting owned by
The Merchants Club, Baltimore.

This Was the Hard Life

BRUTALITY at sea was a common occurrence in the nineteenth century. In some cases it was justified if a mate was to get any work out of a laggard seaman. On the other hand, some officers took advantage of their authority by beating ship's crews unmercifully and gained the title of "bucko."

Many stories have been written about the lot of seamen in the sailing ship era and they seem to stress the ill treatment meted out to the deck hands. Recently, a most unusual pamphlet came into the possession of The Mariners Museum describing brutality on the Baltimore full-rigged ship *Ann E. Hooper* a century ago.

The booklet is entitled, *An Account of the Voyage of the Ship* Ann E. Hooper, *A Tale of Cruelty and Suffering.* This was prepared by one of the ship's seamen, George Claflin, to be dispensed like circulars. The writer hoped to be reimbursed by those who accepted copies. Within its four pages the writer described the beatings dealt him by the *Hooper's* officers and the disastrous results.

The second page, the beginning of the text, is headed, *An Account of the Manner by which the Bearer was Severely Injured and Lost the Use of His Arm.* It began, "Passage from Liverpool to Baltimore, in the American ship *Ann E. Hooper*, 1700 tons burthen, Captain Raines, master; Mr. Johnson, mate. The name of the second mate I do not remember. The carpenter was a son of the captain's. The crew consisted of eleven Germans, five Frenchmen, and myself, the only one before the mast that could speak English.

"On the second day of February, 1857, we hauled out of the Prince's Dock, bound for Baltimore. The steam tug and pilot left us at Holyhead, and we stood boldly on our way with a fair wind after us. But about two bells in the first watch (9 o'clock), the wind chopped round in our teeth,

and we were banging about in the channel twelve or thirteen days, and during that time there were several of the men frozen—two quite severely—but instead of being treated like human beings, they fared worse than brutes.

"The second day out, the officers first showed their colors. Their first act was to put us on short allowance, with the plea of anticipation of a long voyage, when God knew, and I knew, that there was enough to last six months. Acts of cruelty and malice were of daily and hourly occurrence, a few of which I will relate.

"On the 26th of February, between two and three bells in the middle watch (one and half-past one), while we were shaking a reef out of the main topsail, one of the men let the halyards run about two or three fathoms, when the captain jumped afoul of me and kicked me, so that every bone in my body was as sore as they well could be. But was I allowed any kinder treatment or lighter duties? No! If there was any such thing as harder fare or worse treatment, I got it. You may, perhaps, ask why was it? Was it because I could not do my duty? No, it was because I was an American!

"On the morning of the 4th of April, we were all kept on deck, and about 2 bells (five o'clock) we were called into the forecastle, one by one, where the mate and second mate were armed with revolvers and pieces of manila rope, one inch thick and two feet long, knotted at one end and pointed at the other, when they both set upon each of us singly, and beat us to their heart's content. Why was this? Because a tar bucket had been lost, the value of five cents.

"On the 23rd of April, between five and six bells in the morning watch (half-past two and three), we made Cape Henry Light, and if ever a poor mortal was glad at the sight of land, it was your humble servant. We passed pleasantly up the

Chesapeake with a stiff breeze, and we were within sixty miles of our destination when the wind whipped round and blew a gale from the northward, which compelled us to come to anchor and furl sails.

"We had furled all on the fore and main, except the mainsail, when I was ordered below to get some spare gaskets. As I was passing behind the second mate he willfully pushed me off the yard; I caught hold of the buntlines, which partially broke my fall, otherwise I should have been smashed to pieces. I was taken up insensible and hustled into the forecastle, where I lay for three days without

the world and devoted their lives to doing good. To Sister Mary Ann, I feel deeply indebted, for had it not been for her kind and motherly care, and God's goodness, I never could have survived. The above named was nurse of the sailor's ward, having had charge of the sick in that institution, at that time, fifteen years.

"Of the captain and mates, I have but one remark to make concerning them, they were styled bullies in Liverpool, Baltimore, and where ever they were known." (Signed) George Claflin

Whether seaman Claflin received any satisfaction or benefit out of the distribution of these pam-

The *Ann E. Hooper* in the act of rescuing the crew of the bark *Ouzel Galley* in 1859.
This is the painting presented to the *Hooper's* master by Queen Victoria.
Photo: The Mariners Museum

having anything done for me, when at the end of that time a humane person had me conveyed to the Lombard Street Infirmary (Baltimore), where for two weeks, I lay unconscious and very near death's door. I was in the Infirmary about four months, when I went home to my friends, crippled for life.

"I have a word or two to say in praise of the nurses connected with the Lombard Street Infirmary; they are women who have come out from

phlets is not known but he certainly made every effort to publicize the ill treatment he had received at the hands of the ship's officers.

But the *Ann E. Hooper* should not be solely remembered through the brutality of her officers. The ship achieved a certain amount of fame for a humanitarian act. On April 16, 1859, while bound across the Atlantic under the command of Captain Frank B. Hooper, a stricken ship was encountered.

This was the storm-tossed bark *Ouzel Galley* bound from Dublin to Trinidad. As a result of bad weather, three days were required to effect a rescue of all the men on the wreck.

In recognition of this feat, Queen Victoria of England directed one of her country's leading artists to make a painting of the *Ann E. Hooper* in the act of carrying out the rescue work. This was presented to the ship's master along with an engraved telescope. The painting, later in the possession of Captain Hooper's grandchildren in Newport News, Virginia, was recently presented to The Mariners Museum. The telescope has disappeared.

The *Ann E. Hooper* had a relatively brief career. She had been built in Bath, Maine, in 1855 for the Baltimore shipping merchant, James Hooper. In October 1862, while bound from Baltimore to Liverpool with a cargo of wheat and flour, she was approaching her destination as she sailed up the English Channel. At that time she was in command of the pilot and, in spite of severe weather, he assured her master the vessel could be brought into port safely.

A hurricane developed from the WNW and the ship obtained the aid of a tug to tow her into port. But the gale increased and, unable to make headway, the tug was obliged to release the towline between the two lightships at the mouth of the Mersey. The *Hooper* drifted ashore on a shoal known as the Horsebank.

In an effort to lighten the vessel, two of her masts had been cut away. A lifeboat was sent to the scene and twelve of her crew were taken off. Two seamen had been washed overboard the day before and two more lost when they attempted to launch the ship's boat. Of a crew of twenty, four were lost.

The *Hooper* began to break up and wreckage was scattered along the coast. Salvaged from her cargo were 1500 barrels of flour, tallow, and lard. From some of her timbers it was reported that a cradle and a coffin were made. A member of the lifeboat's crew also wrote a poem about the tragic stranding and, in part, it reads:

> 'Neath the thatch of a seaside Cot
> An oaken trestle stands;
> Its burden an oaken coffin
> Wrought by a comrade's hands;
> From the deck of the *Ann E. Hooper*
> Wrecked on Southport Sands.

The *Ann E. Hooper* was one of several sailing ships owned by James Hooper, who was born at Fells Point, Baltimore, on July 5, 1804. The old firm of James Hooper and Company, shipping and commission merchants, was a familiar one for more than half a century on the northeast corner of Gay and Lombard Streets, near Baltimore's waterfront.

His unusual career began during the War of 1812 when, but a boy of 8 years, he took the place of a man aboard the schooner *Comet,* one of Barney's flotilla protecting the port of Baltimore.

Before engaging in the shipping business as a career, James Hooper had accumulated quite a fortune in the wholesale clothing business. In his day he was rated among the wealthiest merchants in Baltimore. It was through his love and knowledge of ships that he became an owner and operator of vessels. He never commanded a ship as did his father, brother, and later, his son.

During the Civil War, Hooper was among the staunch Union men in the State of Maryland. He did not transfer his ships to a foreign flag for protection and gave the strictest orders to the masters of his ships that only the American flag should be displayed. In January 1864, he chartered his bark *General Berry* to the United States Government for transportation of quartermaster's stores from New York to Fortress Monroe, Virginia, for use by the Union Army. On July 10, 1864, the vessel was captured and burned to the water's edge off Cape May.

The *Ann E. Hooper* must have been his favorite vessel. It was named for his wife who was also portrayed in the full-length carving that served as the ship's figurehead. In the figure's hands was carved a bouquet of sixteen roses, representing his sixteen children—nine sons and seven daughters.

According to family papers, Mr. Hooper's *Tennessee* was the first steamer to sail from Baltimore to the United Kingdom. This occurred in June 1855. Forty years after that event on August 29, 1895, Baltimore's mayor, Ferdinand C. Latrobe, acknowledged the importance of the crossing. He also accepted from Hooper a model of the ship and stated, "It will be placed among our most valued archives of the Municipal government." He concluded his letter, ". . . you are, in my estimation, one of the oldest and most valued citizens of Baltimore."

Mr. Hooper died on March 14, 1898, and was buried beside his first wife in his family lot in Greenmount Cemetery, Baltimore.

Sailor Beware

A N OUTSTANDING VIRTUE of Chesapeake Bay is the absence of rock and other formations dangerous to navigation. Instead there are natural sand bars and a few muddy shoals that inflict little, if any, damage when boats come in contact with them. For all this we have nature to thank. Man, not content with having obstruction-free waters, came along and placed a huge obstacle in the middle of the Bay that plagued commercial boatmen and yachtsmen for more than 40 years.

Until 1958, anyone who cruised the length of the Bay was familiar with that menace shown on the charts as the *San Marcos* wreck. This hulk lay in approximately 30 feet of water, southwest of Tangier Island, about 6½ miles east of the main ship channel in the Chesapeake.

The wreck, built in 1889 as the first battleship of the U. S. Navy, was still capable of dealing out deathly blows. It was as deadly as a modern battlewagon to those who were lax in their navigation, for it could destroy with one blow.

On March 22, 1911, a formidable array of American seapower had gathered in lower Chesapeake Bay just south of the Potomac River. The occasion was to witness the shelling of this old battleship that had participated in the Cuban campaign of the Spanish-American War. The vessel was the *Texas* that had become outmoded and considered of no further military value. So she was selected

The battleship *Texas* was a strong arm of the United States Navy. After becoming the target ship *San Marcos* in 1911, she remained a menace to navigation in the Bay until 1959. Photo: The Mariners Museum

as a target ship and given the resisting power of a first-class battleship to determine how much shell fire such a vessel could withstand. She was renamed *San Marcos* and towed to the area southwest of Tangier Island.

Most of the war vessels at the gathering were merely serving as witnesses to the shelling that the battleship *New Hampshire* was to deal out to the *San Marcos*. High government officials, reporters and cameramen were there to get a first-hand view of Navy gunnery.

After 42 salvos from the *New Hampshire,* which was about 7½ miles northwest of the target, the *San Marcos* was boarded to determine the extent of the damage. The vessel was a total wreck—her bottom had been shot away entirely and above deck was a shambles.

It was determined immediately that the old hulk could never be raised and would have to remain where she was. After settling on the bottom in about 30 feet of water, a considerable part of the vessel projected above the surface. At that time it was suggested that she might be blown up with dynamite but, due to the shallowness of the water, it was felt that small vessels would be in danger of having their bottoms torn out should this means be adopted. So it was decided to leave her as is, indicating her position on charts and placing a lighted buoy at the site to mark her as a menace to navigation.

In 1921 the *San Marcos* did further yeoman service for her country by acting as a target in an experiment by General Billy Mitchell to prove that battleships could be sunk by air power. At the same time, the battleships *Indiana* and *Alabama* were also sunk in the Bay. In 1924 the three vessels were offered for sale "as is—where is." The Merritt Chapman Scott Company bid in all three vessels but requested permission from the Army Engineers to remove only the *Indiana* and *Alabama.* The *San Marcos* was returned to the government and the other two vessels were eventually raised and scrapped.

In 1940 some 200 linear feet of the *San Marcos* still projected from 2 to 6 feet above the water. No light was placed upon the wreck but a lighted buoy was situated nearby at varying distances—at times, 500 to 1,500 feet, and again as much as 2 miles from the wreck.

During the winter of 1939-40 there was a severe cold spell that resulted in a great deal of ice forming in Chesapeake Bay. Navigation was seriously impaired and in a great part, halted. On January 28, 1940, the U. S. Coast Guard removed the buoy which marked the *San Marcos* because the light had become heavily encrusted with ice and was practically capsized. An unlighted nun buoy was put in its place to serve as a marker and the change was noted in *Notice to Mariners*. All of this was preliminary to a tragic shipwreck that was to follow.

At that time, the Baltimore, Crisfield & Onancock Line was operating the 120-foot Diesel freighter *Lexington* between Baltimore, Crisfield and Onancock. Due to severe ice conditions, the *Lexington* had been out of service temporarily but, by February 26, she resumed her trade because ice conditions had improved. She made three trips per week, running by night from Baltimore to Crisfield, by day from Crisfield to Onancock, and by night from Onancock to Baltimore.

In late afternoon on March 27, 1940, the *Lexington* departed from Onancock with a cargo of canned goods and general cargo for Baltimore. The vessel was in charge of her mate, I. W. Scott, who, after reaching the buoys at the entrance to Onancock Creek about 7 P.M., turned the vessel over to her master, an old hand on the Bay. The captain set his course expecting to pass about 500 yards southerly of the *San Marcos,* his intention being to reach the main channel in the Chesapeake and run up to Baltimore west of Tangier Island.

It was flood tide, the sky was overcast and visibility poor. Tangier Sound Lighthouse was seen for a time and then lost to view; no other lights to the west were visible. Since the *Lexington* was heavily loaded and it was desired to reach Baltimore in time to connect with the Merchants & Miners steamer, she was pushed at full speed.

After running for about 65 minutes from bell-buoy 2-N, the ship's captain considered that he had run 10 minutes past the wreck. He failed to see a light where the *San Marcos* buoy should have been and was not aware that a nun buoy had replaced the lighted marker.

As he prepared to alter his course to the northward up the Bay, the *Lexington* ran hard upon the wreck. The freighter was badly holed and, within 30 minutes, had disappeared beneath the waters. The crew, however, had lowered the lifeboat and transferred themselves dry-shod to the *San Marcos* from which they were taken by a passing vessel the following morning. The *Lexington* was a total loss, settling alongside the southwest side of the *San Marcos* with 13 feet of water over her highest part.

A suit against the U. S. Government followed the collision. The plaintiff argued that the United

States, as owner of the *San Marcos,* was liable to protect the public from injury by this public vessel. They also claimed further negligence of the United States by the failure of the Coast Guard to replace the lighted buoy within a reasonable amount of time after ice conditions had cleared up.

It was finally decided that the *San Marcos* had lost her identity as a "vessel" and was merely a "pile of junk" on the bottom of the Bay and the government could not be responsible for the wreck of the *Lexington.* As for replacing the light, is was stated that the Coast Guard started in late February to replace many buoys that had been damaged or removed due to ice conditions. Their plans called for restoration of the main channel buoys first and then other buoys in such order as the Commander of the district deemed most wise. The *San Marcos* buoy had not been replaced prior to March 27 when the *Lexington* ran into the wreck. It was actually replaced on April 4, 1940.

The government contended that the navigation of the *Lexington* was exceedingly negligent, resulting in the loss of the ship and cargo. She carried no lookout, her searchlight was inoperative, and she was running at forced speed on a murky night. Her master knew that lights had been extinguished but failed to inform himself about which lights had been extinguished. The suit was dismissed in favor of the government.

In September 1948, the *San Marcos* again figured in the wrecking of a vessel, a yacht from Urbanna, Virginia. The craft was returning to home port after a visit to Tangier Island. She was owned jointly by two yachtsmen who took turns taking the boat out. On this occasion, the operator of the yacht laid out a course from Tangier Sound Lighthouse after assuming a 10-degree error in his compass which would have brought him down to a buoy on the southerly end of the channel.

The day was clear and hot with a glare on the water. Sighting a buoy as he approached the site of the *San Marcos* wreck, he took it to be nun buoy 6; actually, the buoy he saw was the *San Marcos* wreck buoy. Shortly after, the yacht came to a sickening halt as she grated on an underwater obstruction. The yacht was holed and filled.

It developed that the boat had been operating with a 10-degree error on its compass. The other partner had corrected the error but neglected to inform his co-owner that the compass was now accurate. The additional 10-degree correction made in the compass brought the craft down on the *San Marcos* wreck buoy instead of the buoy he had hoped to see. A complaint was registered

but the court dismissed the testimony in the findings.

Following this stranding, it was suggested that the remaining superstructure of the *San Marcos* should be blown away until there was a clearance of not less than three fathoms over it. An employee of the Baltimore District Engineers' office made an inspection of the wreck and recommended the erection of a fixed structure on the wreck. A lighthouse engineer, sent to inspect the hulk, determined that it would not support a lighthouse and it would be necessary to drive caissons in order to display such a light. The estimated cost of such a structure was about $30,000. The wreck was not removed and no lighthouse was constructed at the site.

On the night of October 15, 1949, the 66-foot powerboat *T. H. Anderson,* laden with 2,200 bushels of seed oysters was proceeding from the vicinity of Windmill Point, on the western shore of Virginia, towards Tangier Sound. The master of the vessel, a veteran Bay skipper, had been up the night before, so about 2 A.M., at a point about 1½ miles northeast of Windmill Point, he turned the craft over to his colored mate. Instructions were given him to steer NEbyE and to call the captain at Tangier Sound Lighthouse.

The course would have taken the *Anderson* at least one-half mile southerly of the wreck buoy. As the powerboat approached the wreck buoy from the southwest, the mate identified it. As it was dead ahead, he decided not to go to the south but to the north of the buoy, leaving it on his starboard side, and changing his course from NEbyE to north a little west. After following this altered course for about one-quarter mile and trying to turn back to his NEbyE course, he ran afoul of the *San Marcos.* The *Anderson* was badly damaged and held firmly in place on the wreck. The men were rescued later in the day but the vessel became a total loss.

A suit was brought against the government by the owners of the *Anderson* but they failed to win a claim. It was decided that at the time of the boat's stranding she was not in charge of a competent helmsman and the stranding was caused by the change in course to be pursued. It later developed that the mate was not qualified to read or understand a chart, or to lay out a proper course to be steered. He was cross-eyed and had been rejected by the Army in 1943 because of poor eyesight.

It had been argued that the buoy marking this danger was situated too far from the wreck. In

February 1950, the distance of the buoy was measured and found to be 175 yards, 233 degrees true, from the nearest part of the wreck. The argument in favor of this was that in order to service and replace such a buoy, which weighed from 8 to 10 tons, a large buoy tender about 180 feet in length must approach the buoy against the tide. The vessel must have sufficient seaway in its servicing of the buoy, especially in rough seas and open waters. The *San Marcos* was submerged for a length of 300 feet. After the stranding of the *Anderson,* the buoy was moved closer, within 225 feet of the wreck.

With further deliberation the United States Court of Appeals reversed the original decision of the District Court and held that the United States Government as well as the owners of the *Anderson* was at fault in the loss of the vessel. As a result the damages were assessed and divided between the government and the operators of the powerboat. The court asserted that in the balancing of the two social interests involved, the convenience of the Coast Guard in servicing the buoy and the safety of maritime navigation, they strongly favored the latter.

There was certainly good reason to consider the *San Marcos* a prime menace to navigation. Prior to 1944, about 200 feet of the superstructure of the wreck was well above the surface but in more recent years it was just about submerged, except at low tide. It seemed that since the hulk was fully submerged even more careful navigation was necessary as ships approached the area.

In October 1958 plans were undertaken to remove the hulk. Preliminary tests showed that it could be lowered 15 to 20 feet in the Bay's bottom by using dynamite. After three weeks, having used some 23,500 pounds of explosives, Navy demolition teams failed to achieve their objective.

Efforts were resumed again in February 1959. In one of the last blasts on that try, when about 1,500 pounds of explosives were used, a trench was created on the Bay's bottom in which the remnants of the hulk settled. At that time it was reported that at mean low water there would be 20 feet of clearance above the twisted remains.

The *San Marcos* is said to have been responsible for seven shipwrecks since she was abandoned in Chesapeake Bay. The wreck still appears on the 1962 charts of that area indicating that nun and can buoys mark the presence of the menace. A special note also informs the navigator that the depth is subject to change because of shifting steel and there is danger of unexploded bombs and shells.

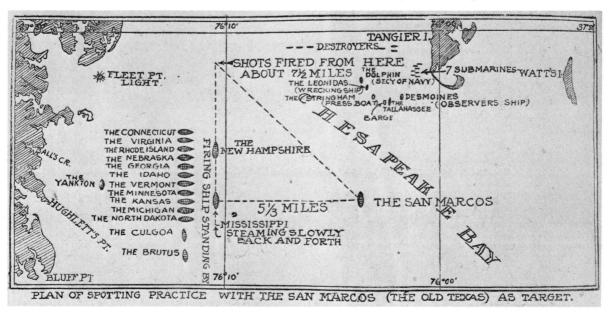

PLAN OF SPOTTING PRACTICE WITH THE SAN MARCOS (THE OLD TEXAS) AS TARGET.

Photo: The Mariners Museum

Nautical Monster
of an Age

IN THE summer of 1860, Chesapeake Bay played host to the largest ship built up to that time. Such a colossal vessel was she that she exceeded anything in size on the seas in displacement tonnage until the ill-famed *Lusitania* was built in 1906. Known as the *Great Eastern*, she was five times the size of the largest vessel then afloat.

As she lay at anchor off Annapolis, countless Baltimoreans were excitedly making preparations to go on one of the many excursions offered to take them down the Bay to see the giant British iron-hulled liner.

The *Great Eastern* was called a screw and paddle bark, having a combination of paddle wheels, propeller, and 6 masts carrying 6500 square yards of sail. One engine turned the 58-foot diameter paddle wheels and another drove the 24-foot diameter propeller, both developing 2600 horsepower. Her massive propeller was only matched in 1958 when a super tanker was launched with one of equal size. *Lloyd's Register of Shipping* indicated that she had a length of 679.6 feet, 82.8 feet in breadth, and 31.6 feet in depth. Over her side-wheel guards she measured 120 feet. She was of 22,500 tons displacement.

The *Great Eastern* was launched in England in January 1858 after several years of building. She was the heaviest object ever moved by man on land up to that time. When she resisted several attempts to get her afloat under normal launching procedures, she was finally pushed into the Thames River by the use of hydraulic rams.

The ship was designed to carry 4,000 passengers, almost twice as many as the liner *Queen Mary* can accommodate today.

Before putting to sea she was opened to sightseers. It was not until September 1859 that she was actually ready for her maiden voyage, but a severe explosion on board delayed her initial sail-

ing. While repairs were being effected, the vessel was again thrown open to the paying public.

In May 1860 the *Great Eastern* lay at Southampton ready to cross the Atlantic. Eight large American cities, including Baltimore, were vying for the honor of becoming her port of entry. New York was selected as her first port of call.

For this momentous voyage she carried but 43 persons as passengers and 418 crew members. In mid-Atlantic a half gale was encountered and despite ominous warnings from many that she would break in half in heavy weather, she only rolled and pitched and continued on her westward passage. On June 28 the ship sailed up New York harbor and was given a rousing welcome. There she was thrown open to the public for exhibition and the metropolitan area seemed to go mad over the monstrous ship.

In late July 1860, the ship advertised a two-day cruise to Cape May, New Jersey, for $10. Two thousand passengers took advantage of the opportunity to go to sea on the iron monster. But on the first night out they discovered that there were sleeping quarters for only 300. Actually, the ship came down to Chesapeake Bay and anchored off Old Point Comfort, Virginia, where she proved to be a great attraction.

Upon her return to New York, it was advertised that she was to make an excursion to Annapolis Roads. This was pushed by a group of Baltimore merchants who wanted to have the huge vessel make Baltimore a port of call.

This second American cruise drew only 100 paying guests. At 6 P.M. on August 2, the *Great Eastern* departed from New York and reached Hampton Roads the next evening after a pleasant run down the coast. Anchored off Old Point Comfort, she again created great excitement.

After a successful stay in Virginia waters, the *Great Eastern* left Old Point Comfort on August

5 for her historic passage up Chesapeake Bay to Annapolis where she was to receive the greatest reception awarded her in American waters. Under the watchful eyes of a Baltimore pilot, the ship steamed out through the Virginia Capes again in order to turn around and get into the proper channel to continue her voyage to Annapolis.

tisements were inserted to tell of excursions by water and rail to Annapolis.

The Baltimore and Ohio Railroad ran three trains daily to Annapolis from Baltimore. It also issued round-trip tickets from all points on the route from Washington and Wheeling at one-half the usual fare, adding thereto $2 for the boat trip

An actual photograph of the *Great Eastern* showing the tremendous size of the ship.
Photo: The Mariners Museum

She had many consorts up the Bay but none could keep apace with her as her huge paddle wheels and propeller threshed the quiet waters of the Chesapeake. Off the Patuxent River the steamer *George Peabody,* one of the latest and fastest steamboats of that time, met the great ship with a large number of passengers and a welcoming committee made up of dignitaries. But the *Great Eastern,* making 15 knots, passed the *Peabody* and left her far astern as she proceeded up to Annapolis Roads.

No Chesapeake maritime event, before or since, has attracted the number of people as did the visit of the *Great Eastern.* During her stay off Annapolis, the Baltimore newspapers, the *Sun* and *Baltimore Daily and Commercial Advertiser,* devoted their lead columns to the ship. Numerous adver-

from Annapolis to the *Great Eastern* and admission aboard the ship. At Annapolis the passengers were transferred to the steamboat *Lancaster* which was gaily decorated with flags and streamers. A company of strolling harpers and other musicians were aboard to delight the passengers. The North Central Railroad also issued round-trip tickets between Baltimore and all points on their run at half fare.

Numerous steamboats took viewers from Baltimore down the Chesapeake. The steamers *George Peabody, Pocahontas, Juniata,* and *Belvedere* of the Powhatan Steamboat Company charged 50 cents for the trip down to Annapolis Roads, circling the *Great Eastern* several times, and return to Baltimore. The steamers *Star* and *St. Michaels* were also employed in this manner. The steam-

31

boat *Cecil* had special excursions at 40 cents a round trip, featured a brass band, and advertised the privilege of their passengers to view the "second wonder of naval architecture," Winan's cigar-shaped steamer then under construction in Baltimore. The *Great Eastern* was considered the "first wonder."

The steamboat *Virginia* advertised the "Great Eastern Concert" with the Union Cornet and Orchestral Band on board, leaving Light Street for the *Great Eastern* and Winan's steamer. Even sailing vessels got in on the act. The fast sailing packet *Joe Hunter* left Brown's Wharf daily at 7 A.M. for the *Great Eastern* at 50 cents a round trip. No consideration was announced in the event of a head wind or calm which might delay its passage.

The best trip offered was that of the Baltimore Steam Packet Company on their steamers *Adelaide, Louisiana, Philadelphia,* and *Georgeanna* from Baltimore. That company had the sole franchise to permit passengers from Baltimore steamboats to board the *Great Eastern*—all for the total cost of $1.50 the round trip. Five trips were made each day from Baltimore by these vessels.

To transfer the passengers to the giant liner the steamboat would lie alongside the ship and place a gangway into one of the lower gangway ports of the *Great Eastern.* As soon as the passengers landed on the big vessel, they were left to shift for themselves since there were no guides.

On August 7 it was reported that between 9 and 10 thousand persons had visited the steamer. A contemporary newspaper describes the scene: ". . . the spacious decks and saloon were as lively as Baltimore Street upon a good promenading afternoon in autumn." Actually, there appear to have been poor regulations concerning the movements of the passengers when they were aboard the ship. The captain was not held to blame but the directors of the company were held liable as they ". . . displayed the ship as would Barnum an elephant." Accommodations were lacking and only warm drinking water was available. Provisions could be secured at advanced rates and ice could be had only if drinks were purchased at the bar.

Each day the number of visitors increased. The excursion steamers were uncomfortably crowded. Trains that left Camden Street had standing room only. One, with 13 cars attached, had 9 of those cars destined for Annapolis with sightseers. Stops were made all along the route and the heavy load delayed the engine. At Annapolis there was only one place to discharge and a panic ensued as the passengers rushed for places on the steamer to take them out into Annapolis Roads.

The master of the *Great Eastern,* Captain J. Vine Hall, came up to Baltimore on the steamer *Philadelphia.* His first visit in the city was to the top of Washington Monument, at his request, so that he could see Baltimore. During his stay there he visited Coleman and Bailey's establishment and Winan's boat. From Baltimore he went over to Washington to call upon President James Buchanan and invited him to the *Great Eastern.*

On August 9 the President of the United States and his suite journeyed to Annapolis by special train where he was greeted by President Garrett of the Baltimore and Ohio Railroad. Then the party proceeded to the Naval Academy to board the steamer *Anacostia* for the *Great Eastern* where they were received by Maryland's Governor Hicks. Captain Hall conducted a two-hour tour of the ship before the President departed for Washington.

The visit of Buchanan had a tendency to draw more visitors to the ship. Daily the ads in the papers increased in number. Page 2 of *The Sun* for August 8, 1860, was a complete ad headed by the slogan—"Ho! For the Steamship *Great Eastern.*" Other ads proclaimed the *Great Eastern* "The Great Maritime Wonder of the Deep," "The Nautical Monster of the Age," and "Possibly the Marvel of an Era Never to Be Equalled Again."

In an attempt to entice the large ship to make Baltimore her American port of call, local capitalists and the Baltimore and Ohio Railroad offered the *Great Eastern* 2500 tons of coal. Of this amount President Garrett of the railroad promised 1000 tons. A fleet of scows and sailing craft were employed to transport the coal to the ship from this port. Laborers then carried the coal aboard the liner in baskets. But the ship never did come to Baltimore.

At 6 A.M. on August 11, the *Great Eastern* departed from Annapolis Roads for New York City. After a brief stay there the steamer left for Halifax, Nova Scotia, a port clamoring to see the big vessel. But port charges there were so excessive the *Great Eastern* departed for England the morning after her arrival.

The *Great Eastern* had a lengthy career but a tragic one. Through the ensuing years, according to a best-seller book about the vessel published in 1953 and entitled *The Great Iron Ship,** she killed

---

* *The Great Iron Ship,* by James Dugan; Harper & Row, Publishers, Incorporated.

her designer, ruined her builder, drowned her first captain, bankrupted 7 companies, survived one of the Atlantic's weirdest storms, lost 2,000,000 British pounds, injured hundreds and killed 35 men, laid the first Atlantic cable and 5 other submarine cables, caused 13 major lawsuits, attracted 2,000,000 visitors, gave New York one of its wildest parties, collided with 7 ships, sinking 4, started international quarrels, made 6 knights, was not outbuilt for 49 years, was auctioned off 6 times and ended her days as a floating circus.

She was finally sold for breaking up and the dismantling began on the first day of 1889, a month short of 31 years after her launching. About two years were required to reduce the vessel to scrap. She was a vessel too far advanced for her day.

Looking aft on the spacious deck of the *Great Eastern*. From *Illustrated London News*, 1859—The Mariners Museum

Parson of the Islands

TO THE natives of the islands of lower Chesapeake Bay—Deal, Tangier, and Smith—the memory of a plain man of great energy and profound faith is revered to this day, although he died more than one hundred years ago. Joshua Thomas was his name.

Thomas is said to have been responsible for establishing Methodism as the deep-rooted faith of the Chesapeake islanders. After more than a century and a quarter, the religious impact he made upon the people is evident today.

Thomas had a humble beginning but he left his mark in the world. In many quarters his name ranks with those of a more illustrious origin. During World War II, when America was in the midst of a huge shipbuilding program, many vessels were given the names of prominent educators, statesmen, and other dignitaries. The name of Joshua Thomas was so highly respected that in 1943 a Liberty ship bearing his name was launched at Fairfield, Baltimore.

Thomas was born in a section known as Potato Neck, Somerset County, Maryland, on August 30, 1776. His father died when Joshua was but a baby and his mother remarried several years later. That second union was not too successful and young Joshua and his brother, having become expert fishermen, helped maintain their home on Tangier Island. Such responsibilities probably molded his character and inspired him to become a leader of the people.

Joshua's mother shared her Christian learning with her children and this had a dynamic effect upon the boy. It is said that he never went fishing without bringing back a good supply of fish. He revealed that his secret was in praying to be directed where the fish might be found.

As he grew older, religion took a greater hold on him. When he was 23 years old, he married, established a home on Tangier Island, and fished and hunted for a livelihood.

At that time Tangier Islanders were attached to the Old Episcopal Church which they attended on the mainland at Annamessex and Pungoteague, Virginia. Methodism began to arouse the people in various neighborhoods and preachers penetrated the Eastern Shore. Revivals were held, prayer meetings started, and societies formed. The islanders, however, held themselves aloof at first and shunned the people called Methodists.

Visiting ministers would preach on the islands and Joshua Thomas was selected to bring a parson over from the mainland on one occasion. Subjected to the minister and his teachings, Thomas gradually became attached to the Methodist Church. He sent to Baltimore for a Bible and after learning to read passages therefrom he became more active in the field.

In 1807 Thomas attended a camp meeting near Pungoteague and was converted shortly thereafter. Later he inaugurated prayer meetings among his neighbors on Tangier and Smith Islands who had now accepted Methodism.

During the War of 1812, the British forces made Tangier Island their center of operations while Chesapeake Bay was being ravaged. When they first landed on the island, they appeared as all invaders—arrogant and possessive. Joshua Thomas represented his people as spokesman and persuaded the commanding officer to forbid his men to molest the islanders or destroy their property. He even ventured to hold a religious meeting in the wardroom of one of the British ships and visited the fleet often while the vessels were moored off Tangier.

In Adam Wallace's *The Parson of the Islands,**

---

* Reprinted in 1961 by Cornell Maritime Press, Inc., Cambridge, Maryland.

34

Thomas' famous delivery before the British Army prior to their departure to attack Baltimore is described. "Towards the close of summer, in the year 1814, we were made aware of some important movement among the forces encamped on the island. Preparations began both on shore and through the fleet in the harbor. . . . Some of the officers told me the cause of all this—they were going to take Baltimore. I told them they had better let it alone; they might be mistaken in their calculations for the Baltimoreans would resist them and fight hard for their city and their homes. . . . Before they left Tangier they sent me word to be ready to hold a public meeting and exhort the soldiers on the campground. I did not like to refuse, and yet I was very unwilling to perform this duty.

"It was arranged to be on the last Sunday they were in camp. Early that morning the flags were hoisted, the drums beat, and every preparation was made for a full turnout. At the hour appointed the soldiers were all drawn up in solid columns, about 12,000 men, under the pines of the old camp grounds. . . . As I looked around on my congregation I never had such a feeling in my life but I felt determined to give them a faithful warning even if those officers with their keen, glittering swords, would cut me in pieces for speaking the truth. . . . I warned them of the danger and distress they would bring upon themselves and others by going to Baltimore with the object they had in view. . . . I told them it was given me from the Almighty that they could not take Baltimore and would not succeed in the expedition."

Thomas persisted throughout his sermon that the British would not take Baltimore even though their forces had met little resistance elsewhere on the Chesapeake. Naturally, the warning had little effect upon the soldiers. The fleet weighed anchor and sailed up the Bay, leaving the islanders to await the outcome.

After their unsuccessful siege at Baltimore, remnants of the British forces returned to Tangier Island. Thomas met some of the officers and asked if they had taken Baltimore. They informed the islanders that their loss was great and the outcome of the battle was just as Thomas had prophesied. Many of the soldiers admitted that all the time they were fighting they thought of Thomas' warning against their attempt to take Baltimore. Psychologically, Thomas' prediction of the failure of the British to take the city may have had a great deal to do with their downfall.

Peace came to the island in 1815 as Joshua Thomas continued his good work. About 1825, he and his large family moved to Little Deal Island, Maryland. By then he had been ordained a deacon in the church and became the successor of a local minister. Thomas extended his visits into the interior of the Eastern Shore delivering his sermons. In addition, he owned a small trading craft in which he made trips to various sections of the Eastern Shore exchanging commodities and seafood.

He assumed more responsibilities in the church and, on occasion, preached in Baltimore before most receptive audiences. But he flourished on the Eastern Shore and the islands of the Chesapeake.

Sketch of the log canoe *Methodist* used by Rev. Joshua Thomas in his circuit of the Chesapeake. From *The Parson of the Islands,* by Adam Wallace

One of the highlights in Thomas' career was his obtaining the log canoe which he named *Methodist,* the most famous craft of its type ever built in the Chesapeake Bay country. About twenty-eight feet long, this was one of two canoes hewed out of a tree that was so large it was considered a curiosity. The tree had long been offered for sale but no one could be found who cared to purchase and fell it. Finally, it was bought for $10 by a man who felled it single-handedly. It is said that as it fell it sounded like the roar and reverberation of heavy ordnance and shook the ground for miles around.

In the *Methodist* Thomas would sail to his circuit of islands in the Bay attending camp meetings and delivering his sermons. His following was tremendous. In 1850 a church was built at Deal Island replacing the campground on that island which had been subject to erosion. Shortly after the erection of the church Joshua Thomas preached his last regular public address.

By then Thomas had become a helpless cripple.

To enable him to attend church a small carriage was constructed for his use and pulled by his family. With the passing years his feebleness increased and, on October 8, 1853, he died at the age of 77, bringing an end to a fabulous career. He was buried beside the little church built only a few years before. That building, now called the Joshua Thomas Chapel, and the tomb can be seen on Deal Island, Maryland, today. In the chapel are the original mourner's bench and pulpit.

Many of Joshua Thomas' descendants still live on the Eastern Shore. At Chance, near Deal Island, is a great-granddaughter, Mrs. Thomas H. Price. In her possession is an armchair that belonged to her renowned ancestor; also an actual photograph of him, said to be the only one in existence.

On Deal Island, Mrs. Robert Jones has the Bible used by Thomas in the chapel and on his trips to the Bay islands. Descendants of Thomas had lived with her father, T. P. Bradshaw, and it was passed on to her. Other descendants live on Deal Island, in Salisbury, Maryland, and in Baltimore.

Down in Onancock, Virginia, another great-granddaughter of Thomas resides. She is Mrs. James N. Belote. A great-grandson, Fred Thomas, lives at Keller, Virginia. Their father fell heir to the famous log canoe *Methodist* and Mrs. Belote recalls sailing in it on Pungoteague Creek when she was a young lady. In her possession is a sail attributed to the *Methodist* when Joshua Thomas sailed the craft.

Mystery surrounds the disappearance of the *Methodist*. Mrs. Belote recalls that her father was asked to send the canoe to Norfolk for display at the Jamestown Tercentenary in 1907. She reports that it reached that area but was destroyed when a warehouse in which it was stored was burned.

The name of Joshua Thomas is still highly revered on the islands of the lower Bay and the immediate mainland of the Eastern Shore. The impression he made upon his followers of a century and more ago has been handed down through the generations. He is spoken of today as though he still moves among the people.

Rev. Joshua Thomas preaching to the British Army on Tangier Island in 1814. From *The Parson of the Islands,* by Adam Wallace

36

Lazaretto Light of Baltimore

LIGHTHOUSES are romantic structures. They are usually the last land-bound objects a seaman sees when his ship makes its departure for an off-shore voyage and keenly anticipated by the in-bound seafarer when his ship approaches a coast.

Baltimore once had a lighthouse all its own. In the mid-nineteenth century many a Chesapeake seaman sailing up the Patapsco River after a long sea passage anxiously sought its beams. This was the lighthouse at Lazaretto Point, built in 1831 and situated in lower Canton, opposite Fort McHenry.

Lazaretto Light, a tapering, cylindrical brick tower, marked the entrance to Baltimore harbor and was once considered a major aid to navigation. The tower stood for 95 years before it was considered obsolete.

In 1911 it was proposed to remove Lazaretto Light and erect a new one at Fort McHenry. The Society of the War of 1812 backed the movement to preserve the old structure if such a move materialized. However, nothing was done other than to change the characteristics of the light from a revolving to a fixed beam.

In 1926 it was announced that the old tower was to be dismantled since factories built in the surrounding area had obscured the range of the light down the Patapsco River. In its place a steel skeleton tower would be erected with a light displayed from its top. The new tower was to be constructed closer to the water's edge. It was stated that space was needed to erect a Radio Laboratory and office building. Plans were formulated that spring and the skeleton tower was completed in the summer. On September 29, 1926, the light from the new tower was displayed for the first time and, after 95 years of uninterrupted service, the light in the old tower ceased to function. With the new light in operation, dismantling of the brick tower began as soon as the lens was removed. The

walls at the base were 3½ feet thick but they soon fell before the wrecker's maul.

Lazaretto had an interesting background. The point got its name from the lazaretto, or pest house, that previously occupied the site and where small-pox patients were treated. In 1801 the Maryland Legislature authorized the building of a lazaretto at what were then the eastern limits of the city.

The property was eventually transferred from the Treasury Department to the Lighthouse Service and at one time the latter organization maintained and repaired navigational aids for the 5th District, made up of the Baltimore, Norfolk, and Carolina Sound areas. It later came under the jurisdiction of the United States Coast Guard and served as a supply depot for lights, tenders, and lighthouses on Chesapeake Bay from the Potomac River to the Chesapeake and Delaware Canal.

Lazaretto Light figured in a hoax believed to have been perpetrated by Edgar Allan Poe. It is said that he visited Baltimore shortly after the light-house was constructed. Word was circulated that a man was to fly the 2½-mile distance between Lazaretto Light and the Baltimore Shot Tower. A crowd gathered to witness the event. After hours of weary waiting, it occurred to someone that it was April Fool's Day. Poe was blamed for the joke on the public. Lazaretto Light is believed to have stirred Poe to write his unfinished story, *The Lighthouse*.

The old tower should have been preserved, if for no other reason than that it was the last such structure intact in the Baltimore area. The old towers at Bodkin and North points, marking the Patapsco River, had been abandoned earlier. Lazaretto Light was the most interesting landmark bordering the harbor, excepting Fort McHenry.

It is interesting to contemplate the old tower's association with the development of Baltimore.

37

Consider the countless vessels, many now famous for the part they played in building up our sea trade, that the lighthouse had guided into the harbor. It could have served as a monument to Baltimore's ships and seamen of the past. Instead it was converted into rubble and a locker room, part of the office building erected on the site, stood where the brick tower once did duty.

The red beam from the tower at Lazaretto was to be seen across the harbor and down the Patapsco River until 1954. The average person would never recognize it as a navigational aid, however, since the skeleton tower bore no resemblance to a lighthouse, and any romance associated with Lazaretto passed on with the old tower.

In 1958 the entire establishment at Lazaretto was sold for commercial use and the navigational aid operations formerly carried on there were transferred to the Coast Guard base in Curtis Bay, Baltimore.

Lazaretto Lighthouse, built in 1831 and in service in Baltimore harbor until 1926.
Photo: C. C. Knobeloch

The *Purnell T. White* Comes Home to Die

FROM 1934 to 1957 a sailing vessel remained in a Locust Point ship graveyard in Baltimore. She was burdened with one of the heaviest loads any ship of comparable size probably has been called upon to bear. Her hold and deck filled to capacity, this vessel had no destination and was never to depart from port. It was the hulk of a once well-known four-masted schooner that lay half buried beneath hundreds of tons of dirt and refuse.

The schooner was the *Purnell T. White*. In 1934, she was dismasted at sea while bound from Georgetown, South Carolina, to New York with a cargo of lumber. That buoyant cargo kept the schooner afloat so that she could be towed to port. It would have been a more deserving fate if the *White* had gone to the bottom of the sea. The indignities the schooner endured after being salvaged were not befitting a vessel of her former beauty.

The *Purnell T. White* was a product of the World War I shipbuilding boom and was one of eight four-masted schooners ever to have been built in Maryland. Constructed at Sharptown, Maryland, the *White* was launched in 1917 for Captain

The graceful *Purnell T. White* discharging a cargo of lumber at Baltimore in 1931.
Photo: Author

R. B. White, of Baltimore. Though small in size for a four-masted schooner, being only 185 feet in length, she was a profitable vessel and never seemed to lack cargoes during her career.

Her maiden voyage was one of her most lengthy ones, taking her across the Atlantic. In the latter part of 1917 she loaded 700 tons of railroad material and a quantity of general cargo at New York for delivery to Boma, Africa. The latter port is situated at the mouth of the Congo River and was the former capital of the Belgian Congo. Ninety days were required to complete that leg of the voyage which was made without mishap.

The *Purnell T. White* running under bare poles before a northeast gale off Cape Hatteras, North Carolina, 1933. Photo: J. S. McCullough

The Congo area had a bad reputation among seafaring men because of the fevers contracted there. Due to poor facilities at Boma, the *White* was in port longer than was good for her crew. After she was unloaded, a cargo of copal—a resin used in the manufacture of varnish—was put aboard for the return trip to New York.

The results of that first voyage were to label the schooner around the Baltimore waterfront as a "jinx ship." After departing from Boma, her master, Captain Ward, died from African fever and was buried at sea. Two days after reaching port, her cook was found murdered in the ship's galley. Within the next seven years, two more of her captains died.

After that maiden voyage, the *White* generally confined her activities to the coastwise and West Indies trade transporting bulk cargoes. Occasionally she would encounter heavy weather which drove her far off her course and caused her to be listed in the local papers as overdue. On February 22, 1924, she left Turks Island, Bahamas, with a

cargo of salt for Baltimore. Weeks passed and she failed to be reported. On April 1, all hope for her safety was abandoned. Two days later, however, she was sighted off the Virginia coast with sails torn and considerable damage to her rigging. After the schooner was towed into Chesapeake Bay, her master, Captain George E. Fleming, told of battles with terrific gales that drove her far to sea.

Two years later she was caught in the path of a hurricane. Before reaching a haven at Morehead City, North Carolina, she had lost a complete suit of sails. In 1930 she experienced a stranding that resulted in minor damage only. That same year a storm drove her 800 miles off her course. But she always managed to make port.

She even made port after her most disastrous encounter with the sea. However, that marked the end of her seagoing career.

Under the command of Captain Charles Nicklas, of Westminster, Maryland, the *Purnell T. White* left Georgetown on January 27, 1934, with a cargo of lumber for New York. Off the Carolina coast she was buffeted by a winter gale that drove her off her course and ripped her sails. Two weeks later a passing steamer sighted her 200 miles east of Cape Fear River, North Carolina. The steamer altered her course to come within hailing distance and Captain Nicklas requested that a radio message be sent at once giving his position and asking for immediate assistance.

The *Purnell T. White* as abandoned in the ship graveyard at Locust Point, Baltimore. At left, dirt fill has covered the stern; eventually, it buried the vessel completely. Photo: Author

The message was intercepted in Norfolk and two Coast Guard cutters were sent in search of the stricken vessel. The cutter *Mendota* arrived on the scene first and took the *White* in tow for the Chesapeake Bay. Even at that time a storm was raging and the cutter and its tow labored in the heavy seas.

About 80 miles southeast of Cape Henry the waterlogged schooner developed a list. Distress flares were observed on the disabled craft, so the *Mendota* put back to take off the crew. Due to adverse weather conditions, which included a snowstorm, it was only with extreme difficulty that the schooner was found. As the cutter approached the stern of the foundering craft, lines were cast to the *White's* deck, one for each of the seven men in her crew.

The extreme cold caused the lines to become coated with ice. Cold and exposure had weakened Captain Nicklas and three of his crew to the extent that they were unable to cling to the lines and were lost over the side in the darkness. A life raft was thrown from the cutter and the three remaining seamen were rescued. A few minutes later, the *Purnell T. White* fell in a trough between two huge seas and capsized.

The *Mendota* raced to Norfolk with the survivors who were in need of immediate medical attention. The schooner was left to wallow in the busy coastal sea lanes, a menace to navigation. Two days after her capsizing the derelict was found by the Coast Guard cutter *Ponchartrain* and taken in tow to Norfolk.

The *White* was almost completely submerged. Only her forecastle head and poop jutted above the surface. After the tangle of rigging and wreckage had been cleared away and her hold pumped free of water, she was towed to Baltimore with her lumber cargo still below deck. Splintered stumps were all that remained of her masts. The after cabin had been swept away and her steering gear reduced to a mass of twisted metal. Fragments of sails and spars littered her deck.

After the lumber was discharged, her hull was surveyed for possible rerigging but the cost proved to be prohibitive. Except for a hole in her port quarter, the result of the cutter making contact with her when removing the schooner's crew, her hull was still stout. If she did not go to sea again under sail, perhaps she would resume her career in the capacity of a barge.

After lying in the harbor for several months, the *White* was sold and taken around to Locust Point. Even though she was in the ship's graveyard, she was not there to be abandoned. Her new owner had plans to fit her out as a barge. Carpenters boarded her and erected a new structure over the gaping hole where her after cabin once stood. For

a while the future looked bright for the old vessel, but the work was called to a halt and never resumed.

Apparently abandoned, the *White* eventually filled with water and settled to the bottom. However, her decks remained above the surface of the harbor. When World War II caused a shortage in shipping, her hull was examined for possible restoration to service. But after seven years of total neglect she was beyond resurrection.

The Locust Point ship graveyard was bounded by property owned by a railroad company which used the area as a dumping ground. When the *Purnell T. White* was towed to that site in 1934,

Figurehead of the *Purnell T. White* after being restored by the author. Photo: Wm. T. Radcliffe

she was some distance offshore and could be reached only by boat. But persistent dumping extended the shoreline out to the hulk, covering over all the other hulks in a line between the *White* and the original land. The dirt fill cascaded into her open hatches until she was completely burdened. Her keel was pressed deeper into the muddy bottom of the Patapsco River. Then the refuse mounted on her deck causing it to collapse in some places as the dirt reached a height of about 15 feet above the level of the deck. Her starboard side was completely buried, leaving a portion of her port bulwarks, poop, and forward sections exposed.

She had been used as a diving platform for neighborhood children who swam in the harbor. Frayed crabbing lines dangled from remnants of her once graceful stanchions. Her bow was set afire by a salvage company intent upon retrieving the huge metal windlass which remained intact.

There was no visible identification on the schooner's hulk—the painted names on her bows had long ago flaked off; the stern transom that once bore her name and home port of Salisbury was below the level of the beach; her nameboards had been removed. Even the one clue to her birthright, her official number #215687, once carved in the beam of her forward hatch, was no longer evident. On this same timber one could barely make out the figures of her tonnage.

In 1957, the Baltimore and Ohio Railroad decided to go ahead with plans to build a Fruit Terminal on that site. This called for a massive dredging job and removal of the hulks. The *White* was patched up, the dirt and debris removed from her

hold and deck, and a battery of gasoline engine driven pumps rigged up to free her of water.

To the amazement of all, the pumps kept ahead of the leakage and the bedraggled hulk became water-borne for the first time in 23 years! A tug then took her over on May 23, 1957, and several more miles of buoyant, if undignified, travel were added to the old ship's itinerary. Taken a few miles down the Patapsco River, a body of water over which she had entered and departed from Baltimore so proudly on countless occasions, she was put ashore at Hawkins Point, on the outskirts of Baltimore harbor, and left in the custody of a shipwrecking firm. Nothing further was done to reduce her timbers after that and she was left to go to pieces of her own accord. Her bones will long lurk beneath the surface.

The *Purnell T. White* is brought into Norfolk harbor—a dismasted hulk after capsizing at sea. Photo: Norfolk Newspapers

The Logwood Trade to the Bay

IN THE last days of coasting schooners operating on the American eastern seaboard, the chief cargoes transported by these vessels were of lumber, with coal and fertilizer acting as occasional payloads. These were unromantic commodities and fit in with the workaday world. But now and then a stray schooner would venture down into the West Indies, either light or with coal, and would return to the States with hold and deck stacked with a heavy, dark, gnarled wood, popularly called logwood.

It is interesting to note that this product which helped to keep some of the last large schooners on the seas was also one of the first valuable exports from the New World. For more than four centuries, logwood, *Haematoxylon campechianum* to druggists and botanists, has sailed the seas destined to be used in medicinal items and as a source of dye.

With the exception of sugar, no single commodity has played a greater part in Caribbean history than logwood.

It seems that logwood did not originate in the West Indies. After Columbus' expedition, grants of territory were issued to individuals. One of these grants on the mainland, within what is now called Mexico, was eventually called Campeche.

Looking forward on the deck of the Baltimore-owned four-masted schooner *Doris Hamlin* bound for Cap Haïtien, Haiti, for a cargo of logwood to deliver to Baltimore.
Photo: Author

43

There the Spaniards found certain trees whose hearts produced a dye. They gathered the wood and shipped it home.

For a long time the wood had no definite name. It was called by variations of its origin, what it was used for, or what it looked like. In the fifteenth and sixteenth centuries, the wood of various tropical trees that yielded a rich, red dye was known as Brazil wood.

Throughout the sixteenth century there was a regular trade in this commodity, especially to the Low Countries where it entered into the composition of most black dyes, particularly for cloth. By the 1550's it had become an article of Spanish contraband.

The best account of the early days of the logwood trade was written by William Dampier, a sailor, explorer, pirate, logwood cutter and, fortunately, a writer. His writings serve both as tales of adventure and as authoritative records of customs and places and are a reliable source of information on logwood.

In 1675 he asserted that after the English had taken Jamaica, they began to cruise in the Bay of Campeche and found many vessels laden with logwood. Unaware of the value of the wood, they either set the vessels adrift or burned them for their iron and fittings until a Captain James took a shipload of the logwood back to England where he planned to fit out the captured vessel as a privateer. The ship's cargo of wood was sold, bringing a handsome price. Thereafter, the English valued the product highly and sought out the wood in the Caribbean area.

Dampier claims that the logwood trade "had its rise from the decay of privateering for after Jamaica was well settled by the British, and a peace established with Spain, the privateers who had lived upon plundering the Spaniards were put to their shifts. Wanting subsistence they were forced either to go to Petit Guavas where the privateer trade still continued or into the Bay for logwood." Here they served as woodcutters.

About 1715 logwood started to appear on Jamaica. Soon after, Haiti and other islands were added to the planted areas to become sources of logwood. And through the years this heavy wood has left the islands in all types of ships bound for European and American ports.

As sail was waning, Baltimore and Chester, Pennsylvania, were usually the ports to which the logwood was taken. The former city offered almost a steady trade in this commodity to supply the huge dye works of the J. S. Young & Company. The four-masted schooners *G. A. Kohler, Doris Hamlin, Albert F. Paul,* and *Herbert L. Rawding* were variously employed transporting logwood into Baltimore during the last decade of coastal sail, 1932–1942. Cap Haïtien, Miragoâne, Port au Prince, and Fort Liberté were the chief loading ports in Haiti, and Black River in Jamaica.

In 1936 the author arrived in Cap Haïtien on the schooner *Doris Hamlin* which was to take on a cargo of logwood for delivery in Baltimore. There were no wharfage facilities at this West Indian port so the vessel anchored in the bay during her entire stay and the wood was lightered out to her in barges. Little time was lost in readying the schooner for her cargo. The crew removed the hatches, brought the dunnage on deck, and prepared the hold for the logwood.

The morning after the schooner's arrival in port a number of natives came alongside the vessel to start the loading detail. Stages were rigged on the starboard side so that the logwood could be passed up to the deck from the deeply laden barges far below the level of the schooner's deck.

During the schooner's absence the logwood had accumulated on shore having been brought to Cap Haïtien from the surrounding area by donkey, oxen, and native sloops. When the time arrived to start loading, the wood was weighed on large scales and then stacked in the barges or lighters. As the *Hamlin's* yawl boat towed the heavier laden barges out to the schooner, smaller, oar-propelled craft would take their positions at the loading site to take on logwood also destined for the schooner.

Alongside the schooner all effort was made to relieve the barge of its burden as quickly as possible to speed its return to shore for another load. As the barge was discharged, the logwood was piled on deck, to be lowered into the hold for proper stowage. The larger, heavier pieces came first, fitting along the keelson. These were followed by the smaller pieces filling all available space for the sake of full capacity and to prevent the cargo from shifting.

When the hold and 'tween decks were full, the hatches were sealed and caulked. Next came the deckload. In preparation for this the deck was swept and boards laid thereon to accommodate the wood. The deckload extended as high as six to eight feet above deck, making up almost a third of the entire load. Shorings came up from the bulwarks extending above the load to keep the wood inboard. When the deckload had reached its limit, heavy chains were placed athwartship to secure the logs for the sea passage.

Naturally, a high deckload would complicate the working of the ship to a certain degree. The fore and main sheet blocks were attached to lengths of chain to bring them up to the level of the deckload. This also necessitated the belaying of the sheets and halliards of the lower sails and topsails higher in the rigging. To ensure even footing for the crew as they went about their duties, planks were placed athwartship and fore and aft on the deckload.

It would require from two to four weeks to load one of these large schooners, depending upon the supply of logwood on hand and weather conditions. During that time, the Haitian natives could be studied with interest. They received about sixty cents a day for working from 6 A.M. to 6 P.M. with an hour for "nooning." Their clothes were a series of patches but their backs were strong and they were willing workers. If their songs and jovialities were indications of their feelings, they were a happy lot.

After a hard day's work they would use the nights for revelry. Into the late night the sound of tom-toms could be heard emanating from the mountains and, as the land breeze carried the sounds over the bay, it also wafted the fragrant, tropical aroma down from the verdant hills. Although but a few hundred miles from the American coast, one could be mentally transported to the darkest regions of Africa.

A cargo of this nature usually contained stowaways in the form of snakes, tarantulas, scorpions, centipedes, and monstrous cockroaches. Whenever the schooner entered colder climes, the tarantulas and scorpions sought the comfort of the after cabin. The occupants of the cabins seldom put on their shoes before shaking them. They knew from experience that a scorpion would often seek the dark recesses of one's footwear.

Cockroaches came aboard with each cargo, and such cockroaches—the flying variety! The sudden turning on of a light would cause a barrage of these insects to fly from all directions, striking anything in their path in an effort to reach a dark corner. Except for these slight discomforts, the trade was a romantic one.

The last schooners to bring logwood to this country were the *Anna R. Heidritter* and *Herbert L. Rawding*. In February 1942, the *Rawding*, in command of Captain Mitchell C. Decker, loaded at Cap Haïtien and left that port for Baltimore. She

successfully ran the screen of U-boats then ranging the east coast and delivered the logwood in good order.

While the *Rawding* was in Cap Haïtien, the *Heidritter* had been taking on logwood at Port au Prince. When loaded, she put to sea and had a good run up to the American coast, putting in at Charleston, South Carolina, about February 10. Her master fell ill and left the ship at that point. Captain Bennett D. Coleman, who had commanded the schooner from 1919 to 1941, joined the vessel to sail her to her destination at Chester.

Haitian natives pass up logwood from a barge to stages erected on the side of the *Doris Hamlin*. Photo: Author

Rounding up a new crew, Captain Coleman made ready for sea and anchored off Charleston Bar on February 25. On putting out to sea, the schooner hugged the Carolina coastline in order to avoid detection by submarines. The weather was against the vessel as she crept up the shore. On March 2, with the wind from an easterly direction and because of her proximity to the beach, she anchored. Heavy weather set in and, though she had two anchors on the bottom, she started to drag toward the shore. One of the anchors parted and it was replaced with a smaller type. But the chains parted under the strain of the heavily laden schooner and the vessel dragged stern to the beach of Ocracoke, North Carolina. The seas washed over her and it was not until the following day that the crew was rescued by breeches buoy. An unfortunate sequel to this event was that, although Captain Coleman survived the stranding, he was killed a little more than a week later in an automobile accident at Newark, New Jersey.

Although the *Heidritter* was a total loss, a portion of her cargo was salvaged. A. W. Drinkwater of Manteo, North Carolina, purchased the cargo of 960 tons of logwood for $50 from the Boston Insurance Company. He recovered about 30 tons of the deckload and reshipped it by boat to Chester, where it sold for $37 a ton. He claimed that about 900 tons remained buried in the sands of Ocracoke beach but it is doubtful if it will ever be salvaged.

Due to the durability of this wood, it has been put to some strange uses along the Hatteras coastline. Some logs serve as fence posts; others for marking graves. One man at Ocracoke had a bed made from part of the *Heidritter's* cargo.

During peacetime these voyages were not out-standingly profitable although the schooners did make money for their owners. With the advent of World War II the freight rates increased enormously. In July 1940, the *Albert F. Paul* took on a cargo of 934.71 gross tons of logwood at Cap Haïtien, for delivery in Baltimore, at $6.00 per ton. In August of the following year, the same schooner loaded 921.80 tons of this product at the Haitian port, for the same destination, at $13.25 per ton. It is reported that the *Anna R. Heidritter*, in March 1941, loaded logwood at Jamaica, probably for Chester, at $16.00 per ton.

With their decks piled high with logwood and their canvas straining under the heavy load, the schooners presented a beautiful picture as the northeast trades sent them on their way from the islands. If luck sailed with them, they reached their American ports with deckloads intact. Often, however, heavy seas boarded them, tearing the wood loose from its chain lashings and washing it over the side.

Logwood now comes to the States by steamers. The sailing vessels are gone, taking with them the romance in the trade.

Looking aft on the *Doris Hamlin* showing the logwood on deck and planked walkway.
Photo: Author

Jones Falls
Protected Wooden Ships

JONES FALLS has probably been considered a scourge since before the town of Baltimore was incorporated. Frequently its waters have gone on a rampage, destroying the bridges spanning it and wreaking flood damage along its course. Entries to this effect in the early records of Baltimore's history are proof of this. Its meanderings through the center of the city have resulted in expense in maintaining bridges and covered roadways to carry traffic over its waters. However, the stream did have one asset other than furnishing power to mills along its banks. This was its invaluable aid in ridding wooden ships of the dreaded teredo, or shipworm.

Teredos have been referred to as "termites of the sea." They have an insatiable appetite for wood, leaving it riddled with cavities resembling a honeycomb. An effective weapon against the pests, once they become embedded in a ship's hull, is immersion in fresh water for a month or more.

Access to fresh water by large seagoing ships frequenting this area is rare except in the headwaters of the Chesapeake's lengthy tributaries. However, a stream having its origin well back in the Maryland hills carried a steady flow of fresh water into Baltimore harbor. This was Jones Falls.

It is not known who first became aware of the worm-killing properties of Jones Falls. The early colonists of the Chesapeake region recognized the threat and the cure of shipworm. The worms were a menace in these waters from their larval rise in June until the first great rain after the middle of July. Then they would disappear until the next summer. If they had entered the wood hull, they did their damage until cool weather came along, but if the ship left the Chesapeake and sailed to warmer waters, the worms would thrive.

Early mariners were aware of the ability of the fresh water of the Bay's tributaries to rid a ship's hull of worms. It is reported that George Washington recommended a creek across from Mt. Vernon as "being out of the way of the ship worm which is very harmful to shipping a little farther down."

Teredos and other species of shipworms have always been a plague to wooden ships that sailed warm salt waters. A coating of pitch, tar, lime, or tallow on the ship's bottom discouraged the teredo attack. Some protection was gained by passing a flame over the ship's bottom to burn the head of the worm. Later, metal sheathing and copper composition paint were effectively employed to protect the hull. But any bare wood exposed in warm, salt water for a short period was sure to become infected.

The accompanying photograph is a scene once typical of Jones Falls. The four-masted schooner *G. A. Kohler* is shown moored there in July 1933 for the sole purpose of ridding her hull of the teredo menace with the help of the Falls. It was the last time a large wooden ship tied up in that waterway for that purpose. The smaller Bay lumber schooners were also aware of the worm-killing properties of Jones Falls but they were not threatened as much as the larger sailing vessels that sailed to the West Indies.

The *G. A. Kohler* was one of the last of the large seagoing wooden sailing ships owned and operated out of Baltimore. She had a regular run between Baltimore and Haiti where she would load logwood for the local firm of J. S. Young and Company. Although her bottom received regular coats of copper paint as a protective measure, complete protection was not assured. If the paint was scraped off the planking, resulting bare wood provided an entrance for larval worms.

At the time the photograph was taken, Captain George H. Hopkins of Baltimore was the schooner's master. The *Kohler* had arrived in Baltimore from the West Indies a few weeks earlier. After discharging her cargo at Young's Boston Street plant, she was towed around to Jones Falls to await her next charter to Haiti. At the same time, the fresh water would help to prolong her life.

After a period in the Falls, the schooner was taken to a local shipyard where her bottom was painted before she sailed into the teredo-infested waters of the West Indies. On August 19, 1933, the steam tug *Radnor* sidled up to her at the Redman and Vane shipyard, Key Highway, Baltimore, to tow her to the open waters of Chesapeake Bay where a fair wind would ease her on her way to Haiti. Two days later she passed out of the Virginia Capes.

Her sojourn in Jones Falls and the new coat of anti-fouling paint on her hull were to be in vain for the *G. A. Kohler* fell victim to a raging hurricane four days after leaving Baltimore. She was driven on the dreaded North Carolina coast, north of Cape Hatteras, where she became a total loss.

The most abundant species of shipworm in Chesapeake Bay waters is the estuarine shipworm. Teredo navalis, the naval shipworm, restricts itself to the saltier waters at the mouth of the Bay. The estuarine worm is common in the Bay from Annapolis south to the Virginia Capes and lower tributaries. This species can drill burrows of a larger diameter and greater length than the teredo and attack any wood in the water, whether it be a ship's hull, piling, or other structure, if it has not been treated. Biologists of the Chesapeake Biological Laboratory, Solomons Island, made a test recently by submerging a wooden panel measuring 2 × 4 × 6 inches from May to early August. At the end of that period the wood was inspected and it was found to contain 22 worms ranging in length from one-half inch to twelve inches.

Jones Falls still retains its worm-killing properties but the remaining wooden hull vessels in the Chesapeake area do not take advantage of them. The principal users of the Falls, seagoing wooden vessels, no longer sail out of Baltimore.

The *G. A. Kohler* in Jones Falls, Baltimore, July 1933.
Photo: Author

Wreck of the
G. A. Kohler

EMBEDDED in the sands of bleak Hatteras Island, North Carolina, are the fragments of a four-masted schooner driven ashore there in 1933. Only those who have followed the vessel's career closely would recognize the timbers. Bleached and weathered, they appear to have been part of that scene for an eternity, and the iron fastenings that had bound the vessel have rusted away to a fraction of their original diameter.

This wreckage represents all that remains of a schooner that had sailed out of Baltimore for ten years, the *G. A. Kohler*. She started her career as the *Charles S. Gawthrop*, having been built at Wilmington, Delaware, in 1919. One of many wooden schooners constructed along the Atlantic coast during World War I and shortly thereafter, she differed from the majority in that she had Diesel engines as auxiliaries. She was also less handsome than the average coasting schooner.

For the first three years of her life she was registered out of New York and was engaged in the South American trade. In 1923 the *Gawthrop* and two other schooners were purchased by a Baltimore syndicate named the Maryland Navigation Company. She was then renamed the *G. A. Kohler* after a Pennsylvania tobacco magnate who had a large interest in the company.

Under her new owners the auxiliary engines were removed, making her a true sailing vessel. After making a few coastwise trips she was put under the command of Captain George H. Hopkins, well-known Baltimore shipmaster, who became her permanent master, except for a few voyages.

She was put on a fairly regular run at this time, loading bricks at Westport, South Baltimore, for Port Tampa, Florida. She would load phosphate rock in Port Tampa for delivery to fertilizer factories in Baltimore.

In 1928, the *G. A. Kohler* and the other schooners of the Maryland Navigation Company, the *B. S. Taylor* and the *Herdis,* were put up at auction at a Pratt Street pier. They were taken over by the Cottman Company as operating managers, thereby retaining Baltimore as their home port. In a short time, the *B. S. Taylor* and *Herdis* were sold to interests in other ports.

On the first trip for her new operators, the *Kohler* loaded a cargo of acid phosphate at Baltimore for discharge at Puerto Rico. While crossing the Gulf Stream on the way south, water entered the schooner's hold through the bow lumber ports and mixed with the phosphate. The mixture seeped into the bilges, hardened, and blocked the pumps. Water continued to enter the hold and, with the pumps useless, the vessel settled by the head. Putting back to the American coast, the schooner anchored near Frying Pan Shoals where a Dutch steamer was hailed and was requested to send a message for assistance. The Coast Guard cutter *Mendota* came to the schooner's aid and took her in tow for Wilmington, North Carolina.

With great difficulty the mass in her hold was eventually discharged. She was then sailed to Norfolk where she lay idle for several months before being sold at a Marshal's sale to R. B. White and W. B. Vane, veteran Baltimore sailing ship operators.

The schooner was then taken to the Baltimore shipyard of Redman & Vane, situated at the foot of Federal Hill, where the bilges were cleared sufficiently to allow water to circulate to the pumps.

The *Kohler's* new owners had little difficulty in finding cargoes for her. Her usual practice would be to load coal at Hampton Roads for West Indian ports. Then she would go to a Haitian port to take on a cargo of logwood for the Baltimore dye firm of J. S. Young & Company, in Canton. It was while on such a voyage that she met her tragic end. However, at that time she was sailing light direct to Haiti.

Prior to sailing she had been dry-docked to have her bottom painted. For a month or so previous to this, after having discharged her cargo, she

49

had been tied up in the fresh water of Jones Falls at Pratt Street in order to kill the marine worms in her planking.

On Saturday afternoon, August 19, 1933, the tug *Radnor* came alongside the schooner at Redman & Vane's to tow her down to Sandy Point. There she would be released to sail on her own. Lines were passed aboard and the tug attempted to back her away from the slip, but she failed to respond.

fair and light but huge swells were coming from the direction in which the threatening cloud was observed. At first it was thought that it was just another squally condition found over the Gulf Stream, but this cloud bank extended across the southerly horizon as far as the eye could see.

Orders were given to take in all of the schooner's light sails in anticipation of a blow. By this time, the vessel was off the North Carolina coast on the

The *G. A. Kohler* sails down the Chesapeake on her last passage, 1933. Several days later she was a total wreck on the North Carolina coast. Photo: Fred Tilp

She was touching bottom and seemed reluctant to leave port. However, after some maneuvering, the tug and its tow finally backed out and pointed their bows down the Patapsco River. Upon reaching Sandy Point, the *Kohler* was anchored to await a fair wind for the passage down the Bay.

The breeze finally came from a favorable quarter and the schooner weighed anchor. The wind held fair all the way down the Chesapeake and the *G. A. Kohler* passed out of the Virginia Capes at 8 P.M. on August 21.

At 4 A.M. on the 22nd, the mate called Captain Hopkins on deck to look at an evil looking black cloud hanging over the horizon. The wind was

landward side of the Gulf Stream. The swells continued to increase in size even though the wind remained light. This was a good indication that they were preceding a terrific storm. In fact, the motion of the sea interfered with the progress of the schooner.

As the wind veered around to the southeast quarter, the *Kohler* came about on another tack in an effort to get away from the treacherous coast. But shortly after a new course had been set to take her out to sea, the wind shifted around to the east. The seas had built up to such an extent that they prevented the schooner from making headway in any direction that would keep her away from the beach.

At 9 A.M. Captain Hopkins decided to anchor. An anchor with 120 fathoms of chain was dropped in 30 fathoms of water. Everything on board was made secure in preparation to battle the gale. The wind continued to increase in force and huge seas caused the high-riding schooner to drag anchor. Another anchor with 120 fathoms of chain was released and the dragging halted temporarily.

The seas became so heavy that as they swept by the schooner her entire forward section would be lifted clear of the water, causing her to strain on her chains and expose long portions of their length above the surface of the sea. As the giant waves passed on, her stern would be lifted high and her bow would be buried in the furious waters.

When the first anchor was released, the *Kohler* was about 12 miles offshore but she was slowly decreasing this distance as she dragged toward the sands. Everything that was humanly possible had been done in an effort to save the ship. All hands on board could only await their fate.

During the entire day and night of the 22nd she fought the storm, which proved to be a hurricane that had swept up the Atlantic coast without warning and hurled itself against shipping and shore alike. She touched bottom early on the morning of the 23rd, sending a sickening shudder throughout her length. Then a sea would lift her clear of the bar and carry her farther in.

At 4 A.M. she dragged stern-first onto the beach near the Gull Shoals Coast Guard Station, located between Wimble Shoals and Cape Hatteras. Her bow was carried around to point in a northerly direction as she came to rest parallel with the beach.

Succeeding waves hit her broadside, sweeping over and pushing her higher up the shelving beach. The steering gear on deck was smashed and her rudder was carried away. With the exception of a broken stem and sternpost, her hull and rigging were intact.

The stranded vessel's crew of nine and Mrs. Hopkins sought shelter under the forecastle head as the waves crashed aboard. When the storm had abated to a degree, Coast Guardsmen, who had manned a vigil for hours after the schooner was first discovered struggling offshore, brought all hands to safety in a breeches buoy on the afternoon of the 23rd.

The schooner was washed high up on the beach and her hull buried deep in the sand. All hopes of her salvage were dismissed. Her sails and gear were removed to be used on the other schooners owned by White and Vane. The slightly damaged motor yawl boat was sold and the wreck was disposed of for a few hundred dollars.

In 1938 the wreck of the *G. A. Kohler* was the only complete hulk left on the North Carolina coast. Even then her masts and jib boom had been cut away. Since she was located within the bounds of the National Seashore Development, a movement was started to purchase the hulk and preserve it as a landmark, but her owner had other ideas. He figured her metal fittings would bring more at a scrap price. The best way to get to these was to burn her. As the flames consumed the timbers, the fittings fell into the sea to be recovered later. Today, only a few of her stern timbers remain above the surface of the sea and sand.

After the hurricane the *G. A. Kohler* lies cast up on the beach, a total loss, with her anchor chains stretching seaward. Photo: Captain George H. Hopkins

The pathetic remains of the gallant *G. A. Kohler* lie almost buried in the sand of the North Carolina coast after being burned for her metal fittings. Photo: Jack J. Zehrt

A Quaint
Baltimore Shipyard

As A RULE, shipyards have an air of hustle and bustle about them. Action, noise, clatter and confusion fairly describes the average shipyard. Therefore, one would not expect to find a shipyard that could be described as quaint and serene. Yet there was such a yard in the middle of all the waterfront activity at the port of Baltimore.

It was the site of the Redman and Vane Shipyard, specialists in repairing wooden ships. Perhaps it was due to this specialty that caused many of the Bay's and coastwise sailing craft to take advantage of the yard's facilities. Those vessels probably gave the shipyard that quality associated with a slower but more pleasant way of life.

Redman and Vane's was situated on Key Highway, at the base of the eastern side of Federal Hill. That stretch of Baltimore waterfront was formerly a continuous row of shipyards. There were Booz Brothers, McIntyre and Henderson, J. S. Beacham and Brother, and Skinner's. Some of these firms built steamboats and sailing vessels and many of these vessels returned to them for repairs.

McIntyre and Henderson later became the Baltimore Ship Repair Company; Skinner's was renamed the Baltimore Dry Dock and eventually became the Bethlehem Shipbuilding Company.

In 1917 Redman and Vane's was established on the site of the old J. S. Beacham yard. John Clarence Redman, his son W. Carroll Redman, Allen P. Vane, and William B. Vane, were the owners. The elder Redman and the Vane brothers had that "know-how" that insured a successful future for their new yard; they had owned and sailed vessels on the Chesapeake. Carroll Redman joined the firm after service in World War I and remained with it throughout its period of activity.

There was more maritime lore centered in that yard than in any other single place in Baltimore harbor. Artists found it an ideal location for marine subjects. Unlike most shipyards, there were no restrictions to visitors so long as they did not interfere with the workmen, and the officials of the firm were always ready to talk ships.

One of the most interesting buildings on the property was the spar shed where masts and other spars were shaped. Scented shavings, excess wood removed by the spar maker's tools, were ankle-deep on the ground. At the end of one of the long piers was the tall pair of "shears," a two-legged affair used to remove and install masts in the sailing vessels.

Although Redman and Vane specialized in wooden ship repairs, they also serviced many of the Bay steamboats. The yard had two marine railways. The largest was 235 feet in length and capable of handling vessels up to 1200 tons. The cradle of the smaller railway was 165 feet in length. It was always interesting to see the big side-wheel steamers hauled free of the water. The underbody of a ship has a certain attraction because it is rarely seen. The sailing vessels were even more intriguing. The hulls of the bugeyes, pungies, schooners, and rams all differed, each type having its own distinct hull form.

Redman and Vane also operated the Maryland Block and Pump Works. As the name implies, ship blocks and pumps were manufactured there. Wooden steering wheels also were made in the shop. The yard carried in stock a large supply of lignum vitae and was one of the chief sources for this durable wood in Baltimore. The rigging shop of William F. Wilson was on the property, also.

With clouds of World War II hovering over the harbor, the maximum output of the port's ship repair facilities was needed, and the colorful Redman and Vane shipyard was swept away virtually overnight.

On January 20, 1942, the Navy Department

52

issued condemnation proceedings calling for the immediate acquisition of three long-established ship repair firms adjoining the Key Highway plant of Bethlehem Shipbuilding Company. They were Booz Brothers, the Baltimore Ship Repair Company, and Redman and Vane. Their combined facilities sprawled over ten acres of land with about 1,000 feet of waterfront.

The Navy Department's action came as a complete surprise to the heads of the smaller yards. The first knowledge they had of the Government's intent was the appearance on January 19 of a United States Marshal who posted in the offices of each firm the legal order acquiring the properties.

This brought an end to the reign of the smaller independent shipyards along what has been termed "shipyard row." Old buildings were leveled, the waterfront dredged, new piers constructed, and tall masonry buildings erected. The Bethlehem Shipbuilding Co. expanded, engulfing the little yards.

Now steel seagoing ships dominate that part of the waterfront behind guarded gates. Hydraulic riveting and chipping hammers have replaced the ring of the caulking hammers. The pungent odor of oakum and marlin went with the sailing vessels. The old-time shipyard, as Baltimore once knew it, ceased to exist.

Booz Brothers and the Baltimore Ship Repair Company, the latter assuming the new name of the Baltimore Marine Repair Shops, resumed business on the site of the old Woodall shipyard adjoining the American Sugar Refinery, Key Highway. Redman and Vane passed out of the Baltimore picture. And it was just as well, since the steamboats and sailing craft that yard had serviced were no longer a part of the harbor scene.

The Redman and Vane Shipyard in 1936, a peaceful looking setting in a busy port.
Photo: Author

Sailing Coal Out of Hampton Roads

O N JULY 3, 1948, the British wooden three-masted schooner *Frederick P. Elkin* sailed from Cape Henry for a West Indian port with the last cargo of coal to leave Hampton Roads in a sailing vessel. The demand for coal has not lessened, as evidenced by the number of steamers usually anchored in the Roads awaiting this cargo. The *Elkin* has joined the scores of other abandoned sailing vessels that formerly carried coal to all ports of the world because they could not compete with steamers.

Prior to World War II, schooners were constant visitors to Newport News and Norfolk. Vessels of three, four, and five masts were common. In the early years of this century, six-masted schooners and the *Thomas W. Lawson*, only seven-masted schooner ever built, made Hampton Roads a regular port of call. All were after coal cargoes.

In the 1930's, the four-masted schooners *Edward L. Swan, Doris Hamlin, Albert F. Paul, Purnell T. White, Velma Hamlin, Ida S. Dow,* and the five-master *Edna Hoyt,* were as familiar to these waters as are the colliers now steadily employed in the coal trade.

These schooners were products of the World War I shipbuilding boom when scores were constructed to ease the shipping crisis of that period. The majority had brief careers due to acts of war, founderings, or being forced into idleness because of lack of cargoes. A few, however, properly managed, found bulk cargoes such as lumber, coal, bricks, fertilizer, and fish scrap to enable them to keep active and show a profit for their owners. Most were handsome, displaying lofty masts and pleasing sheers, those graceful curvatures of a ship's deck lines.

This type of vessel has always fascinated me and well I remember the four-masted schooner *Sally Wren.* She was brought to the attention of the public in a most spectacular manner when, in the 1920's, she collided with the old Berkley Bridge in Norfolk, causing considerable damage to her forward rigging. She was repaired and went to sea again, finally being abandoned at Bermuda about 1930.

My interest in these ships increased as the years went by. As they dwindled in number, I resolved to make a voyage on one to try to record on film life aboard the last of the large wooden sailing ships. My ambition was realized in October, 1936, aboard the four-masted schooner *Doris Hamlin* when she took a cargo of coal from Newport News to Bermuda.

The *Doris Hamlin,* built in Harrington, Maine, in 1919, was sold to Baltimore owners in 1930. My voyage originated in Baltimore on October 15, 1936. The crew was made up of 9 men—captain, bosun, engineer, cook, and 5 seamen. Only a small crew was needed to handle this 200-foot wooden sailing vessel because most of the heavy lifting, such as weighing anchor, pumping, and hoisting the sails and the yawl, was done by a donkey steam engine.

Her 16 sails were the *Hamlin's* only means of propulsion. A motor yawl was carried in stern davits to be used as a shore boat when anchored and to tow the schooner to open water.

For two days the *Hamlin* swung at her anchor awaiting a favorable wind. On the third day a brisk nor'wester arrived and the lower sails were raised, the anchor was weighed, and the schooner followed the channel out to the Bay. The *Hamlin* was light and sat high in the water, causing her to heel over considerably as the pressure of the wind bore upon her sails.

The wind remained fair throughout the day permitting the vessel to hold to her course. At 4:30 the following morning, after an 18-hour sail down the Chesapeake, the *Hamlin* came to anchor near

Thimble Shoal Lighthouse at the entrance to Hampton Roads.

For two days she waited for proper wind and tide conditions to enable her to negotiate the channels leading into the Roads under sail.

Finally, she got the right slant of wind and eased towards Old Point. This proved to be an interesting maneuver in such confined waters.

She cleared the busy channels and came to anchor off the Virginian Railway coal piers near the Naval Operating Base. Later, the tug *D. J. Harahan* came alongside and towed her to the loading berth.

After loading, the vessel was towed to an anchorage in the lower James River where the coal dust was hosed through the scuppers into the river. The next day the *Hamlin* was readied for sea.

Looking forward on the deck of the schooner *Edna Hoyt* as she loaded coal at Newport News in March 1937. Photo: Wm. T. Radcliffe

On October 26 the weather forecast predicted northerly winds. This was just what the heavily laden schooner needed to drive her across the Gulf Stream to Bermuda. At 10:30 that morning the lower sails were raised and the anchor was weighed.

When her bow swung out into Hampton Roads the voyage had finally started. As we passed down the channel three topsails were put on and her speed increased. Passing Old Point we observed storm signals displayed from the staff.

Within four and a half hours we had passed out of Cape Henry and picked up the motion of the sea. To prepare for the predicted blow the captain ordered the topsails taken in and the lower sails

The British schooner *Frederick P. Elkin* departing from Newport News, July 3, 1948. This was the last sailing ship to carry coal out of a Hampton Roads port. Photo: Wm. T. Radcliffe

reefed. Gradually the Virginia shoreline dropped astern as a southeasterly course was set for the islands.

That evening the wind increased in force and it started to rain. Instead of coming out of the northwest quarter as predicted the wind roared from the northeast. The *Hamlin* was able to hold her course but the wind from that direction caused heavy seas to build up in the opposing Gulf Stream. The schooner had a tendency to roll violently and with a jerky motion. The most serious accident to occur as a result of this rolling was the carrying away of the two lead blocks attached to the spanker boom. This sail had been furled and the boom secured earlier but, with the failure of the lead blocks, this massive timber cut a swath across the deck with each roll of the ship. All hands were called in an effort to secure the boom that threatened to do away with the helmsman. This was accomplished with some difficulty as the schooner ploughed through the foam-topped seas making good time toward her destination.

Schooner *Doris Hamlin* anchored in Hampton Roads to take on a cargo of coal for Bermuda, October 19, 1936. Photo: A. Aubrey Bodine

As the evening wore on, I was to become convinced that a ship at sea, especially a sailing ship, was a thing alive. I had visited many large schooners at their berths in placid waters where they looked gigantic and seemed able to withstand anything the sea might hurl at them but the *Doris Hamlin* looked rather small that night with the seas boiling all around her. At the crest of a huge wave the schooner seemed poised before sliding downhill into the trough. The seas swept past, lifting her bow high. Then another would follow, lifting the stern as the ship raced on.

There were varied noises never heard on a schooner in port. The sounds of the surging seas dominated but the roar of the wind in the rigging lent an eerie tone, especially as she rolled to windward. The big wooden vessel seemed to creak and groan at every joint due to varying strains and stresses placed upon her by wind and sea.

The next morning revealed an overcast sky, rolling white-capped waves on to the horizon, and a strong northeast wind. Far behind us were the greenish waters of the coast. The sea had now taken on a deep blue hue and was remarkably clear.

The schooner was taking in some water although not at an alarming rate but when an attempt was

made to free the bilges, only a trickle of water emerged from the pumps. The rolling and pitching had stirred up in the bilge bits of coal and wood that had clogged the pump strainers. The engineer had to go down in the hold to dismantle and clean the strainers.

For two days the heavy weather continued with the wind out of the northeast and east forcing us to sail under reduced canvas. On the third day, blue skies replaced the overcast and the wind subsided but the surface of the sea continued to roll, making it even more uncomfortable aboard ship since we had lost the cushioning effect of the wind's pressure against the sails.

The sails were left raised, hoping that the wind soon would pick up again. Examination showed that the slatting of the sails and wear on the gear had taken its toll. The most vulnerable part of the gear seemed to be the jaws of the gaffs. As the sails swung from side to side with each roll, the jaws would chafe against the mast, the weaker fittings giving way. Finally the sails were lowered so that repairs could be made and not raised again until later that evening when a favorable wind picked up.

There followed days of fair winds, head winds, and calm. Life aboard the schooner fell into a routine pattern of standing watches, handling sails, and painting. The meals were good and the food

The four-masted schooner *Doris Hamlin* bound for Bermuda with coal from Newport News in 1936. Looking aft from the jib boom. Photo: Author

plentiful, which is more than could be said of the sailing ships of earlier days. There was no means of refrigeration aboard so the food was either canned, dried, or salted. Fresh vegetables were carried but they did not last long. Eggs, a Sunday-morning delicacy aboard the *Hamlin*, were preserved by packing them in a barrel of salt. This was accomplished by covering the bottom of the barrel with salt and then placing the eggs on end in the salt. Alternate layers of eggs and salt were repeated.

On the seventeenth day out of Hampton Roads, just before dark, a beam of light was observed ahead. Referring to a chart, the beacon proved to be the Gibbs Hill Lighthouse on Bermuda. We hoped to be at anchor in the harbor of St. George the next day but this was not to be our luck. As we approached the island under darkness, an arched, black cloud accompanied by lightning and thunder swept down on us, driving strong north-east winds before it. The topsails had been furled and the schooner was sailed by the wind so as not to be blown away from the land. But by daybreak Bermuda was astern.

The wind held strong from the northeast and the seas had built up. Under these conditions the *Hamlin* could not approach the islands but could only hold courses to keep the land near. This she did for the next two days, sailing back and forth waiting for the seas to moderate sufficiently to permit a tug to come out and tow her into port.

On the twentieth day out, the wind shifted around to the southeast and allowed us to sail toward the island. We were close to land when we observed a tug coming through a cut to tow us in. As she drew alongside, a line was passed aboard and we were taken in tow. In the harbor

of St. George we went through quarantine and the *Hamlin* was tied up alongside the hulk of the old iron sailing ship *Duncrag*, into which we were to discharge our cargo. After nearly three weeks of sailing and drifting, we had finally reached our destination.

Discharging the cargo was quite a contrast to the way the coal had been loaded. Huge reed baskets were lowered into the hold and a gang of laborers filled them with shovelfuls of coal. The baskets were hoisted by a steam donkey engine on a lighter alongside and emptied into the hulk. In this primitive manner, a week was required to clear the *Hamlin's* hold.

When she put to sea again, her destination was Cap Haïtien, Haiti, where she was to take on a cargo of logwood for Baltimore. Almost two months were to pass before she was back in Chesapeake waters.

Time was closing in on the career of the *Doris Hamlin*. In 1939 she changed owners and once more was in Norfolk for repairs at Colonna's Shipyard at Berkley and later to load coal there for the Canary Islands. That was to be her last voyage. She set sail in the early part of 1940 and has not been heard from since.

The coal schooner has passed from the American scene and with it has departed much of the color that was instrumental in building up the Hampton Roads coal trade.

Schooner *Wyoming* towing out of Hampton Roads, February 6, 1920. Photo: Robert T. Little—The Mariners Museum

Tugs Once Raced
for Their Tows

IN 1951 Captain Joseph Herbert Mullen, a veteran tugboat operator in Baltimore harbor, was in a reminiscent mood and related the following description of tugboating on Chesapeake Bay around the turn of the century.

"During my strolls around the waterfront these days I am most impressed by the change that has come over the tugboats in Baltimore harbor. This is only natural since I have spent all of my working life on tugs in those waters and operated a fleet of four. But the Diesel-driven, streamlined, welded hulls of today lack the character of the wooden-hulled steam tugs that served me from way back in 1888 until I put my last vessel aside in 1939.

"1888—that's when I was in my second year at Baltimore City College. During that Christmas vacation I went on my father's tug *Easby,* built that year by Wm. E. Woodall & Co. Little did I realize it then but that was to be the start of my tugboating career. While I was on the *Easby,* someone turned steam on in the pipes without first letting out the condensed vapor. This burst a pipe, permitting live steam to fill the engine room. In an effort to permit fresh air to enter, I broke the glass out of a cabin door with my bare fist. As a result I spent the next six weeks in the hospital nursing a bad cut. After my recovery I felt that I had lost too much time from school so I quit and signed on the *Easby* as cook.

"During an extremely rough trip on the Bay, a pot of hot water spilled over me so I gave up the galley and signed on as deck hand. Within five years I had my captain's license. In 1892, my father had the tug *E. W. Marts* built at Woodall's, here in Baltimore. Upon her completion he took her over and I stayed on the *Easby* as master.

"As I look back now, those days were full of excitement. Our tows took us all over the Bay and its tributaries. In 1900, I was towing the barkentine *Hattie G. Dixon* down the Potomac River for Baltimore. At Cedar Point, on the Potomac, fog closed in and I didn't see another object until we reached Ober's Wharf in Baltimore. This is one instance where the knowledge of the Chesapeake's navigation aids paid off.

"The trips down the length of the Bay were made when we towed the large sailing vessels out the Virginia Capes where they would pick up the wind and have sea-room to maneuver. After dropping our tows, we would cruise around just inside the capes waiting to sight an inward-bound sail over the horizon. We were not alone in this field.

The *Radnor* hauled out at the Chesapeake Marine Railway, Baltimore, in 1936. Photo: Author

Competition was stiff and when a sail was sighted, the tugs raced to be the first to put a line aboard for the long tow up the Chesapeake to Baltimore. Many times our tugs towed the vessels of the famed South American coffee fleet. Schooners bound for Curtis Bay to load coal also kept us busy. The tugboat operators had an unwritten law that once a tug had her lines aboard a ship, it was her tow. Sometimes it would require some dickering before the sailing craft would accept a tow at the tug's rates. For towing a large ship up the Bay we received $90.

"In 1899, we sold the *E. W. Marts* and, through the years, added the *Emily, Jesse Tyson,* and *Radnor* to our fleet. In 1916, I saw the possibilities in oil engines and paid a visit to a Danish ship at Locust Point to inspect one. The chief engineer of the vessel told me that he would not give one reciprocating steam engine for all the Diesels in the world. That's the opinion I formed that day and still cling to it. I never did change over from steam.

"However, I discovered that Diesels were cutting inroads into my business as the years went by. In 1934, I had the contract with the Old Bay Line to handle their steamers and lighters. Along came the Diesel craft with fewer in crew and cheaper to operate and I lost my contract to them. As a result, my *Emily* and *Jesse Tyson* were tied up. I had put the *Easby* to rest about ten years before in the ship graveyard at Locust Point.

"I sold the *Emily* in 1939. That same year the *Jesse Tyson* was tied up at Jenkins' Wharf when an excursion steamer passed by and created a huge wash. The *Tyson* was knocked up against the wharf causing her seams to open. She sank and I sold her as she was for $100.

"The little steam tug, the average length of mine being 61 feet, had a chance of survival in the old days when sailing craft and the Bay steamboats dominated the harbor. We were kept busy shifting scows and schooners to various berths around the harbor.

"I handled the majority of the last large coasting schooners that came to this port, meeting them down the Bay and towing them to local piers. Or I would take them down to Sandy Point where they could take advantage of the wind and wide waters as they were bound out.

"In 1939 I beached my lone tug *Radnor* at Swan Creek, near Rock Hall, on Maryland's Eastern Shore. This brought to an end my career as a tugboat operator. Sail is gone for good and the big steamships that have taken its place need the services of powerful Diesel craft. But none of them for me."

The *Doris Hamlin* being towed down Chesapeake Bay by the tug *Radnor,* November 1933. Photo: Author

The Story of The *Katherine May*

ON JUNE 18, 1931, the British four-masted schooner *Katherine May* sailed from Devonshire, Bermuda, for Baltimore, Maryland. As the island dropped astern it is unlikely that anyone interested in the vessel considered the fact that she would never see those shores again, nor that this would be her last departure from any port. She was well found and good for years of service.

While the schooner was anchored in Granaway Deep undergoing preparation for her departure from Bermuda, people referred to her as the "honeymoon ship." The newly married couple aboard were the captain, O. G. Lindley, and his bride. It was rather unusual for a vessel of 896 tons to be carrying a cargo away from Bermuda. Many American coasting schooners called at Bermuda at that time to discharge lumber and coal but the island had little to export.

The cargo of the *Katherine May* consisted of 366 tons of scrap iron consigned to the Boston Iron and Metals Company in Baltimore. Most of this material probably was the remains of vessels that had made Bermuda their last port of call. In years past, many sailing ships found in distress in that section of the Atlantic were towed to the island. The majority were converted into storage hulks or abandoned and broken up later.

The schooner made good time on her passage to Chesapeake Bay and on June 28 anchored in the Patapsco River, Baltimore. This type of vessel was not a rarity in Baltimore but she attracted attention for she was flying the British flag.

The *Katherine May* went through the necessary procedure for her entry into Baltimore and then was taken to her berth to discharge. The hold of the schooner was soon cleared of its meager cargo of scrap and she was in readiness for sea again—but there was no cargo for her. The depression years of the early 30's were particularly lean for shipping. Since many American coasters were available for charter, chances of an alien schooner receiving a cargo were slim.

The *Katherine May* was towed to an empty berth at the old Woodall shipyard in Baltimore to be tied up. In November 1931, a caretaker, with his wife and two sons, moved aboard and set up quarters in the after cabin. While making use of the schooner as a home, the occupants kept the vessel in order so that if a cargo became available she could be made ready for sea with little difficulty. An almost steady stream of water emerged from the scuppers as the pumping engine relieved the leaking hull of its burden.

In February 1934, a group of Baltimore business men planned to send the *Katherine May* to South America on a trading venture. She was to carry machinery, shoes, and clothing and in return she would accept as payment, coffee, sugar, and other items in demand in the United States. A Norwegian skipper, Captain Wiik, would command the vessel. With her hull painted dark green, and deckhouses and fittings white, she made a presentable and seaworthy appearance. Evidently her registry remained British for BERMUDA was painted on her transom in large letters to designate her home port.

The schooner was towed to the Maryland Dry Dock Company, Baltimore, to be dry-docked for survey and repairs. Examination of the vessel disclosed that she would need three new masts, along with other repairs, at an estimated cost of $10,000. This was too much for the backers of the venture so she was towed back to her berth at Woodall's.

A vessel needs more than paint and pumping out to keep her afloat. When a schooner fails to earn her keep, she requires more than faith to keep her in a seaworthy condition. It was reported that Captain Lindley occasionally visited the schooner but considered her too far gone for restoration.

The caretaker's wife died in 1935. His pay stopped, the pumping engine broke down, and water crept up in the vessel's hold. The schooner filled and settled to the harbor's bottom, with a good portion of her hull and decks remaining above water.

The caretaker left the listing hulk the following year. To satisfy a libel against the vessel, filed for wharfage charges, the United States Marshal took over the abandoned schooner to sell her at auction. The top bidder offered $405 with the understanding that the vessel be refloated and taken out of the harbor. The proposition was accepted and workmen with salvage gear moved aboard.

The pumping engine was repaired and once again the *Katherine May* was waterborne, but she was a dejected sight. Fragments of sails and sail

shipping. The story circulated around the Baltimore waterfront about 1941 that a prospective buyer, with plans to restore the vessel to service as a barge, offered the owner of the schooner $10,000 for the waterlogged wreck. Anticipating that the shipping crisis might enable him to net more, the owner held out for $20,000. The story goes that the buyer was murdered that same night in a Baltimore hotel and robbed of the funds with which he had planned to purchase the hulk. So the *Katherine May* remained in the graveyard to die.

The *Katherine May* ready for sea after discharging her cargo. Photo: Dwight Foster

covers clung to her spars; frayed running rigging whipped in the breeze. Her new owner probably had no intention of sending the schooner to sea. Instead, he hoped to make a profit on what little scrap metal the vessel and her fittings would yield.

While still at Woodall's, her bowsprit and jib boom were sawed off even with the longhead. Then her four masts were removed, leaving a gaunt hull that still retained a smart sheer. Thus stripped, the *Katherine May* was towed around to a ships' graveyard in Curtis Creek, near Baltimore, where a number of wooden hulks found refuge. Here the schooner was permitted to fill and settle to the bottom, leaving her deck clear of the water. Time and weather took their toll, robbing the vessel of her last vestige of seaworthiness.

World War II brought with it a shortage of

Years of exposure to the elements and vandals have left their mark on the hulk that remains in the graveyard. Her deck is spongy and sagging; the after cabin has collapsed. Her starboard quarter is a complete shambles, showing the damage caused by a steamer that broke loose from a tow and drifted down upon her. However, on her stern one may still read her name and BERMUDA as her home port. These are the remains of virtually the last large, wooden sailing vessel to fly the British flag.

This 192-foot schooner was constructed of hard wood and pine in 1919 by the Bangor Shipbuilding Corporation, East Hampden, Maine, for their own use. She is said to have cost $175,000 to build. In September 1919, she had a charter to carry 850 tons of coal from Norfolk to Lisbon. That may have been her first voyage and probably her only transatlantic trip. Her master was Captain F. P. Hardy, who bought the schooner around 1921.

It is reported that Captain Hardy lost a considerable amount of money on the schooner. About 1929, she was sold to Captain Lindley for $300 after having stranded off Bermuda. She was registered out of Halifax, Nova Scotia, and Hamilton, Bermuda, under the British flag. Further reports state that her new owner spent $30,000 on the vessel's restoration. It is unlikely that he realized but a fraction of that amount from freight profits.

The *Katherine May* was one of those unfortunate schooners built a little too late to profit from the freight boom created by World War I. As times became lean, there were too many of her kind for the limited cargoes available.

As one looks at the schooner today, rotting in the putrid backwaters of a creek far from her home port, it is difficult to imagine that she was ever a seaworthy ship capable of making a voyage to any part of the globe.

The *Katherine May* as an abandoned hulk in Curtis Creek, Baltimore. Photo: Author

Waterlogged and rotten, this once fine schooner presents a sad picture in her Baltimore graveyard, 1956. Photo: Author

Looking forward on the starboard deck of the *Katherine May* while tied up at Woodall's Shipyard in Baltimore. Photo: Author

The Last Voyage

SOME OF THE most dramatic views portraying the fierceness of the sea from the deck of a large wooden sailing ship have been captured with an ordinary box camera. The accompanying deck scenes show a large commercial schooner caught in turbulent seas. The humble box camera not only did a magnificent job of recording the angry mood of the ocean, but also portrayed the end of an era in American shipping. The seas proved to be more than the schooner could endure and resulted in the final voyage of one of the best known latter-day commercial schooners on the American east coast.

Until the late 1930's, American coasting schooners might be encountered anywhere along the coast as they plied their trade of hauling lumber, coal, or guano. A particular schooner was likely to be as familiar to yachtsmen in the Chesapeake area, where it took on a cargo of coal, as to boatmen in Nantucket Sound, near its point of discharge. This was true in the case of the *Edna Hoyt*. She had ports of call in Florida, Virginia, Maryland, New

The *Edna Hoyt* at Baltimore, January 1933. Photo: Author

York, Massachusetts, and Maine, and seemed to be more regularly employed than most vessels of her kind.

The *Edna Hoyt* was a five-masted schooner, the last to be built on the American east coast and the last of that rig in service on those waters. She was built in 1920 by Dunn and Elliott, Thomaston, Maine, at an approximate cost of $280,000.

The *Hoyt* was small for a five-masted schooner, having a gross tonnage of only 1512. The largest five-masted schooner, the *Jane Palmer,* was built in 1904 and measured 3138 gross tons. The *Hoyt's* longevity was partly due to her small size. While larger schooners were idling in port awaiting car-

Chesapeake area to some northern port, returning to her accustomed routes when the greatest danger from storms was over.

The *Edna Hoyt* had her share of mishaps and minor troubles at sea, but none was serious. Around 1936 she began to experience competition from the smaller Scandinavian steamers that were accepting charters in the West Indian region. Anticipating fewer trips to Venezuela, she entered the coal trade between the Chesapeake and New England.

Captain Robert Rickson skippered the *Hoyt* almost the entire time she was operated by Foss and Crabtree. However, in 1937, a new hand took over the helm of the schooner. He was Captain

Looking aft on the deck of the *Edna Hoyt* as the schooner battled the Bay of Biscay storm in November 1937. Photo: Captain George H. Hopkins

goes, the smaller, handier schooner kept busy. It is said that she never was laid up for a lengthy period from the time of her launching until her last voyage 17 years later.

Her builders operated the schooner until the mid-1920's when she was sold to the Superior Trading and Transportation Company. This firm sold the schooner to Foss and Crabtree of Boston in 1929. For 7 years the new owners operated the *Hoyt* in the fertilizer trade between Venezuela and North Atlantic ports. She enjoyed great success, finding general cargoes outbound for West Indian ports and guano for the return trip. Occasionally, during the hurricane season, she would accept a charter to carry lumber from Jacksonville or coal from the

George H. Hopkins, who had spent virtually all of his seagoing career in sailing ships.

Captain Hopkins' first voyage in the *Hoyt* took him to the West Indies with coal from Hampton Roads, Virginia. At Martinique, he loaded scrap iron for Puerto Rico. Then he sailed light to Turk's Island to load salt for Boston.

After an uneventful passage to Boston, requiring 17 days from Turk's, it was announced that the *Hoyt* had obtained a charter to carry a cargo of lumber from Halifax, Nova Scotia, to Belfast, Ireland. The schooner was dry-docked at Boston to prepare for this voyage.

Seventeen years of lugging heavy cargoes along the east coast caused her to develop a pronounced hog. Observers claimed that it was possible to place a yardstick upright amidships between her keel and the keel blocks, but she was tight. She left Boston light for Halifax after a thorough overhaul.

On August 9, 1937, she sailed from Halifax to Belfast with hold and deck stacked with 1,350,000 feet of lumber. This was a history-making voyage. She was to be the last wooden five-masted schooner to cross the North Atlantic.

Ten days out of Halifax she encountered a severe gale that shifted her deck load. She hove to and rode out the storm.

Her first European landfall was Fastnet Light, Cape Clear, on the Irish coast, 17 days out of Hali-

great that she carried away a number of her shrouds. Captain Hopkins refused to continue loading in Newport so the schooner was towed to Cardiff, where she would remain afloat at low tide, to complete her cargo.

On November 2, the *Edna Hoyt* left Cardiff for the long passage across the Atlantic to Venezuela. This was probably the longest leg over open water she had undertaken during her entire career. With no propulsion other than her sails and no wireless to keep the outside world informed of her position, she would be on her own as her predecessors had been 100 years earlier.

While making her way south and west across the

The fury of the wind and sea is evident as the *Edna Hoyt* runs before the gale. Photo: Captain George H. Hopkins

fax. There she picked up a pilot for the Irish Channel. Her first day up the channel was plagued by a calm and the next four by head winds. When within 8 miles of her destination, she accepted the services of a tug and was towed into Belfast.

Three weeks were required to discharge the lumber. Early in October the *Hoyt* sailed for Newport, Wales, and took a week to complete the passage. Here she was to take on a cargo of coal briquettes for delivery to La Guaira, Venezuela, but extreme difficulty was experienced in loading. Due to the drop in the tides, the *Hoyt* rested on the bottom. Her tremendous hog caused her to straighten out. Strain on the wooden hull was so

Bay of Biscay she encountered one of those raging gales for which that body of water is noted. For almost three weeks she battled the storm. The strain on her hull while on the bottom at Newport had weakened her structurally. Portions of her 'tween decks collapsed, causing her cargo to shift. She took in water and had to be pumped constantly. All she could do was run before the gale with only a rag of sail exposed.

It was under these conditions that Captain Hopkins attempted to record the scene with a box camera. The technique of picture taking was not one of his accomplishments but he knew he was experiencing a storm of such proportions that some

65

pictorial record would be of extreme interest.

The *Edna Hoyt* was 224 feet in overall length. She gave the impression of being a large wooden vessel in port but she seemed small against the backdrop of the turbulent Bay of Biscay. In the view looking astern on the port side, a big sea is sweeping by, lifting her forward section and allowing her stern to fall in a trough. A pooping seems imminent but she still retains buoyancy and lifts

and forestaysail seem insignificant on such a large vessel but it was all she could handle.

The pumps were barely keeping up with the water entering her hull. The schooner's course was taking her farther out in the Atlantic and away from possible salvage. Several ships had been sighted on the horizon and the inverted American ensign had been hoisted in an attempt to attract their attention.

Looking forward along the deck of the *Edna Hoyt* as she runs before her last gale under forestaysail and reefed foresail. Photo: Captain George H. Hopkins

her stern to the next wave. She wallows as she barely makes headway under the reefed foresail not even visible in the picture. Her timbers creak and groan as she works in the undulating sea.

To further record the scene, Captain Hopkins climbed up on the starboard bulwarks, grasped the foreshrouds, and aimed his camera aft again. This time he devoted more of the film to the surface of the sea yet kept the deck of the schooner in the finder. Anyone who has experienced a terrific storm at sea can feel the fury of this gale. The heads of the larger seas have been beaten down by the wind and it, in turn, is driving the water before it.

A more tranquil scene is the one looking forward on the starboard side, only because it was taken from a lower point of vantage. The raised poop is in the foreground and evidence of boarding seas can be seen gathering in the waterways as the schooner lists to starboard. The reefed foresail

Twenty-one days out from Cardiff, the Norwegian steamer *San Amigo* sighted the schooner with its signal of distress and stood by until the seas diminished. She took the sinking *Hoyt* in tow and, when the storm had passed on, the tow made good progress. On Thanksgiving Day, 1937, the *Edna Hoyt* dropped anchor in the port of Lisbon —a fitting time to be delivered from imminent disaster.

The schooner and crew stood by in Lisbon for 5 weeks. The vessel was surveyed and condemned as being unfit to go to sea again. The underwriters took her over and she was sold for $3500 to Lisbon interests for conversion into a coal hulk. Thus, the last five-masted schooner in service on the North Atlantic was stricken from the records.

As a raging gale brought the *Edna Hoyt's* active life to a close, the camera captured for posterity the end of an important phase in American shipping.

Baltimore to Richmond by Water and Rail

AT ONE TIME Pier 19, Light Street, Baltimore, was the point of departure for the most pleasant means of travel between that city and Richmond, Virginia. Passengers could leave there by steamer and enjoy a comfortable trip down Chesapeake Bay and up the York River, disembarking at West Point, Virginia. From this point, a train could be boarded for Richmond and all points south.

The accompanying reproduction of a contemporary print shows Pier 19 in its heyday. Horse-drawn traffic dominated Light Street and the piers were piled high with freight.

The company operating from the pier at that time was the Chesapeake Steamship Company whose house flags are displayed from the two steamers and the pier. This flag consisted of a field divided diagonally into blue and red. The letter R, for Richmond, was on the blue; the letter N, for Norfolk, on the red.

Just below the flagpole atop the pier appears a rectangular sign reading: BALTIMORE, CHESA-

The steamers *Baltimore* and *Atlanta* of the Chesapeake Line at Pier 19, Light Street, Baltimore. Photo: Eldredge Collection—The Mariners Museum

PEAKE & RICHMOND STEAMBOAT COMPANY 1874–1889. This company occupied the premises before the Chesapeake Steamship Company took over.

The predecessor of the Baltimore, Chesapeake & Richmond Steamboat Company was the Powhatan Line, formed in 1845 to operate between Baltimore and Richmond via Chesapeake Bay and the James River. In 1854 a railroad had been projected to connect Richmond with West Point. About the time this was completed, the Civil War started and the line was totally wiped out. When hostilities ended, the railroad was rebuilt. In 1870 the Powhatan Line alternated triweekly service from Pier 10, Light Street to the James and York Rivers. Due to the expense of its rebuilding, the railroad found itself in such poor financial condition that it was sold to Philadelphia interests.

In 1874, the Baltimore, Chesapeake & Richmond Steamboat Company was incorporated by the Maryland Legislature to connect Baltimore and West Point. One of the first vessels operated by this company was the *Louise,* a favorite of Baltimoreans at a later period when she served as an excursion steamer of the Tolchester Line.

The newly formed company ventured into the Baltimore-Norfolk trade in 1876, organizing the People's Line. However, the Baltimore Steam Packet Company objected to the Norfolk competition, so an agreement was reached in 1877 and the People's Line steamers withdrew.

When Pier 10 became too small for the company's operations, Pier 2, Light Street was taken over. The line suffered from growing pains again so it moved to the more commodious Piers 18 and 19 in 1889. The two steamers appearing in the accompanying view are identified as the *Baltimore* at the left and the *Atlanta* at the right. Actually, an earlier version of the print identifies the vessel at the right as the *Danville,* which she more accurately depicts.

Competition loomed again between the Baltimore Steam Packet Company (Old Bay Line) and the Baltimore, Chesapeake & Richmond Steamboat Company with the latter entrenched on the Baltimore-Norfolk run and the former entering the York River trade.

In 1900 the Chesapeake Steamship Company, consisting of the York River Line operating between Baltimore and West Point, and the Chesapeake Line sailing between Baltimore, Old Point Comfort, and Norfolk, managed by the Southern Railway, was organized and acquired the assets of the Baltimore, Chesapeake & Richmond Steamboat Company.

Over the years various vessels were built for the Chesapeake Steamship Company and they were able to hold their own against the competing Baltimore Steam Packet Company until 1941, when the Interstate Commerce Commission approved the plans of the Baltimore Steam Packet Company to take over the Chesapeake Steamship Company. This brought to an end the many years of rivalry between the two organizations.

The scarcity of ships during World War II caused the government to acquire four steamers of the merged companies, leaving only two of the older, former Chesapeake Steamship Company vessels to handle heavy wartime traffic—the *City of Norfolk* and the *City of Richmond.* They served commendably during one of the Baltimore Steam Packet Company's busiest periods. The York River service was dropped in 1942, ending a link between the cities of Baltimore and Richmond.

In the early 1950's Pier 19 was deserted, awaiting the arrival of wreckers who were tearing down the wharves along Light Street to make way for a park in memory of General Sam Smith.

68

Steamboats Cause
Traffic Jam in Baltimore

BALTIMOREANS are familiar with the constant traffic congestion occurring at the intersection of Light and Pratt Streets prior to 1954. In that year the Calvert Street extension across General Sam Smith Park was opened and one-way traffic was introduced on Light Street. This helped to expedite traffic and alleviate the condition.

If we of the motor-driven age have experienced traffic jams at that intersection, a glance at the accompanying illustrations will show what horse-drawn vehicles encountered around the turn of this century. One view looks south on Light Street, taken from a point just below Pratt; the other looks west on Pratt Street from the point where Light crosses it.

No mechanized vehicles appear in the scene except a few street cars caught in the Pratt Street jam. Wagons and carts waiting to move are lined up for many blocks.

What patience the drivers of the wagons had in those days! Finding himself in a line of traffic like this, one could do nothing but endure the delay. It is evident that the side streets had their own traffic problems, so there was no way of getting out of line.

One compensation was a total absence of blaring air horns heard nowadays when traffic slows down. In their place were the "Gees" and "Haws" of the draymen as they encouraged their horses and mules to inch along when the opportunity was presented.

In the view of Light Street, all wagons and carts either are backed up to the steamboat wharves or in a single line headed in a northerly direction. Even in those days there may have been a plan to expedite traffic along that street comparing with our one-way system.

The Light Street view is one of the most interesting of that thoroughfare to come to light. In an effort to date it I have concluded that it is of the decade 1894–1904 for several reasons. The pier immediately to the left is Pier 4 of the Baltimore, Chesapeake and Atlantic Railway Company. In 1894 the B. C. & A. was organized after taking over a number of steamboat companies that operated from Light Street. The original photograph shows B. C. & A. on pier fronts, indicating that it was taken sometime after 1895.

On Pier 7, the name of Chester River Steamboat Company can be seen and, since that line was not absorbed until 1904 by the Maryland, Delaware and Virginia Railway Company, we can be sure that the photograph was made prior to that date.

Looking west on Pratt Street, Baltimore, at its junction with Light Street, about 1903. The Philadelphia steamer *Anthony Groves, Jr.* is at left, at Pier 1, Light Street.
Photo: The Peale Museum

The stack of a steamboat bearing the letter W is visible at the adjoining pier. This was the insignia of the old Weems Line and was evident in Baltimore harbor until March 1905 following the sale of that line to the M. D. & V. The two steamboat pilothouses extending above the wharves belong to the former Wheeler Line's *Chesapeake* and the Chester River Line's *Corsica,* both active during that period.

A tall tower-like structure in the background marked the terminal of the Old Bay Line and was a prominent landmark on Light Street until 1950 when it was dismantled.

In 1898, fire destroyed the Old Bay Line's establishment at the foot of Concord Street and the company moved to Pier 10, Light Street. Shortly thereafter they acquired the property and erected a pier marked by that tower.

In front of that pier is a bridgelike affair crossing Light Street. This was truly a bridge, erected for the convenience of the patrons of the Old Bay Line.

The Baltimore fire of 1904 changed the profile of that area. In 1905, it was decided to widen Light Street by condemning real estate on the west side. The Old Bay Line's bridge was dismantled at that time.

Federal Hill can be seen in the left background of the photograph. Prominent on that hill is a tower which was erected in 1887 and used as a signal station to report the arrival of ships to Bal-timore merchants by means of flag signals. On July 20, 1902, this building was demolished during a squall. Thus, the date of the photograph is pinpointed between 1899, the date of the erection of the Old Bay Line's pier, and 1902.

The Pratt Street view is approximately of the same period. Light Street is still unwidened, indicating that it was taken prior to 1905. The vessel at Pier 1, Light Street, on the left, is the Baltimore-Philadelphia steamboat *Anthony Groves, Jr.,* built in 1893.

Steamboats were the basic cause of the congestion on Pratt and Light Streets. They were the chief means of transportation between tidewater Maryland and Virginia. Most of the goods used in the Chesapeake country were funneled down to the city wharves via thousands of wagons and teams. Seafood and farm products came to the city on steamers and wagons were called upon to disperse these items to various parts of Baltimore.

Steamboat traffic waned as the years went by but tie-ups continued on Light and Pratt as automobiles and trucks increased. The streets were arteries leading to the growing industrial sections of Baltimore.

Looking south on Light Street, Baltimore, showing the steamboat wharves and congestion of traffic, circa 1900. Photo: C. C. Knobeloch

Eagles
Over the Bay

THERE WAS a time when giant eagles, with wingspreads up to six feet, soared over Chesapeake waters. Their breasts bore the design of the American shield and in their talons olive branches and arrows were clutched.

They were the carved wooden type that served as a theme for paddle-box decorations on the numerous side-wheel steamers operating out of Baltimore.

The arc-shaped paddle boxes, housing the steamer's side wheels, were usually fluted except for a small semicircle at the center reserved for the decoration. Flutes radiated outward from the carving like rays and the huge paddle boxes appeared to have a lacelike quality when viewed from a distance.

Paddle box of the Weems Line steamboat *Lancaster* that plied the Rappahannock River route from Baltimore for many years. Author's Collection

A spread eagle was the favorite motif for this decoration. Some steamboats on which this design appeared were: *B. S. Ford, Avalon, Lancaster, Annapolis, Kitty Knight, Westmoreland, Emma A.*

Ford, and *Joppa.* Gold leaf and bright colors made the carvings extremely attractive and greatly admired when vessels bearing them were in port. Shipbuilders employed the finest skilled craftsmen to fashion these designs. Though the carvings were covered with many coats of paint as the years went by, the stately splendor represented by the eagle was not concealed.

The last examples of paddle-box decorations of this type around the Bay were those on the Tolchester ferry *Annapolis* and the excursion steamer *Federal Hill.* The former was dismantled at the old Woodall Shipyard in Baltimore in 1935. The fine carvings were probably broken up for firewood.

The *Federal Hill* was originally the *Avalon* that operated to Maryland and Virginia tidewater ports. She was stripped down to a bare hull at Curtis Bay, Baltimore, in 1940 and converted into a barge.

The side-wheeler *Eastern Shore* simply carried a small semicircle bearing the letters USM carved in relief, boasting that she transported the mails. When the *Ida* first came out, she bore the profile likeness of a girl, probably the one for whom she was named. The old Tolchester steamer *Pilot Boy* merely had a carved wooden star in position. The designs were varied but the spread eagle was universally popular. However, they have taken wing along with the steamboats they decorated.

Another favorite perch for carved wooden eagles was atop pilothouses of steamboats and tugs. Gilded and with wings spread as though about to take flight, they were part of any well-dressed ship. Most of the Bay steamers and tugs carried them.

The pilothouse eagles were rather vulnerable in their exposed positions, however, and few lasted the life of the steamer they adorned. In later years, the searchlight took this position on the pilothouse and the tradition became outmoded. The last of these carvings on Bay vessels were on the tugs *August A. Denhard, Porter, Jesse Tyson,* and *Huntington.*

The eagle has long graced the bows and sterns of Chesapeake commercial sailing craft. It has also been worked into the design of the trailboards with wings spread behind draped flags and cannon. Examples of these carvings may still be seen on some of the craft in Maryland's oyster dredging fleet and a few of these vessels bear crude representations of eagle figureheads.

Large seagoing merchant sailing ships used the spread eagle as a stern decoration. Builders of the smaller Bay vessels were not to be outdone, however, and many Chesapeake schooners carried carved wooden eagles on their sterns. The last Bay schooner decorated in this manner was the *Mattie F. Dean.* During heavy weather in the 1940's, a sea tore the carving loose and destroyed the last local example of this nautical tradition. It is doubtful whether beautifully carved decorations will ever again adorn commercial craft.

Carved wooden eagle paddle-box decoration on the Chesapeake Bay steamboat *Avalon*.
Photo: Author

Steamboat Reveries

ON MARCH 2, 1932, as two trim Chesapeake Bay steamboats sailed into Baltimore harbor, they approached their Light Street wharves with whistles playing a mournful dirge. Those familiar with waterfront affairs understood as the doleful tones echoed from the warehouses and factories bordering the harbor. They were bemoaning the end of a phase of Chesapeake steamboating that had had its inception as far back as 1817.

These were the last arrivals of the Baltimore & Virginia Steamboat Company's fleet after that organization had declared bankruptcy a few days previously. One of the steamers, the *Anne Arundel,* had left Washington, D.C., two days before,

bidding farewell to her twenty-four Maryland and Virginia landings on the Potomac River and its tributaries. The other vessel, the *Potomac,* was arriving from Tappahannock and other wharves on the Rappahannock River in Virginia.

The grief these vessels expressed was shared by other steamboats of the defunct company already tied up at their Baltimore piers. They were the side-wheelers *Talbot, Eastern Shore, Virginia,* and *Dorchester,* and the propeller-driven *Northumberland, Calvert,* and *Piankatank.* Their crew members, many of whom could count their service on the various steamers in decades rather than years, had already departed. When the crews of the two

The *Anne Arundel* at Cambridge, Maryland in 1935. Photo: Author

most recent arrivals walked off their ships for the last time, a total of approximately four hundred men had joined the growing ranks of unemployed in that depression year.

Baltimore's principal marine link with the famous tidewater country was terminated. The last survivors of the once-thriving Bay steamboat trade could not compete with truck, bus, automobile, and powerboat.

Although the Baltimore & Virginia Steamboat Company had only been in existence since 1923 (originating as a result of the foreclosure of the Maryland, Delaware & Virginia Railway Company, and, a few years later, absorbing the holdings of the Baltimore, Chesapeake & Atlantic Railway Company), it was the descendant of a long line of famous Chesapeake steamboating names. Some of the forerunners were the Weems Line, Maryland Steamboat Company, Eastern Shore Steamboat Company, Chester River Steamboat Company, Wheeler Line, and Choptank Steamboat Company.

No longer would the daily procession of steamboats be sailing out of Baltimore harbor for coun-

The *Calvert* sails down the Potomac River while on the Baltimore-Washington route. Hollerith Collection

try landings down the Bay, a sight that had been familiar to waterfront spectators for generations. Around 4:30 P.M. every afternoon a long blast on each steamer's whistle would signify that they were backing out from their piers. After skillful maneuvering in the confines of the upper harbor, their bows would be pointed toward open waters. Reaching the Patapsco, the faster steamer would pull out of line and forge ahead. As she steamed by her slower partners, the stevedores of the victor never hesitated to jeer those on the vessels left in her wake.

These steamers offered varied cruises. On the Eastern Shore of Maryland and Virginia, one could sail up the Pocomoke, Occohannock, Wicomico, and Nanticoke Rivers, pathways to the strawberry and potato lands. A shorter trip to the Eastern Shore was up the Choptank River to Cambridge. If the Western Shore was favored, a cruise up the Rappahannock or Piankatank Rivers of Virginia would always assure a scenic, restful voyage. The most popular of them all, however, was the Baltimore-Washington trip which the company advertised as "a dip into the pages of the chronicles of a nation in its making—a little journey through a country teeming with riches of history and tradition."

Although the land distance between these two cities can be covered by car in an hour, the water route required the steamer to spend about thirty-seven hours traversing Chesapeake Bay and the Potomac River and its tributaries, making numerous landings on the way.

It was a real experience to lose one's self in the echoes of the past as the steamers penetrated the historic waters of Maryland and Virginia. In an attempt to recapture those days, let us take an imaginary trip from Baltimore to Washington on the paddle-wheel steamboat *Dorchester*, say, in 1931, the last summer the steamers operated for the Baltimore & Virginia Steamboat Company.

Pier 3, Light Street, the *Dorchester's* berth, is a center of activity as stevedores truck the last bit of freight on board; we nimbly jump out of their way as we make for the gangplank. That odor permeating the Light Street area is a part of the steamboats—the aromas of spices and freshly roasted coffee blending with those emanating from the varied freight, engine room, and salty, tar-sodden rope give one the feeling that he is about to embark on a real voyage.

After purchasing a ticket and receiving a stateroom key at the purser's office we go on deck to watch last-minute activity before sailing. Over at Pier 1, Pratt Street, Eastern Shore steamers are preparing to leave. In the slips near us are the Rappahannock and Piankatank River steamers. All are glistening white in the midsummer sun with all visible brass fittings shining to the utmost. Those scheduled to sail alternately blow their whistles to announce that departure time is at hand.

Lines are cast off and the first thrust of her paddle wheels backs our steamer out into the harbor. The *Calvert* has already left her Pratt Street pier and is bound down the harbor. We will soon follow in her wake.

A wide, white trail of foam is made as the paddle wheels surge the steamboat forward in rhythmic motion. Astern of us is the squat side-wheeler *Virginia* bound for Crisfield. The *Piankatank* is following her and she will go farther down the Bay than any of the steamers. She will turn off into the Great Wicomico River and later proceed down the Bay for Freeport and other landings on the Piankatank River. Bringing up the rear is the *Potomac,* bound for Rappahannock points.

What is that bell we hear? The tone is not as deep and mellow as that of the bell buoys we have

ington. If one knows the captain well enough, he is sure of an invitation to join him for dinner—a singular honor.

After dinner, we come on deck again and find that we are almost abreast of Annapolis. The sun is sinking behind the city in a blaze of color, promising fine weather for the next day's passage up the Potomac. Relaxing in a deck chair and inhaling the pine-scented air blowing from shore, we watch the lights come on along the shoreline.

We notice the *Calvert,* ahead of us, is veering toward the Eastern Shore. She has reached the buoy marking her turning-off point for the Choptank River, and will have docked at Cambridge and started to make her other landings on the return trip to Baltimore before we enter the Potomac River.

Before midnight, most of the passengers have trailed off to their respective staterooms to sleep until awakened by the steamer's whistle blowing for the first landing at Potomac View, on Smith's Creek, in southern Maryland.

Reference is made to the little folder, *Vacations and Outings in the Chesapeake Bay Country* and the pamphlet, *A Little Cruise Through Historic*

The *Piankatank* idles away at Baltimore after service to the Piankatank River ended. Photo: Author

The *Northumberland* at Coan Wharf, Virginia. Photo: Author

been passing, but its source is soon revealed as a white-coated waiter approaches, ringing the dinner bell and announcing, "Dinner is now being served."

For $1.00 we indulge in the finest foods that the Chesapeake Bay and its surrounding counties produce: Maryland-style fried chicken, fish or deviled crab, corn bread, and all the extras prepared as only the steamboat cooks, in their inimitable style, can prepare food. We may look forward to four more meals like this before the steamer docks in Wash-

Waters. They are typical of the advertising leaflets passed out to prospective vacationers, attempting to give brief lessons in history along with a description of the steamer's voyage.

The *Dorchester's* first landing, Potomac View, is a small settlement centering around a fish-packing cannery but it stands on historic ground. Behind the village is "Calvert's Rest," represented by a fine old dwelling, Calvert Hall, the home of William Calvert, son of Maryland's first governor. Few people are astir on shore at this early hour but there is always someone present to catch the heaving line. A little freight is trucked off and a few passengers disembark.

After leaving Potomac View, the *Dorchester* begins a day of calling at numerous landings in Maryland and Virginia. She proceeds to St. Mary's City (or, rather, to the wharf known as Bromes, near the site of Maryland's ancient capital) where Leonard Calvert and his little group of English Catholics settled to establish towns and proclaim religious liberty throughout the colony. It is too early in the morning to go ashore for a visit but, on the return trip from Washington to Baltimore, the vessel docks here about 6 P.M. Then, while freight is being handled, the passengers will have time to climb

The *Virginia* at Baltimore shortly before being cut down to a barge in 1936. Photo: Author

the bluff from the wharf and wander around through old St. Mary's. A focal point is the 36-foot-high granite shaft marking the site of the mulberry tree under which Calvert and the Indian king signed a peace treaty in 1634.

The next landing is Porto Bello. The folder explains that it derives its name from the fact that three Potomac River lads sailed as midshipmen with British Admiral Vernon in his campaign against the Spaniards in the West Indies where they took part in naval engagements at Porto Bello and Cartagena. Day is just beginning to break and fowl and cattle on nearby farms lend their crowing and lowing, respectively, to the sounds of escaping steam and stevedores' trucks rattling down the wooden gangplank.

As the lines are cast off, the *Dorchester* steams across St. Mary's River to Grason's Wharf, located on St. Inigoes Creek. The folder reminds us that this creek's name is derived from St. Ignatius. The landing is quite unimpressive but if one walks to the top of the hill behind the landing, he will find

hidden among the trees the oldest house in Maryland, Cross Manor. When the steamer has completed its business here, it departs and leaves St. Mary's River astern as it crosses the broad Potomac for the Virginia shore. It requires about an hour for the *Dorchester* to cover the 7-mile-wide body of water and when one looks to the east, beyond the mouth of the Potomac River, he observes the sun rising over the distant Eastern Shore of Chesapeake Bay.

Coan Wharf is the first landing on the Virginia side, the schedule calling for arrival there at 5 A.M. Coan River wends through rich farm land. Near its head is the landing, made up of a general store, hotel, and tomato cannery. Behind the buildings is

The *Eastern Shore* leaves Baltimore in 1927 bound for Eastern Shore landings. Photo: C. C. Knobeloch

a dirt road winding through large trees, a gateway into one of Virginia's loveliest tidewater counties, Northumberland.

The next landing is but a stone's throw away. This is Bundick's, directly across the narrow river from Coan Wharf. The channel is narrow here and expert maneuvering is required to keep the vessel from running aground.

The channel to our next landing, Lake Wharf, remains narrow, marked only by a bush on a stake. From Lake Wharf, our steamer heads across the river to Walnut Point. No walnut trees are in evidence but there are many tall, graceful poplars. This is a busy landing with store and canneries, and several large sailing craft are moored on the opposite side of the wharf. A profusion of oyster shells proves it to be an important oyster and fish center.

The next landing is Cowart's, up an arm of the Coan River, known as The Glebe. Few of these landings can boast of more than a freight shed, packing house, and general store, and this is a perfect description of Cowart's. Each has its own unspoiled atmosphere, an air of charm and serenity. Spectators on the wharf seem interested in the steamer and its passengers and are eager to hear news from Baltimore.

The last landing in Coan River is Lewisetta. As at previous landings, the stevedores truck freight on and off the steamer in their own individual style. They do more than push the hand trucks laden with boxes or bags of fertilizer. Their bodies go through a strutting motion which seems to have had its origin at some tribal gathering in darkest Africa. When they attempt to bring cattle aboard for shipment to the market, the onlookers are treated to all the thrills of a rodeo show. A particularly balky calf will require three or four pairs of hands and feet to encourage him up the sloping gangplank. Sheep are carried bodily.

Departing from Lewisetta, the *Dorchester* heads up the Potomac leaving a wide, foamy path astern

a delay but it never seems to bother the passengers on board or those awaiting the steamer at the next landing. They relax in chairs on the canvas-shaded, breeze-cooled deck and enjoy the scenery.

The morning is getting on and Kinsale is the next wharf. The steamer is scheduled to arrive there at nine. This is a brief passage up another branch of the Yeocomico but a scenic one. We see the wooden buildings marking the landing; packing plants and a rickety bridge crossing the stream are beyond. Behind the wharf is an oyster-shell road climbing the hill to the town. Kinsale has a hotel and a bank, and is marked off in streets. Here in the Yeocomico we are likely to meet the *Talbot*, the *Dorchester's* running mate during summer months. She will be bound for Baltimore, having left Washington the previous afternoon.

Having completed her business at the landing, the *Dorchester's* lines are let go and she maneuvers until her bow is pointed downstream. She is

Foredeck and pilothouse of the *Eastern Shore* at Pier 1, Pratt Street, Baltimore. Photo: Author

The side-wheelers *Virginia, Talbot,* and *Dorchester* tug at their lines at Baltimore in 1936 after their passenger and freighting days on the Bay came to an end. Photo: Author

as her paddle wheels surge her forward to the next river up the Virginia shoreline. That is the serene Yeocomico, an Indian name meaning "Tossed to and fro by the waters." At Lodge Landing the whistle echoes through the surrounding forests as our vessel blows for the wharf. Lodge is just a small village but postmark stamps used by the U. S. Post Office are made in a plant located here.

The steamer must steer down the Yeocomico River again for her next landing. A brief sail brings her to Mundy Point. This is a prosperous looking community and boasts of a tomato cannery, a herring packing plant, and the usual general store and post office. During the height of the tomato canning season many cases of canned goods may be expected as freight for the city. This causes

bound for Maryland once more to spend the day wandering up and down the bays, creeks, and rivers in the southern part of the Old Line State. Piney Point is our destination as our steamer plods across the Potomac.

Piney Point is a summer resort and there are many people on the dock—some fishing and crabbing, others garbed for a swim. These pastimes are abandoned as the steamer sidles up to the wharf and the activity of handling freight occupies the spotlight. It is now 10 A.M. and at this point we are about seven miles by land from Porto Bello, one of our landings before daybreak. After a brief stay at Piney Point, our steamer continues up the Potomac to Leonardtown at the head of Breton Bay.

It is a two-hour sail up to Leonardtown, the most historic site in Southern Maryland with the exception of St. Mary's. It has been a progressive town ever since it was laid out in 1708 and has been the county seat since 1710. The steamer is scheduled to arrive at noon and while the freight is being handled, we enjoy our midday meal. On steamboats this is called dinner, and for good reason, considering all that is placed on the table. The evening meal is referred to as supper.

Before passing out of Breton Bay we make a brief stop at Abell's, marked by a wooden shed on a sandy point with gently rising hills behind it. This is decidedly rural and it is not unusual to see an oxcart coming down the sandy road. We continue on to St. Clement's River to St. Clement's, Cobrum's, and Bayside—all quaint landings.

Bushwood and Rock Point, on the Wicomico River, are the next wharves on the steamer route to Washington. By the time Rock Point is reached, the afternoon is well spent. Leaving Rock Point,

Alexandria is reached in the early morning. Most of the passengers are out on deck by now to view the approach to Washington, the end of the voyage and 40 miles by land from our departure point two days ago. Our steamer has traveled about 320 miles and touched at 25 landings between the two major cities.

After breakfast and a personal goodbye to each passenger from the captain, we are off to the railroad station to catch a train for a forty-five-minute trip to Baltimore.

At the time of our imaginary trip, the Potomac River steamers left Pier 3, Light Street, Baltimore, on Mondays, Wednesdays, and Saturdays at 4:30 P.M. They arrived at Washington early in the morning on the following Wednesday, Friday, and Monday. Steamers also left the 7th Street Wharf, Washington, the same days at 4 P.M. and arrived at Baltimore the following Wednesday, Friday, and Monday.

Circle-tour tickets included the fare between

The *Dorchester* at Lodge Landing, Yeocomico River, Virginia. Photo: The Mariners Museum

The *Talbot* at Piney Point, Maryland.
Photo: The Mariners Museum

the *Dorchester* steams out into the Potomac River again to cross its breadth to Colonial Beach, Virginia.

Supper is over by the time we reach this popular summer resort and the passengers sit on deck to watch activity on the dancing pavilion, the walks, and the dock. Darkness has descended and a cool breeze sweeps across the deck. Presently the gangways are hauled aboard, the lines cast off, and strains of the music on shore are muted by the sound of paddle wheels slapping the water's surface.

We head back across the Potomac again to land at Liverpool Point and Glymont on that river.

Baltimore and Washington via train, taxicab transfer at either Baltimore or Washington, steamer fare, stateroom, and meals. The cost was $12.12 for one person; when two people occupied one stateroom, the charge was $11.00 per person!

When the Baltimore & Virginia Steamboat Company ceased operations, a way of living vanished. Today we are asked, "What has happened to the tidewater landings?"; "Where are the steamboats?"

Many of the landings have been deserted and have fallen into disuse. Others, relying on shipments by water to some extent, are being kept in repair to cater to powerboats. None, however, are as they were when steamboat time was at hand—an event that never grew monotonous to the tidewater folk.

How could the steamboats have disappeared so completely and in such a short time after their disposal by the Baltimore & Virginia Steamboat Company? There were many years of service left in each one but they had outlived their usefulness in the trade for which they were designed originally. They were all put up for sale immediately after the bankruptcy announcement; some were destined to leave the Bay forever, and others were to be converted into excursion steamers or cut down to barges.

Several of the vessels were given a new lease on life. In May 1932, the Western Shore Steamboat Company was organized under the guidance of Captain James W. Gresham. Captain Gresham had been a skipper of one of the Baltimore & Virginia steamboats and had first-hand knowledge of the vessels and their routes.

This new company began by operating the little steamer *Hampton Roads* on the abandoned Cam-

bridge route. Business increased and this vessel was disposed of and the *Virginia* and *Potomac* were added to the roster. During the summer of 1932, the famous Chesapeake cruises were revived on a small scale. The *Virginia* made two trips each week to the Piankatank River and a weekend trip up the Patuxent River. The *Potomac* serviced the Rappahannock River landings. The management endeavored to offer the public the most for their

Steamboat time at Lodge Landing, Virginia, on the Potomac River route. Countryfolk come down to the wharf to witness the scene. The steamer's passengers take time out for a stroll up the sandy road to the town as stevedores truck the freight.
Photo: H. Graham Wood

money. For as little as $7.00, all-expense trips (including passage, outside stateroom, and four meals) were offered. However, an inviting offer like that failed to entice many travelers.

By the next year, the *Virginia* was replaced by the *Anne Arundel*. The *Potomac* and the *Anne Arundel* operated to the Choptank, Patuxent, Potomac, Rappahannock, and Piankatank Rivers for several years after that. In 1936, the *Potomac* was rammed by another steamer and stricken from the active list. The Western Shore Steamboat Company suspended operations the following year.

In July 1933, the steamers *Eastern Shore* and *Piankatank* were being operated by the Baltimore,

79

Crisfield, and Onancock Line to the Eastern Shore of Maryland and Virginia. This organization also offered reduced rates to encourage travelers, but with little response, and in 1939, ceased operations.

The steamboats had made a game but vain try at a comeback. There was no place for them in the modern transportation trend. Trucks and buses could handle the business with greater speed and this is what the public was demanding. However, there was work for them to do in less romantic fields.

Several years after the Baltimore & Virgina Steamboat Company's failure, the *Northumberland* came under the Buxton Line, a Norfolk firm. She was renamed *Norfolk* and operated as a freight vessel between Norfolk and Richmond. She enjoyed a few years of activity but finally burned in September 1945, while tied up at Claremont, Virginia, on the James River. *Calvert* was the next to go. She was taken to New York and later remodeled, dieselized, and operated as a car ferry out of New London, Connecticut, until the Navy took her over in 1942. After a long period of idleness, she was broken up in 1957.

In 1936, the sister ships *Talbot* and *Dorchester* left their Boston Street berths in Baltimore and went separate ways. The *Talbot* was taken to New York, converted into an excursion steamer, and renamed *City of New York*. After a face-lifting,

the *Dorchester* went to Washington, D.C., as the excursion steamer *Robert E. Lee.* They were broken up in 1951 and 1953, respectively.

The end of the *Virginia* and the *Eastern Shore* as side-wheelers came about in 1936. The former was converted into a barge. The latter, after being stripped, emerged from the shipyard as a Diesel freighter, but retained her original name. She continued to operate on the Bay until World War II, when she was taken over by the Government for service in the Hampton Roads area. She burned at Great Bridge, Virginia, April 26, 1949.

The *Potomac* was cut down for a barge in 1938 and broken up in 1954. The *Anne Arundel* was renamed *Mohawk* in 1938 and operated as an excursion steamer to Fairview Beach. Later she plied to Tolchester Beach. In 1943, the Government acquired her for use in the Hampton Roads area. After World War II, she was taken to Boston to sail between that port and Nantasket Beach. She was broken up in 1952. The *Piankatank*, the last of the group, was scrapped in 1940.

The grand fleet of the Baltimore & Virginia Steamboat Company is but a memory now. The beauties of the tidewater country remain the same and beckon to all, but its scenic waterways and bordering shorelines, once available to all, are limited to the minority—the individual boatowners.

The *Middlesex* at Irvington, Virginia. Built at Philadelphia in 1902, this steamer was a favorite on the Rappahannock River route plying between Baltimore and Fredericksburg. In 1929 she went to Boston and was renamed *Plymouth*. She was sold to New York owners in 1939, renamed *Manhattan,* and burned at Tottenville, New York on March 12, 1939.
Photo: The Mariners Museum

Norfolk to Baltimore - the Long Way

NORFOLK steamboating is usually associated with the James River, Hampton Roads, and routes in the immediate vicinity, such as the lower part of the Eastern Shore of Virginia and the Mobjack Bay area. The Rappahannock River service out of Norfolk is probably the least known of steamboat routes of that area, yet it lasted longer than some of the others.

The *Potomac* was typical of the freight and passenger steamboats that once plied Chesapeake Bay and its tributaries. She was a 176-foot, propeller-driven vessel, built in 1894 by Neafie and Levy, in Philadelphia, for the Maryland and Virginia Steamboat Company, to serve between Baltimore and the Potomac River.

Through the first quarter of a century of the *Potomac's* career she operated under several owners but always confined her activities to the Chesapeake region. It was while managed by the Baltimore and Virginia Steamboat Company that she last served on the Norfolk-Rappahannock River-Baltimore route.

The *Potomac* would arrive in Norfolk on Sunday evening, having left Baltimore at 4:30 P.M. on Friday. On her way down the Bay from Baltimore she would steam directly for the mouth of the Rappahannock River.

During the early hours of the following morning she would arrive at Westland Wharf, at the very tip of Lancaster County. This was the beginning of an all-day procession up the Rappahannock, the vessel making landings at a total of 21 country wharves, finally arriving at Fredericksburg, 95 miles above the river's mouth, at 8 P.M. on Saturday.

There was no long layover period for the little steamer. By 9 P.M. she had discharged her passengers and freight and was ready to depart from Fredericksburg for Norfolk. On the way down the river she would make stops at 10 wharves, be-

tween Tappahannock and Fredericksburg, having by-passed them on her way up. Below Tappahannock she would omit stops at five of the wharves she made while bound up the river. She would make a total of 23 landings, however, before leaving the Rappahannock astern to head south down the Chesapeake. Arriving at Norfolk on Sunday evening, 50 hours had been consumed from the time she left Baltimore until she reached her destination.

Tying up at the Pennsylvania Railroad pier, the *Potomac* would discharge and take on freight and passengers. At 2 P.M. on Mondays she would depart for Tappahannock, halfway up the Rappahannock to Fredericksburg, en route to Baltimore. As on her southbound trip from Baltimore a few days earlier, her initial landing on the Rappahannock River would be Westland.

Again a whole day would be required to make the landings up the Rappahannock, reaching Tappahannock late Tuesday afternoon. At 7 A.M. on Wednesday, the *Potomac* would depart from Tappahannock for Baltimore, making eight landings down-river before putting out into Chesapeake Bay. Her next stop would be Baltimore, her home port, on Thursday morning. Almost a whole week was required for the completion of the round trip.

The Rappahannock wharves were picturesque parts of tidewater Virginia that are virtually non-existent today. The landings on the river proper reached far offshore in order to accommodate the *Potomac* in deep water. In waterways like Carters and Urbanna Creek, the wharves were built close to shore because the water was deep near the land.

At all of the landings, especially those made in daylight hours, there were crowds waiting for the arrival of the steamer. People would come from the surrounding countryside to meet passengers, to pick up freight consigned to them, or merely to gossip with friends and members of the steamer's crew. Some of the landings were locations of good-sized towns, like Irvington, Urbanna, and Tappahannock; others consisted of a general store and post office, a few houses, and a cannery. However, all were centers of activity at steamboat time.

Many of the passengers used the steamer as a means of transportation and a large percentage were vacationists. With comfortable staterooms, good meals, and an ever-changing panorama as the steamer threaded its way along the rivers and creeks, a trip on the *Potomac* was an ideal vacation cruise eagerly anticipated by city dwellers.

the remote necks and peninsulas closer to city markets.

As steamboat companies struggled against this competition, many landings were abandoned and some of the older vessels were laid up or sold. Steamboating, as Chesapeake Bay once knew it, was on its way out. Nevertheless, the little *Potomac* carried on, her coarse whistle reverberating around Norfolk harbor and the Rappahannock countryside as she blew for her landings.

In February 1932, during the depth of the depression, the Baltimore and Virginia Steamboat

The *Potomac* served landings on the Rappahannock River and was long a favorite.
Photo: The Mariners Museum

The Rappahannock River trip out of Norfolk was extremely popular because that river offered varying scenery. Near its mouth the river was wide, the water clear, and the surrounding countryside low. About halfway up to Fredericksburg, the river became muddy and narrow and the shoreline high. It was so narrow at some places on the upper river, and the channel came so close to shore, that the steamer's stack almost touched the branches of the overhanging trees.

By the late 1920's, inroads in the steamboat's business were being made by automobiles, buses, trucks and powerboats. Good hard-surfaced roads were penetrating the tidewater sections and bridges were being built across many of the rivers to bring

Company declared bankruptcy. The *Potomac* was on her Rappahannock route at the time and, when she arrived in Baltimore, she found the company's other steamers tied up at their piers. That brought to an end the service between Norfolk and the Rappahannock River.

Little is left along the Rappahannock to remind one of steamboating days. Virtually all of the wharves, except those in towns like Urbanna and Tappahannock, have vanished. When steamboats left the Rappahannock, trucks and buses took over the trade. The wharves were neglected and finally abandoned. In some cases, it is even difficult to find traces of their pilings. That way of life in the tidewater country belongs to the ages.

A Shipshape House

KEEPING a house shipshape is the aim of most homemakers, but keeping a ship "house-shape" is a new approach along this line. This complete turnabout applies to a dwelling over-looking the Rappahannock River in Virginia. There on the river's shore stand the pilothouse and officer's quarters of the former Baltimore steamboat *Potomac*. They have served as a residence since 1938.

It is most fitting that this cabin structure be located in that area. For 42 years, the *Potomac* linked Baltimore with the Northern Neck of Virginia, that peninsula between the Potomac and Rappahannock Rivers. When she ceased operation as a steamboat, she was not broken up for scrap as so many of her kind were. Remnants of the steamer serve useful purposes ashore today.

Like a vessel still in service, the pilothouse and cabins undergo their annual overhaul. The exterior is a glistening white; the canvas-covered deck is scraped and repainted; life preservers, bearing the name *Potomac* with the home port of White-stone, are relettered and attached to the railing. Atop the pilothouse, the name boards, in which the incised letters POTOMAC are carved, appear fresh in their new paint.

Outwardly, the appearance of the structure has not changed since its removal from the steamboat. The interior of the pilothouse remains intact with the steering wheel, binnacle, and engine-room gong pulls in their original positions. This now serves as the living room.

An inside door connects the pilothouse with the officer's quarters. The captain's cabin is now a

Pilothouse and officer's quarters of the *Potomac,* erected on the beach at Whitestone, Virginia. Photo: Author

bedroom for its full width. Abaft this are two cabins divided by a partition; one has been converted into a bath, the other remains as it was when the *Potomac* was sailing the Bay. It has its original upper and lower berths. An aroma that was always connected with steamboats can be detected here, one that revives fond memories in anyone who knew the old vessels.

Another full-width bedroom joins the bath. The last cabin has been converted into a kitchen and dining room with electric range and icebox. Hot and cold running water complete the homelike qualities of the dwelling. Including the spacious decks on all sides, the overall measurements of the structure are approximately 50 feet in length and 25 feet in width.

The front yard of the house is the sandy beach of the Rappahannock. Sitting in a steamer chair on its deck, one gets the feeling that he is actually on the *Potomac* under way. The sound of the waves on shore can be accepted as the bow wave made by the steamer's cutwater as she wends her way about the tidal rivers of Maryland and Virginia.

It has been a long time since the *Potomac* coursed the Chesapeake as a steamboat. Her activities came to an abrupt end on February 27, 1936 while she was being operated by the Western Shore Steamboat Company. On that date, the steamer was

The *Potomac*, as a Weems Line steamer, tied up at Pier 7, Light Street, Baltimore, in 1902. Photo: The Peale Museum

bound out of Baltimore for down-the-Bay ports. Near Seven Foot Knoll, while caught in an ice jam, a tramp steamer came up from astern and rammed the *Potomac,* cutting into her wooden superstructure and opening her hull above the water line. The *Potomac* returned to Baltimore under her own power—her last passage as a steam vessel. Her owners were awarded $8000 in damages as a result of the collision and they, in turn, sold the steamer for $5000 for conversion to a barge.

The *Potomac* was towed to a shipyard at Norfolk to be dismantled. The owner of the shipyard felt that the pilothouse and officer's quarters would make an ideal dwelling if placed on property he owned on the Rappahannock River. Huge timbers were placed beneath the structure and, while supported by a crane, the adjoining beams were cut away. The pilothouse and cabin were then lowered onto a scow and shored in place for a passage up the Chesapeake.

In tow of a tug, the scow had an uneventful trip up the Bay. Upon reaching its destination near Whitestone, the scow was maneuvered into positon. This location was one of the few low-lying sections along that part of the river. The structure was eased ashore and placed on a permanent foundation not far from the water's edge.

Now owned by the Menhaden Products Company, Inc., Whitestone, the shorebound *Potomac* is regularly occupied by the officials of that company who use it for vacations during the summer months and winter holidays. After the superstructure was removed from the steamboat, the hull was acquired by the Chesapeake Corporation of Virginia, operators of a pulp mill at West Point on the York River. Retaining the name *Potomac,* this vessel was towed along many of the same Chesapeake tributaries that she had frequented as a steamboat. The barge was finally broken up in 1954.

The pilothouse dwelling is the sole reminder in the Bay area of one-time numerous smaller freight and passenger steamboats that were such an important part of Chesapeake tidewater life.

Last of the
River Boats

RECORDS indicate that in 1852 the 258-ton paddle steamer *Wilson Small* inaugurated steamboating from Baltimore to the Wicomico River. For more than a century, river boats maintained scheduled sailings between Baltimore and Salisbury —Maryland's largest cities on their respective sides of Chesapeake Bay. On December 17, 1954, this maritime connection was severed as the Diesel freighter *Victor Lynn* fell victim to the bridges, ribbons of highways, and faster means of transportation that had penetrated the Bay country.

treasurer of that company had been in favor of establishing a route up the Wicomico to tap the rich resources of the area. His fellow officials were of the opinion that it would be too difficult for a steamer of any size to negotiate the narrow, winding waterway. On one occasion, when the president of the company was out of town, a group expressed a desire to charter a steamer to take them to Salisbury to attend a camp meeting. Against the advice of many, the ambitious treasurer decided to accept the charter and attempt the run. The 160-

Lighthouse tender *Jessamine* was converted into the power freighter *Victor Lynn*. Photo: The Mariners Museum.

The *Victor Lynn* at Pier 4, Pratt Street, Baltimore. Photo: Author

The *Wilson Small* made her Wicomico River landing at Cotton Patch, a wharf east of Shad Point and about two miles below Salisbury. At that time the river's depth would not permit navigation of larger vessels to the city proper. Almost a quarter of a century was to pass after the *Small* started her trips before a channel was developed to make Salisbury accessible to larger steamers.

The Maryland Steamboat Company is credited with opening the Wicomico River to traffic of larger steamboats. For a number of years, the

foot paddle steamer *Champion* was selected for the trip and the services of two of the best Wicomico River pilots were secured.

At the last minute, the charterers could not raise sufficient funds to pay for the trip but the *Champion* sailed, anyway. The passage was completed successfully and the steamer was welcomed at Salisbury. A group of citizens of that city persuaded Enoch Pratt, the largest stockholder in the steamboat company, to establish a regular steamer run between Baltimore and Salisbury. The side-wheeler

Kent opened the route; one source places the date as 1883. Additional landings were built along the river and the trade prospered. To accommodate the increase in business, the more commodious side-wheeler *Enoch Pratt* replaced the *Kent,* leaving Baltimore three times a week. In 1903, the side-wheeler *Virginia* was built for the route, then operated by the Baltimore, Chesapeake & Atlantic Railroad Company. She was to become the best loved of all steamboats associated with the Wicomico River and operated there until about 1929, when steamboats left the river for good.

Buses, trucks, and powerboats had taken most of the business away from the Bay steamboats by that time. The Victor Lynn Line was operating a small powerboat named *Victor Lynn* that burned at Whitehaven, Maryland on March 10, 1924. The company purchased another vessel to replace her and named her *Victor Lynn* after the son of the firm's founder.

The latter *Victor Lynn* had quite an honorable past. She had been built in Baltimore in 1881 as the side-wheel lighthouse tender *Jessamine,* and had serviced the buoys, lighthouses, and other navigational aids in Chesapeake Bay and adjoining waters for 40 years. When she became outmoded in the eyes of the Lighthouse Service, she was sold to private parties, renamed *Queenstown,* and freighted on the Bay.

When the Victor Lynn Line acquired the vessel, they powered her with what was said to be the first pair of direct-reversible Diesels ever built. She was employed in carrying freight between Baltimore and Salisbury, and vice versa, where it was transferred to trucks for further distribution. For many years she worked in conjunction with the other vessels of the company, the *Henrietta Frances, Red Star,* and *Clio.*

In 1938, the *Victor Lynn* was placed in a "coffin"; that is, her iron plates were sheathed with wood planking. During World War II, when the coastwise and Caribbean trade was stripped of its vessels, freight rates soared. The *Victor Lynn* was sent south, operating under the Miami Lines, and sailed between Florida and the West Indies. On her first trip from Cap Haïtien, Haiti, to Miami, she carried 14,000 stems of bananas at a freight of $1.00 per stem. It was a rugged trade for an old vessel, so in September 1944, after freights had dropped and repair bills increased, the *Victor Lynn* returned

to the Chesapeake and took up the route to Salisbury that had been maintained by other vessels of the company.

For some time the officials of the Victor Lynn Line could foresee the end of their river boat service. For sentimental reasons, among others, they were reluctant to abandon the route. With a new terminal in Baltimore and increasing demand for motor truck service, withdrawal of the *Victor Lynn* was inevitable. Her last trip was a special one, leaving Pier 4, Pratt Street, at 5:45 A.M. and arriving at Salisbury at 4:05 P.M. She normally made the passage at night, departing from Baltimore about 6 P.M. and arriving at her destination the next morning. On her last run she carried officials, special guests of the management, and newspapermen.

Seventy-six-year-old Captain Charles B. Wilson, skipper of the *Victor Lynn* for many years, admitted that he would miss the vessel and the run up the Wicomico. He started his steamboating career in 1901 on the side-wheeler *B. S. Ford* and spent most of his time on the Chester River and Choptank River routes. When the Baltimore & Virginia Steamboat Company ceased operations in 1932, Captain Wilson joined the Victor Lynn Line and remained with them until the *Victor Lynn* was tied up. At that time, he retired to his home in Cambridge, Maryland.

When Captain Wilson started steamboating there were scores of steamboats operating out of Baltimore to all parts of the Chesapeake country, and they were the chief means of transportation between Baltimore and the Eastern Shore. Passengers were accommodated in comfortable staterooms and served delightful meals. Farm produce and seafood reached the city markets on steamers; farm implements and merchandise were transported to country towns in the same manner.

Compared to today's standards, the steamboats offered slow transportation. For instance, in 1928, just before the steamers halted operations on the Wicomico River, a vessel would leave Salisbury at 10 A.M., touch at ten landings on the Wicomico, Nanticoke, and Honga Rivers, and arrive in Baltimore the following morning after more than 15 hours en route. Since construction of the Bay Bridge, the distance between the two points can be covered in 3 hours—faster, but less comfortable and scenic.

A Picnic
at Fairview Beach

IT IS PLEASANT to recall the days when a steamboat trip to Fairview Beach, on Rock Creek in Anne Arundel County, was the event of the summer.

This brief voyage was the only opportunity for many Baltimoreans to get away from the city via steamer to a spot which, though near Baltimore, resembled the more remote tidewater sections.

get the choicest deck space because the trip down the harbor and the Patapsco was always interesting.

In a little more than an hour, the steamer would enter Rock Creek, a tributary of the Patapsco River. Her whistle would resound throughout the countryside announcing her approach. That landing smacked of all the atmosphere once found around tidewater steamboat wharves—just a few

Steamboat wharf at Fairview Beach, Rock Creek, Maryland. Photo: Charles F. Efford, Sr.

That special occasion was usually the annual Sunday School picnic, when the whole family (or, in fact, the whole neighborhood) took off for the day. For several days prior to the outing, Mother would be occupied with preparing the perfect picnic lunch basket.

The steamer's pier in Baltimore was originally at the foot of Broadway. In later years the boat departed from Pier 6, Light Street. The object was to get aboard as early as possible in order to

pilings, roughly planked wharf, and shed. Long before the steamer's lines had been heaved to the wharf, the boys would crowd around the gangway, anxious to get off and race for the most suitable lunch tables—those with roofs. A full day of swimming, rowing, or enjoying various games and sports events followed.

Having discharged her early-morning passengers, the steamer would cast off for Baltimore to bring down the afternoon crowd. They would return about 3:30 P.M. in time for a swim, a few games, and what was left in the lunch baskets.

Tired and sunburned picnickers would board the steamer for the trip back to the city about 6:30 P.M. The whistle would have to be blown to hurry along the stragglers. When all were aboard, the steamer would back away from the landing and it would be another year before most of its passengers would return for another picnic.

Fairview Beach came into being in 1892. Its founders were George W. Efford and Captain Octorus Hudson. The former was a marine engineer and the latter held a master's license. Both knew steamboating from all angles and interested Robert Chard and James McCubbin, large land-owners in Anne Arundel County, in forming a steamboat line for passengers and freight from Baltimore to Rock Creek.

Known as the Rock Creek Steamboat Company, their first steamer was a 75-foot vessel named *Falcon,* which carried about 100 persons. The first landing was a farm called Fairview. Impressed by the ideal location, James Marsh built a small hotel on the point and encouraged family parties on a small scale.

Eventually other landings were added, such as Colonial Beach, Fox Point, Jenkins, Club House, and Head of Rock Creek. The Stony Creek route was added at a later date and these landings were Stony Beach, Landings, Thomas', Altoona Beach, Weedon's, and Head of Stony Creek.

Following the *Falcon* in succession, the boats operated by this company until 1924 were the *Petrel, Thos. L. Worthley, Tourist, Rock Creek, Clio, Severn, Kitty Knight,* and *Riverside.* The Stony Creek run and the *Severn* were sold out to a corporation named the Stony Creek Steamboat Company which later purchased the little steamer *Huntington* and renamed her *Stony Creek.*

The Rock Creek Steamboat Company sold out in 1924 and Mr. Efford's sons, Charles and Harry, formed a new company, purchasing the Fairview tract. After the Stony Creek line failed, the Effords purchased the *Stony Creek* and renamed her *Fairview.* They continued to improve the park and add

new attractions. In 1932, the *Tred Avon* was added to the run. By this time Fort Smallwood was also a stop for the steamers. Both of these vessels were disposed of in 1938 and the former Chesapeake Bay steamboat *Anne Arundel* was purchased, remodeled, and renamed *Mohawk.*

Around this time the old landing was abandoned in favor of a new pier on the opposite side of the point. Due to action of wind and tide, the sand on the point had encroached upon the wharf, causing the water to shallow. A new pier, jutting out into Rock Creek, was built to replace the old one.

For several years, Fairview and the *Mohawk* fought a losing battle. Then war conditions finally sealed the company's fate and the steamer stopped operating after 1941. For the first time in almost half a century, Fairview and Rock Creek were without a steamboat.

Kitty Knight and *Severn,* Rock Creek and Stony Creek steamers, at foot of Broadway, Baltimore. Photo: Charles F. Efford, Sr.

In 1945, the Maryland Yacht Club leased the park for its summer quarters. Slips for yachts were built out into Wall Cove, once a favorite anchorage for weekend yachtsmen. Many changes took place on the grounds, too, but a few of the old landmarks remained. The hotel served as the clubhouse.

The area where steamers had tied up in the old days was paved and became a parking space for cars and boat trailers. Pilings that had fended steamers off the old landings reached up out of the sand, many feet from the water.

Louise, Belle of the Bay

IF EVER a steamboat endeared itself to the people of Baltimore, it was the side-wheeler *Louise*. She was associated with Chesapeake Bay for more than half a century. The greater part of that time she served as an excursion steamer between Baltimore and Tolchester Beach and was considered the largest excursion steamer in the South.

The *Louise* played a prominent part in the courtships of several generations of Baltimoreans. Many will recall with fond memories the moonlight excursions on this veteran steamer. Her departure in 1926 was mourned as the loss of a good friend.

It has been estimated that during the 43 years the *Louise* plied between Baltimore and Tolchester she carried an average of 300,000 persons a season, totalling 12,900,000 during her operation under the Tolchester Line. That is a conservative figure because she made numerous trips under special charter before and after the regular excursion season.

It is doubtful if many of her passengers were familiar with the background of the ship, her original route, and her participation in the Civil War. The *Louise* was built with an iron hull at Wilmington, Delaware, in 1864. Named *Louise* for the daughter of her original owner, Charles Morgan, she plied between New Orleans and Mobile at the outset of her career. From December 1864 until after the close of the Civil War, she was chartered by the United States Government, earning $600 a day for her owners.

In 1874 the *Louise* was purchased by the Baltimore, Chesapeake and Richmond Steamboat Company to carry freight and passengers between Baltimore and West Point, on the York River, Virginia. She made her first trip to West Point on June 17, 1874, and was described as a fine steamer equipped with 50 staterooms and 60 berths.

The Tolchester Company acquired the *Louise* to take care of their expanding business in 1885. She was rebuilt and emerged as an excursion steamer with a capacity of 2500 persons as compared to the 900 carried by the side-wheeler *Nelly White,* her predecessor on the Baltimore-Tolchester route.

Year after year the *Louise* served as a sure sign of spring around the Baltimore waterfront as she was overhauled to transport thousands across the Bay for another season. She was rebuilt again in 1899 and little of the original vessel remained. New steamers came on the scene in Baltimore harbor and served their normal time before being replaced by others, but the *Louise* was there before they came and continued to carry on after many left.

Her first captain under the Tolchester flag is recorded as Captain James H. Truitt, who commanded her for 25 years. Captain John Harris followed him for a short period. Then Captain F. W. Kolb took her over as master for 16 years, until she left Baltimore.

Considering the millions of passengers she carried, the *Louise* was relatively free from mishap and is said to have figured in only one accident. In 1890, while returning to Baltimore from Tolchester, she was rammed by the steamer *Virginia,* resulting in 15 deaths and injuries to many passengers. The *Louise,* however, managed to come on to Baltimore under her own power and, after repairs were effected, she resumed her trips across the Bay.

Sunday school picnics and club outings were the mainstays of the *Louise.* Many local citizens of today had their first salt-water boat ride on this veteran during the early years of the twentieth century.

By 1925 the automobile had gained prominence

and the Tolchester Company realized the value in operating a car ferry between Baltimore and Tolchester but none of their boats were suitable for the purpose. Consequently, the *Louise* was sold to C. L. Dimon, of New York, after being rebuilt. For a brief period she ran as an excursion steamer between Bayonne and Coney Island under the name of *Express*.

The former Staten Island double-ended ferry *Castleton* was brought down to Baltimore to replace the *Louise* and, coincidentally, was renamed *Express*. This side-wheel steamer had a good passenger capacity in addition to being able to transport a large number of automobiles.

After a short career as a Coney Island steamer, plans were completed to convert the old *Louise* into a $100,000 dining palace to be moored off Manhattan Beach, New York. On May 11, 1933,

the vessel developed a leak and sank as the conversion was in progress. It was suspected that she was scuttled because the townspeople had violently opposed the project, fearing that she would become a noisy dance hall. The steamer was never salvaged and her bones still lie beneath the waters of Long Island Sound.

One thing about the *Louise* that is remembered by most people who knew her was her distinctive whistle. Its deep, hoarse tones could be identified above those of any other steamer in the harbor. It is said that when she left Baltimore, the Tolchester Company kept the whistle and placed it on the ferry *Express*. When that vessel was replaced by the steamer *Tolchester* in 1933, it was reported that the whistle was transferred to that vessel. The *Tolchester* burned in 1941 and we may assume that this brought an end to the whistle.

The *Louise,* long-time favorite of Baltimore excursionists, steams out of Baltimore harbor bound for Tolchester Beach. Photo: C. C. Knobeloch

Tolchester on the Bay

TOLCHESTER PARK, on Maryland's upper Eastern Shore, is no longer an amusement center but there is a mute reminder of those days still plying the Bay. This is the barge named *Tolchester,* which, as the steamboat of that name, once carried thousands of Baltimoreans to the popular Eastern Shore resort.

One would hardly associate the barge with the former steamer. All that exists today is a stripped hull on which a pilothouse and living quarters are mounted aft. As a steamboat she was the queen of the excursion vessels operating out of Baltimore between 1933 and 1940.

There have been three vessels named *Tolchester* that operated between Baltimore and the amusement park. The first was an iron-hulled side-wheeler built as the *Samuel M. Felton* at Chester, Pennsylvania, in 1866. She was brought from the Delaware River, rebuilt, and renamed *Tolchester* in February 1889. She was transferred to New York owners around 1890 and was abandoned in 1914.

The second *Tolchester* is the vessel now serving as a barge. The last steamer of that name to operate to the park was built as the *City of Philadelphia* at Wilmington, Delaware, in 1910. She was brought

Tolchester Beach, popular resort for Marylanders, awaits the steamer. Photo: Author

to Baltimore in 1948 to replace the *Bear Mountain* and renamed *Tolchester.* When her service out of Baltimore ended, she began a varied career. She sailed out of Boston, was a gambling ship named *Freestone* on the Potomac River, and was later renamed *Potomac,* returned to Boston, and continued in service.

Of the three, the "barge," the second *Tolchester,* had the most colorful career. She was built at Wilmington, Delaware in 1878 and christened the *St. Johns.* This iron-hulled side-wheeler first operated between New York City and a pier outside of Long Branch, New Jersey, in the summer season.

The *St. Johns,* shown as a Potomac River excursion steamer, finally became the *Tolchester.* Hollerith Collection

During the winter months she traveled between Charleston, South Carolina, and Jacksonville and Palatka, Florida. In the early 1880's she ran between New York and Connecticut River points before being placed on the New York-Sandy Hook, New Jersey route.

The *St. Johns* came down to the Potomac River around 1909 to serve between Washington, D.C., and Colonial Beach, Virginia, as an excursion steamer. During World War I the government used her to transport ammunition and sailors from the Yorktown naval site to Hampton Roads.

In June 1919, this steamer was used to inaugurate freight service between Baltimore, Newport News, and Norfolk on a short-lived run. She then went back to the Potomac River excursion trade before departing for New York in 1926. After being refurbished she emerged as the *Bombay,* catering to the excursion trade.

The Tolchester Lines bought the steamer in 1933, renamed her *Tolchester,* and placed her on the familiar run down the Patapsco and across the Chesapeake to the favorite waterside amusement

park of countless Baltimoreans. With her spacious decks, speed, and easy motion, she was second in popularity only to the old *Louise* as a Tolchester excursion vessel. For seven years the *Tolchester* did the summer daytime stint of making two trips across the Bay in addition to "moonlight" passages in the evenings.

On May 14, 1941, the steamer had been returned to Pier 16, Light Street, after shipyard repairs. The 1941 excursion season was approaching and only some final touch-ups were required to ready her for the opening date.

Shortly after midnight a fire was discovered aboard the vessel. Alarms were sounded but by the time the first piece of fire-fighting equipment arrived, the flames had reached from the steamer to the wooden pier. Six alarms brought 28 pieces of equipment to battle the flames on the *Tolchester,* the smaller *Southport,* the Tolchester Line's pier, and the Chesapeake Line's pier. It was not until two fireboats arrived on the scene, however, that any appreciable headway was made in combating the flames. One fireboat battled the pier fire while the other one towed the two steamers out into the harbor and concentrated on their fires. After the fires were extinguished, the *Tolchester* was found to be severely damaged.

The barge *Tolchester,* formerly the steamer of that name that burned at Baltimore in 1941, still sees service in Virginia waters. Photo: Author

Plans were made to rebuild the *Tolchester* but shipyards failed to respond to bids due to defense orders as a result of World War II. In the fall of 1941 she was taken to a Key Highway shipyard where torches cut up her engines, walking beam, and side-wheels. Only the bare hull remained.

She was acquired by the Chesapeake Corporation of Virginia, at West Point, for use as a barge.

While many of the barges employed by that firm were former steamboat hulls and were renamed, the name of the *Tolchester* was retained.

She was towed by tug to various sections of the Chesapeake to load pulp wood for making paper. One of her running mates was the barge *York River,* the former double-ended ferry *Express,* another Tolchester Beach steamer. This barge was broken up in 1954.

The aging barge *Tolchester* has served admirably recently by carrying finished paper products from the West Point mill to Hampton Roads ports.

The *Tolchester,* built as the *St. Johns,* approaching her Baltimore dock in 1936.
Photo: Author

Palace Steamer *Pocahontas*

RESIDENTS of the lower Bay area used superlatives to describe the steamer trip on the James River between Norfolk and Richmond.

When steamboating reached its zenith at the turn of the century, the line operating on the James River, Virginia Navigation Company, distributed a descriptive and historical booklet to the traveling public. It was entitled *Afloat on the James, The Historic River of the South, The Palace Steamer POCAHONTAS of the Virginia Navigation Company,* and presented a vivid account of the trip.

of a day, while local travel and freightage has depended upon the *Ariel* for transit at nearly 30 landings along the river.

"Recently the Virginia Navigation Company, owners of the *Ariel,* was reorganized. Plenty of capital was enlisted and the splendid new steamer *Pocahontas,* a veritable princess of the river, was built and placed in service. The increase in first-class and local travel was large and immediate.

"No steam vessel so entirely suited to first-class travel in points of elegance, speed, safety, and comfort, in all weathers, as the new *Pocahontas* has ever before been

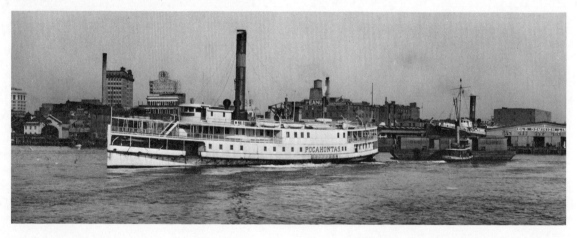

The *Pocahontas* in Norfolk harbor. Photo: H. C. Mann—The Mariners Museum

To capture some of its spirit, let us read some excerpts from the text of this typical brochure of the steamboat era:

"For many years a single steamboat, the staunch old *Ariel,* has maintained a regular tri-weekly route between Richmond and the ports upon Hampton Roads. From her decks tens of thousands of old soldiers of both armies have looked again upon the scenes of battle and march in which they once participated. Numerous tourists hibernating to the resorts of Old Point Comfort, Virginia Beach, and the far South have gone or returned by this pleasant voyage

seen in southern waters. This steamboat was built by Harlan and Hollingsworth, Wilmington, Delaware, in 1893, at a cost of $150,000. Upon the main deck, in addition to the freight and baggage space forward, are the social hall and separate parlor rooms for lady passengers and servants respectively. The purser's office and mail agent's room are also upon this deck. The large dining room below is furnished in exquisite taste and the menu equals in quality and variety that of the best hotels.

"The promenade deck is open fore and aft, the enclosed portion forming large elegantly furnished saloon finished in ivory and gold, to which is added during the winter season a roomy sun parlor covering a portion of the forward deck and giving a protective outlook upon either side and in front. A range of staterooms, large and richly furnished, extend upon either side. Private card-rooms, suggestive of the cozy comfort in a palace car smoking compartment, are also part of the conveniences which will win the praise of many travelers. Upon either side of the grand stairway are pretty semi-circular private parlors, draped with silk curtains.

"The central feature of the steamer is the large and costly electric orchestrion, upon which the choicest selections of popular composers is performed during the trip with the excellence and effect of a band of thirty pieces. The hurricane deck is open to passengers, where plenty of seating room is provided. An electric searchlight apparatus crowns the pilot house."

The *Pocahontas* would leave Richmond at 7 A.M. on Monday, Wednesday, and Friday and arrive at Norfolk at 5:30 P.M. She would leave Norfolk at 7 A.M. on Tuesday, Thursday, and Saturday and reach Richmond at 5:30 P.M., touching at intermediate points along the James River en route. The fare was $1.50 one way, $2.50 round trip, and $1 second class.

"History begins to unroll her time-stained scroll when the hawsers of the *Pocahontas* are cast from the wharf. She beckons the traveler astern for a backward look along the slopes of Richmond glowing in the morning sunshine."

Leaving Rockett's Landing, just below Richmond, the *Pocahontas* would start her day-long shuttle down and across the James. Warwick Park, the first stop, served as a destination for Richmond excursionists via steamers of the Virginia Navigation Company. Successive landings were made at Fort Darling, Varina, Meadowville, Deep Bottom, Curle's Neck, Malvern Hill, Shirley, Bermuda Hundred, Berkeley, Westover, Weyanoke, Upper Brandon, Brandon, and Claremont.

"The passing traveler, observant of the varied onlookers thronging the rude wharves as the steamer comes and goes, may find much to interest and amuse. All of Kemble's types, in both white and black, are there. But one's admiration is provoked for the handsome planters, brown and athletic, and for the slim, pretty girls who come down the winding roads from unseen domiciles, for the mail, or to welcome schoolgirl friends to some Utopia of Old Dominion hospitality. . . . Building materials, new farm machinery, furniture, and similar freight landed all along the river from the steamer proclaim present prosperity."

Jamestown was one of the historical highlights on this trip and while the steamer was busy loading

or unloading freight, the passengers had an opportunity to go ashore and view the ruins of the old church and graveyard.

"When the steamer turns away from Jamestown she heads across the river to the landing of Scotland where extensive wharfage, great piles of lumber, cordwood, and pyramids of barrels account for the presence of a group of vessels, large schooners, barges, and tugs. The prongs of a railway, the "Surry, Sussex, and Southampton," lead out upon the wharves, either side of the warehouse, and connect tidewater with the three counties in its title.

Scotland Wharf, James River, Virginia. The *Pocahontas* (her funnel visible in the background) is lying at the end of the wharf. Hollerith Collection

"This place as well as many others along the river must suggest to the passing traveler who is of a practical nature, the abundant and varied opportunities for profitable investment in cheap forest lands, in fruit-preserving plants, building material establishments, and varied industries for which the raw material is close at hand and which the facilities for cheap water carriage place in close touch with the centers of traffic. Labor is low priced and plentiful, the entire region wonderfully healthful, and so easily reached that the business man leaving New York at 8 P.M. may arrive at river points (upon alternate days at present) as far as Jamestown before 12 o'clock next day."

Proceeding down river the steamer touched at Kings Mill Wharf, originally the mail landing and stage route for Williamsburg, Homewood on Hog Island, Fergusson's, and later Newport News, Old Point Comfort, and Norfolk.

Along the entire route, the distinctive steam whistle of the *Pocahontas,* made up of three individual whistles of different tone to create a chord, announced her approach to the landings. This would bring the farmers and hands from the fields and nearby homes and stores. The steamer was welcomed for more reasons than the fact that she was a link with the outside world. It was said that, suddenly out of nowhere, here was an oasis to the thirsty who could come aboard at the landings and indulge in some thirst-quenching at the ship's bar.

The booklet concludes with:

"It is earnestly hoped that the traveler over the James River route who has by aid of these pages, learned something of the storied past, the busy present and the roseate future of this fruitful region and its historic river, will feel so well repaid for the tour he has undertaken that it will lead him to commend its thronging attractions to many others who as yet know only of its charms 'dimly as seen or heard from afar.'"

On the night of April 30, 1904, a disastrous fire devoured the *Pocahontas* while she was tied up at Rockett's Landing. A watchman discovered the fire but by the time firemen arrived on the scene the flames were beyond control. The wooden superstructure and furnishings went up like tinder. She sank at her pier as firemen pumped water into her. She was raised and within a year was rebuilt according to her original plans.

The Old Dominion Line took over the Virginia Navigation Company in 1906. The *Pocahontas* remained on her James River route with triweekly sailings. Later on, she substituted as a spare boat on the Mobjack Bay run.

On November 29, 1919, the Old Dominion Line abandoned several of its feeder lines in the Hampton Roads area and the James River Day Line was one to be discontinued. The following year the *Pocahontas,* with her running mates *Smithfield* and *Mobjack,* was sold to the Keansburg Steamboat Company. For 15 years she plied between Keansburg, New Jersey and lower Manhattan. In November 1939, she was broken up for her metal content.

An interesting sidelight into the career of the *Pocahontas* was revealed when the *City of New York* (her replacement on the Keansburg-New York route and the former Chesapeake Bay steamboat *Talbot*) was dismantled in the New Jersey marsh where she had been blown in 1950. Her pilothouse nameboards were salvaged by the Perth Amboy engineer and steamboat enthusiast, Louis P. Booz. It was found that the boards had the name *Pocahontas* carved on their reverse sides and were more suited to the lengthy name *City of New York* than the original boards of the *Talbot.* By exchanging another ship's nameboard with Mr. Booz, the author was able to secure one of the *Pocahontas* nameboards to add to his collection of Chesapeake Bay memorabilia, returning it to the Chesapeake area.

The *Pocahontas* served as a spare boat on the Mobjack Bay route and she is shown here at the New Point Comfort Wharf. Photo: Hollerith Collection

Louise of the C & O

FOR MANY years a reminder of steamboating days in Hampton Roads hung under an ivy canopy in a yard on Riverside Drive, Norfolk.

It was the bronze bell from the side-wheel steamboat *John Romer*. Under the name of *Louise* she had served the Chesapeake and Ohio for almost 20 years, carrying passengers, mail, and freight between Newport News and Norfolk.

The owner of the bell was Harry Barghausen who was long associated with several well-known Hampton Roads steamboat lines. Aware of the nostalgic appeal of the bell in his possession and wishing to preserve it, he constructed a belfry from which it could be hung. When he sold his home and moved to a downtown Norfolk apartment, the property was sold with the stipulation that the bell was not to be included in the sale. Mr. Barghausen made an effort to find a suitable home for the relic and eventually it came to The Mariners Museum.

Before Mr. Barghausen acquired the bell, it had been mounted atop the river end of old Pier A in Newport News, where it had served as a fog bell to guide steamers into their berths. The pier, used as a terminus for the steamboats of the Buxton Line, finally became unsafe for use and was dismantled. Mr. Barghausen, an official of the Buxton Line at the time, salvaged the bell.

It is fortunate that the bell came into the possession of someone who was interested in local shipping and the steamboat's past. The *John Romer* had an interesting past, almost a quarter century of which was devoted to service in Hampton Roads' waters.

Appearing in relief on the surface of the bell are the name of the steamboat *John Romer* and the maker's name and date: "Meneelys, West Troy, New York, 1863." Her builder was B. C. Terry, Keyport, New Jersey. For several years she ran between New York and Greenwich, Connecticut, until she was acquired by the Boston and Hingham Steamboat Company in 1866 and placed on the run between those two cities.

An anecdote about this steamer appeared in a story by John Lochhead, published in *The Tiller* in 1948. It reported that Collis P. Huntington, the builder of the Chesapeake and Ohio Railroad, saw the *John Romer* steaming up the Hudson River on one occasion. Struck with her fine appearance, he bought her as a connecting link for his railroad between Newport News and Norfolk. In any event, the steamer was acquired by the railroad in May 1884 and Captain James H. Topham was sent to Boston to bring the steamer to Newport News. After a stop at Jersey City for an overhaul of her machinery, she set out for Newport News to start her career in those waters. On June 7, 1884, she made her first trip from Newport News to Norfolk and thereafter maintained a schedule of two trips a day in each direction for almost two decades. During her entire life of operation in that area, Collis P. Huntington was listed as her owner in the *Record of American and Foreign Shipping*.

Considering the numerous passages this little steamer made between the two Hampton Roads cities, in all kinds of weather, she had a relatively uneventful life. A few months after assuming her new duties, she collided with a mud scow and sank in 15 feet of water off Atlantic City, Norfolk harbor. But she was raised without difficulty and resumed service.

She suffered another collision four years later when the Old Dominion Line steamer *Guyandotte* rammed her in the center of her starboard paddle box while the *Romer* was trying to effect a landing alongside the Old Dominion steamship *Old Dominion,* just below Craney Island.

The *John Romer* was towed into port and later taken to Baltimore to undergo repairs. While the collision damage was being repaired, considerable changes were made in her construction. Her main deck was raised to lift her guards higher out of the water. Her machinery was rebuilt and a new boiler was installed.

On May 20, 1889, she returned to her old run,

completely refurbished and bearing a new name, *Louise,* after the daughter of M. E. Ingalls, president of the Chesapeake and Ohio at that time.

The *Louise* carried on for 13 more years, when she was replaced by the new propeller-driven *Virginia* that had been built in Richmond in 1902 expressly for the Newport News-Norfolk route. For a short while thereafter, the *Louise* made excursions to Smithfield, Jamestown, and Yorktown. She also filled in as a spare boat when the *Virginia*

steam whistle. The whistle was mounted on the *Virginia* along with her regular whistle. When broken up in Baltimore in 1952 several items were salvaged from the *Virginia* and presented to the museum. The whistles were included. They were later attached to a steam line and a tape recording was made of their tone for preservation in the museum's library.

Another relic of the *Louise* in Newport News is the carved wooden eagle that had graced the top

The *Louise,* formerly the *John Romer,* in dry dock at the Newport News Shipbuilding and Dry Dock Company. Photo: The Mariners Museum

was taken off her run for overhaul. Finally moored at the south side of the Chesapeake and Ohio's Pier 7, Newport News, she served as a storeroom, a dormitory for extra crews of the company's tugs, and as an office for Captain J. N. Cooksey, Superintendent of Floating Property for the railroad. There she sank and was broken up about 1905–06, being listed in the shipping register as having been abandoned.

In addition to the bell, The Mariners Museum contains other items that serve to prolong the memory of the *John Romer's* activities in the Chesapeake area. In its collection are an oil painting of the steamer, a series of photographs of her, and her

of her pilothouse. About 1910, Captain Cooksey presented the eagle to T. W. Ross, Assistant Superintendent of Repairs at the Newport News Shipbuilding and Dry Dock Company. The carving was mounted atop the cupola of the superintendent's old office, then located between Dry Docks 1 and 2 and now the site of Building 66. It was subsequently moved and placed over the entrance of the west end of Building 77. A later move placed it on the top of the porch entrance to the lobby on the southeast side of the Superintendent's Building, No. 77. Periodically, the carving is repaired and gilded. R. E. Holzbach, of the Ship Repair Sales Department, prepared a descriptive label for it.

98

The huge bronze bell of the *John Romer,* later renamed *Louise,* as found in a Norfolk garden where it had been mounted and preserved by Mr. Harry Barghausen, shown standing beside it. Photo: Author

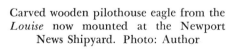
Carved wooden pilothouse eagle from the *Louise* now mounted at the Newport News Shipyard. Photo: Author

The Veteran
C & O Steamer *Virginia*

IN LATE summer 1949 the Chesapeake and Ohio passenger ferry steamer *Virginia* was approaching the day of her last run. She had faithfully connected the ports of Newport News and Norfolk, Virginia, for almost half a century. An overhaul was now due and she was taken off her route. As the fires died beneath her boilers that September, they were destined never to be lighted again. After two years of idleness at her Newport News pier, her next move was to a scrap-yard.

There never will be a genuine replacement for the *Virginia*. Perhaps bridges and tunnels offered quicker connections between the Hampton Roads cities, but the trip across the mouth of the James River offered relaxation and cool breezes after a confining rail trip down from Richmond. Many Norfolk and Newport News residents made the round trip on the steamer as an excursion. She endeared herself to everyone who had an interest in steamboating.

One of the *Virginia's* most distinctive features was her shrill whistle. Heard throughout the community and easily identified, it marked her punctual arrivals and departures. She was dubbed "Smoky Joe" because black smoke belched from her stack. This may be remembered by many as being her most significant characteristic.

The *Virginia* was launched by the William R. Trigg Company, Richmond, on November 12, 1901. It has been reported that her construction

The sleek *Virginia* approaches her pier at Newport News after a run from Norfolk, April 1941. Photo: Author

was the result of a most unusual swap. The Trigg Company had contracted with the United States Government to build several light naval vessels, but additional land was needed to expand their facilities. The most logical site was on the right-of-way of the Chesapeake and Ohio Railroad. At that time the railroad was in need of a modern steamer to replace the veteran wooden-hulled side-wheeler *Louise,* employed at that time on the Newport News-Norfolk route. To the advantage of both organizations, a swap was arranged. The shipyard would construct a steamer for the railroad and acquire the desired property in exchange. This was to be the first commercial ship ever built by the Trigg yard that had previously constructed only government vessels.

was left in her wake in a race on local waters while carrying out her daily routine. She retained this speed throughout her career.

The number of her daily crossings between Newport News and Norfolk depended upon train schedules and it has been suggested that she logged enough miles to equal 50 or more trips around the world. Most of these daily trips were uneventful but she did send at least one vessel to the bottom as a result of a collision. It was the powerboat *Nettie B. Greenwell,* off the Newport News coal piers in May 1948. The *Virginia* was held blameless.

In World War II the *Virginia* repeated the good work she had done during the 1917 conflict—transporting thousands of service men between the two strategic cities on her route. She plied this run

Backing out of her Newport News pier, the *Virginia* starts a passage to Norfolk in 1947. Photo: Author

The *Virginia* was a twin-screw steel vessel, 191 feet long on the keel. She was propelled by two 3-cylinder triple expansion engines. On a four-hour trial run in Chesapeake Bay on February 5, 1902, she attained a speed of 18½ knots over a measured mile. At the conclusion of the trials it was found that her funnel was so hot the adjacent woodwork had almost ignited. Eventually, adequate casing was built around her funnel to afford the protection needed for forced draft operation.

Placed into service by the railroad, the *Virginia* soon proved to be the fastest steamboat in Hampton Roads. In May 1902, she beat the N.Y.P. & N. steamer *Pennsylvania,* previously considered one of the speediest in the area. The side-wheeler *Hampton,* another steamer respected for her speed,

alone throughout most of her career, but was given a running mate in 1944. In July of that year the steamer *Wauketa* that had been tied up with the James River idle fleet after serving for the government in harbor transport work, was acquired by the C & O and given a new lease on life. She was 175-feet long, built in 1909 at Toledo, and had served in the Great Lakes, New York, and Baltimore before coming to Hampton Roads.

By the spring of 1946, as the movement of troops dwindled, the *Wauketa* was tied up at the Newport News C & O pier. Then, on July 12, 1947, a change in the train schedule required the services of both the *Virginia* and *Wauketa.*

In September 1949, the sleek, white *Virginia* was withdrawn from service to await an overhaul. The

Wauketa continued in her place. At that time there was talk that the steamers were to be replaced by buses, so work was held up on the *Virginia* as she tugged at her lines in the Newport News slip.

On June 2, 1950, the Chesapeake and Ohio was granted a trial period by the Virginia State Corporation Committee to use buses instead of a steamer to transport passengers between Newport News and Norfolk.

On the night of June 4, 1950, the *Wauketa* departed on her regular trip to Norfolk. This proved to be the last sailing of a Chesapeake and Ohio passenger steamer between the two ports, and brought to an end the service that the railway had carried on since 1884. Before that time, steamers of the Old Dominion Steamship Company handled the run for the railroad. Several disputes arose over the use of buses but, in December 1950, the railroad was authorized to discontinue steamer service.

The *Virginia*, once kept spotless as a yacht, became streaked with grime and her formerly brilliant brass work was discolored. Many hoped that when she was offered for sale she would be purchased to resume service, even if in waters other than Hampton Roads. When that time came, however, the best offer was submitted by a Baltimore scrap firm. Her only value was the metal content in her hull and engine.

On July 3, 1951, the Diesel tug *Sophia* arrived at Newport News to tow the *Virginia* on her last trip. As she was backed out into the James River, no shrill whistle sounded to announce her departure. Among the few who witnessed this event, the dock workmen, who had handled her lines for years, seemed to be most affected. A note of sadness could be detected in their expressions as the steamer, her bow pointed down the river, gradually disappeared behind a jutting pier.

At the yard of the Patapsco Scrap Corporation little time was lost in dismantling the *Virginia*. Her wooden superstructure was ripped off and torches cut into her metal. The few relics salvaged from her were presented to The Mariners Museum. Two large saloon mirrors, steering wheel, whistles, capstan head plate, pilothouse nameboard, engine-room gauge board, and clinometer joined her flags and logbooks which were already in the museum's collection.

The *Wauketa* soon followed her running mate and was dismantled at the same scrap-yard. Being an out-of-state product and a virtual newcomer to the area, little sentiment was attached to her passing. On the other hand, the *Virginia* was all Virginia, though she was not named after the Old Dominion state, as many believed. She was named for the wife of George W. Stevens, a former president of the Chesapeake and Ohio Railroad.

As this photograph was taken, the long familiar sound of the *Virginia's* whistle was reverberating around Newport News. Photo: Author

The Schooner on the Chesapeake

IN THE JANUARY 1911 issue of the British historical marine publication *The Mariners Mirror,* appeared a view of an engraving after a painting entitled "A Fresh Gale," by the Dutch artist, W. Van de Velde. The purpose of its reproduction and description was an effort to disprove the claim that the first schooner was built at Gloucester, Massachusetts, in 1713.

In the illustration, two vessels with an embryonic schooner rig can be seen. Since some knowledge of the artist exists, the painting and the vessels can be assigned to the last quarter of the 17th century. Further evidence that the schooner rig was not uncommon in England during that time, and had been used in Holland earlier, is given by reference to other early marine scenes in which schooner-rigged vessels are portrayed.

Regardless of the schooner's origin, this rig enjoyed its greatest popularity under the American flag. The schooner is said to have appeared in this

The *Lula M. Phillips,* rebuilt in 1913 at Bethel, Delaware from the *Annie M. Leonard,* which was built in Oxford, Maryland in 1877, still serves on the Chesapeake as a power-boat. Photo: Levick Collection—The Mariners Museum

country by 1700 or shortly thereafter. Here it underwent many changes. During the second half of the 18th century the schooner displaced the sloop as the principal coasting vessel and became the most distinctive American rig during the Revolutionary War.

By the 1730's, local shipbuilders, having admired and studied the fast Bermuda sloops that visited the Bay, were turning out a much improved model.

The schooners developed rapidly and were in demand because of their speed. The type was referred to as "Virginia-built" or "Virginia model," even though Maryland contributed to its development. By 1780 shipbuilders along other sections of the east coast recognized the superiority of these fleet schooners and built similar vessels. The majority of the early seagoing schooners carried square topsails in addition to the fore-and-aft rig.

The *Lula M. Phillips,* former schooner converted into a powerboat, at Humphrey's Shipyard, Weems, Virginia in 1951. Photo: Author

The Revolution and the period thereafter had a decided influence on further improvement in the design of these craft. The schooners were employed as privateers, and, to some extent, as blockade runners. The chief requisite for a vessel so engaged was speed. These forerunners of the Baltimore Clipper were extremely sharp and fine-lined and their large spread of canvas enabled them to outsail anything on the seas at that time.

During the first decade of the 1800's, the terms "Virginia-built" and "Virginia model" began to fall into disuse when referring to these outstanding Chesapeake designs. In their place "pilot boat" and "pilot-boat construction" became more popular. Many of the vessels were employed as pilot boats off our coast and their fame became wide-

spread. During the War of 1812 the type reached the point of near-perfection, and was considered the best all-around sailer ever produced. The term "Baltimore Clipper," by which this class of vessel was best known, is said to have become most common after the type was on the decline and had been modified as to hull and rig.

While these speedy seagoing schooners were in the limelight, the work horses of the class—the smaller, slower, full-bodied schooners, designed primarily for cargo carrying—were active on the Bay in the passenger and freight trade. They were ably assisted by sloops. Roads were scarce and poorly constructed; waterways were the main arteries of trade and travel.

During the first part of the 19th century shoal-keel schooners were common on the Bay. The continuous silting of the Chesapeake's tributaries, however, demanded even shallower draft vessels. Soon after the War of 1812 centerboards were introduced to the Bay schooners. This new model was of shallow draft and broad of beam. By 1850 they had almost replaced the older type. The first of these new models had round stems, but the handsome clipper bow gradually gained favor.

Prior to the use of steam as a means of propul-

The *Harriet C. Whitehead,* built in Connecticut in 1892, was one of a number of schooners built in New England and brought to the Chesapeake. She was converted to power during World War II and lost at sea in 1944. Photo: Levick Collection—The Mariners Museum

104

sion, sailing packets were used on the Chesapeake to carry passengers and freight between Baltimore and the nearby ports of Frenchtown, Chestertown, Annapolis, Alexandria, and Norfolk. They were called water stages and were usually owned by individuals. The packets also maintained a regular service between Baltimore and the Eastern Shore points of Easton, Oxford, St. Michaels, and Wye Landing. This trade proved profitable, even after the advent of steam, until the Civil War interrupted. Some of the vessels managed to carry on after the war, but the steamboats gradually put them out of business.

To supplement the fleet, schooners were brought down to the Chesapeake from New England waters. These sturdy vessels fit into the Bay trade very well, but were a decided contrast to the smaller locally-built schooners. Some of these former coasting schooners, the names of which should strike a familiar note to those who may have seen them in Bay ports, include the *Abel W. Parker, Florence A., Harriet C. Whitehead, Annie E. Webb, Brownstone, Lucy May, Black Bird, John W. Bell,* and the last to be brought down, the *LaForrest L. Simmons.*

Some of the schooners were individually owned,

The New Jersey-built *Anna and Helen,* the last commercial schooner on Chesapeake Bay, on the oyster dredging grounds in 1951. Photo: A. Aubrey Bodine

The Bay schooners had a virtual monopoly on Bay freighting until the advent of the powerboat. Many of the smaller schooners were used in the oyster and fishing trades. Coastwise and West Indian voyages were part of the routine for the larger two- and three-masted schooners. These vessels often got into trouble at sea; their names appeared frequently in the records of the Lifesaving Service.

Although the powerboat had gained a foothold in the Bay trade, the schooners continued to be regularly employed, but their ranks grew steadily thinner. Few were constructed after the start of the 20th century and the older ones were retired.

with the owner usually serving as captain. Others were operated by such firms as C. C. Paul & Company, W. B. Vane, Lottie V. Wathen, and R. B. White, all of Baltimore.

As late as the middle 1930's there were some rather ancient schooners still finding work to do on the Chesapeake. The oldest then employed on the Bay was the two-masted schooner *Federal Hill* which had been built in Baltimore in 1856, and had plied the Bay for 84 years with varied cargoes. By 1940 she had earned her rest and was abandoned in Monroe Creek, behind Colonial Beach, Virginia.

Until the beginning of World War II, the Bay

schooners did remarkably well in holding their own against progress but were almost limited to hauling one type of cargo—lumber. It kept them active, made money for their owners, and, for the sentimental, retained an air of the past on these waters. With war came the usual shortage of bottoms and the Bay schooners were called on to play their part. Most of the larger two-masted schooners were either converted to powerboats or sold for trading in the Gulf of Mexico or the Caribbean.

A number of smaller schooners were also sold or converted to power and by the end of the war, few of this type of craft remained on the Chesapeake. After the war their value as carriers had ceased. Trucks, with their simplified methods of loading and unloading, took over the lumber trade.

The *Maggie, Ida May,* and the *Chesterfield* had been sold out of the Bay for conversion into "dude cruisers," former commercial sailing craft fitted out to carry tourists and vacationists. The *Bohemia* carried on in the Chesapeake until 1947 under her long-time owner, Captain Edgar B. Riggin. He then sold her and she remained active on the Bay for several more years. Old-timers like the *Kate Darlington, Kate H. Tilghman, Thomas A. Jones, Florence,* and *William J. Stanford* were abandoned.

The last commercial schooners on the Bay were the *Annie C. Johnson, Mattie F. Dean,* and the *Anna and Helen.* The first of these to be abandoned was the *Dean,* in 1954; the *Johnson* was next, in 1956. The *Anna and Helen* carried on until she was abandoned in Crisfield harbor after she sank there, in 1958.

So the commercial schooner has disappeared from the Chesapeake. The hulls of those converted to powerboats—the *Ida B. Conway, Sarah C. Conway, Ruth Conway, Betty I. Conway, Lula M. Phillips, Flora Kirwan, Gussie C., A. Victor Neal, John Martin, Mildred, Minnie May Kirwan,* and *W. J. Mathews*—still serve on the Bay. All are former two-masted schooners; some have been renamed; most have retained their original names.

Hulk of the *Anna and Helen* in Crisfield harbor, June 1960. The loss of this vessel brought an end to the commercial schooner on Chesapeake waters. Photo: Author

The Chesapeake Bay Bugeye

CHESAPEAKE BAY is well known in shipping and yachting circles for the commercial sailing craft that have been developed on its waters. The log canoe, bugeye, pungy, skipjack, and ram were all built to suit the trade in which they were to engage and the waters in which they were to sail. Each was unique in design and attracted the attention of the yachtsman and casual traveler, as well as the veteran seafarer.

The best known of the Bay types is the bugeye. Those who have only a speaking acquaintance with the Chesapeake sailing craft may refer to the ram as a 3-masted schooner, a pungy as a 2-masted schooner, and a skipjack as a sloop. In proper marine terminology, as far as rigs are concerned, they would be correct. Due to its singular design, the bugeye would rarely be referred to by any other name.

The bugeye emerged in the early eighteen sixties as a result of the development and growth of the log canoe. Previously, these forerunners of the bugeye used Chesapeake Bay as a proving ground, in all kinds of weather, to develop and test the most efficient sailing vessel for these waters.

In the latter part of the eighteenth century the taking of oysters had become an established industry on Chesapeake Bay and the craft most frequently used to catch and transport the oysters were log canoes, similar in design to those we know today. While the demand for this Bay delicacy was slight, they were taken by tongs in comparatively shallow waters, and these small boats (between 18 and 25 feet in length) were adequate. When the demand increased, longer trips to the market had to be made and it was necessary to increase the size of the carrier.

By using more logs, larger in size, a craft 35 to 40 feet in length was constructed and referred to as a "coasting canoe." This remained in popular use until the early eighteen fifties. Afterwards the canoes continued to increase in size in order to accommodate the larger loads harvested by the "scrape," a form of dredge used in the taking of oysters. This implement had been made legal in several counties of Maryland's Eastern Shore.

The next step in the development of the bugeye was the "brogan." This boat was built like a canoe and measured between 40 and 50 feet in length. There was a fixed bowsprit, a cabin forward, bulkheads, permanent fittings, and standing rigging on the foremast. The mainmast, like that of the coasting canoe, was removable. Sails were identical with those of the present-day bugeye: jib, leg-of-mutton foresail and mainsail.

A bill passed in Maryland toward the end of the Civil War period permitted the use of the dredge in all Chesapeake waters over 15 feet deep. This necessitated a further increase in the size of the brogan. The pungies, schooners, and sloops had certain disadvantages which made them ill-suited for dredging. The brogan was ideal for that operation, provided it could be built large enough to

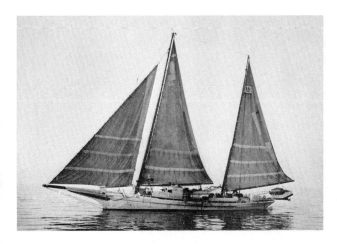

The *Edna E. Lockwood,* one of the last of the bugeyes in Maryland's oyster dredging fleet, on the Choptank River, November 1962. Photo: Author

handle the dredge. This was accomplished by adding 2 wing logs, a deck, and increased sail area. This process of evolution produced the first of the bugeyes.

The term "bugeye" was not immediately used to identify the craft. Several interesting explanations of how the name originated are to be found in *Chesapeake Bay Log Canoes and Bugeyes,** by M. V. Brewington, an excellent account of the development and history of this vessel.

The bugeye increased in use and popularity, and was preferred by watermen over the other types of dredging craft. The middle eighteen eighties saw the peak of their construction. Later the skip-

* Published by Cornell Maritime Press, Inc.

jack was developed because it was cheaper to build and more suitable to the smaller catches of that period. The demand for bugeyes steadily decreased.

Near the turn of the century the gasoline engine began to replace sails as a means of propulsion in Bay craft. The vessels operated by gasoline power usually had their longhead, bowsprit, and main-mast removed and the foremast shortened. An engine was placed in the after cabin area; a super-structure to serve as cabin and pilothouse was built over this. The resulting powered vessel continued to ply the Bay and tributaries for many years.

A state law later prohibited the dredging of oysters in Maryland waters by all except those pow-ered by sail. Consequently, several bugeyes may

Round-sterned, gaff-rigged bugeye *Catherine* on marine railway at A. Smith & Son's Shipyard, Curtis Bay, Maryland, 1939. Photo: Author

Conversion to powerboats was the fate of many bugeyes. The *Gladys L.* is shown hauled out at Humphrey's Ship-yard, Weems, Virginia, July 1951. Photo: Author

The *Mollie V. Leonard* is eased through a calm on the Choptank River by her auxiliary engine, 1935. Photo: Author

still be seen at work on the dredging grounds.

The bugeye has been used by yachtsmen for pleasure and has proved notably worthy. The simple rig requires few hands and it sails well under any two of its three sails.

Among the last bugeyes to join the ranks of those converted to pleasure craft were the *Agnes C. Leonard, Dorothy A. Parsons* (now preserved as an exhibit at Mystic Seaport, Mystic, Connecticut), *Little Jennie, Sanxton Hubbard,* and *Florence Northam.*

The craft remaining, commercial and pleasure, are proof that these renowned workhorses of yesteryear are far from extinct, and that the remaining ones have many years of service left in their sturdy frames.

Even after a life under sail and then power, further use is found for the hull of the bugeye *Mary Sue,* serving as a home on Sarah Creek, Virginia, June 1951. Photo: Author

The Skipjack

OLD-TIMERS on the Bay claim that the picturesque Chesapeake sailing craft known as the skipjack derived its name from the species of fish known as skipjack, that spring from, or skim over, the water. There is no proof of this but it is presumed that Bay watermen likened the lively movements of the vessel to that fish, known locally as the bluefish.

The skipjack, a centerboard craft, is beamy, has a raking mast, jib and leg-of-mutton mainsail. It is dead-rise or V-bottom and is of shallow draft. Although at one time it was an all-purpose vessel used for transporting watermelons, hay, and other farm products when not engaged in the oyster trade, the skipjack is now used entirely as an oyster dredger.

The vessel has been a favorite of oystermen for dredging since its perfection, because it is economical to build, is fast and able, and ideally suited to the smaller oyster catches and shallow waters of the Chesapeake.

The ancestry of the skipjack, as with all the Bay's commercial sailing craft, is interesting. It is presumed that the type developed in the early 1890's from the earlier enlarged types of flat-bottom or V-bottom skiffs once so common on the lower Eastern Shore of Maryland.

A little later the graceful longhead, with its decorative trailboards terminated by a little figurehead, was adopted. Just when the craft acquired the name skipjack is not known.

Improvements followed, one of which was the introduction of the self-bailing cockpit. On some skipjacks the hand winders for bringing in the dredges were located in the cockpit and forward of the cockpit was the hatch, except on small craft, where the cockpit was extended forward. Normally the cabin trunk was forward of the hatch but on larger skipjacks the deck was flush.

In the first decade of this century the flush deck was generally adopted. This was probably due to the increased use of the power winder. The early

Skipjack *Ethelyn Dryden* reefed down as she makes a "lick" over the bottom of the Choptank River, 1948. Photo: Author

skipjacks had no shrouds but with the additional strain and weight of the power winder they came into use. The cabin was eventually placed aft.

Various sections of the tidewater country have their own names for a particular type of craft and the skipjack has received its share. On the lower James River in Virginia, when the skipjack first became popular, it was referred to as a "Crisfield flattie or sharpie" since the majority hailed from that Maryland port. Also, the watermen in that area of Virginia did not recognize a craft by the name skipjack unless its bottom was planked fore-and-aft instead of athwartship. In certain sections of the Eastern Shore of Maryland the term skip-

Hand winders on the deck of the skipjack *Ella* at Oxford, Maryland, 1936. Photo: Author

jack refers only to the rig rather than the type of craft. The boats themselves are known as two-sail bateaux; a bateau is a V-bottom or dead-rise hull larger than a skiff.

Three-sail bateaux were also built on the Eastern Shore of Maryland, in the Bishop's Head area of Dorchester County. Their hulls were similar to the two-sail bateaux but had a little less beam in proportion to length. They generally carried the sail plan of the bugeye but one of them, the 44-foot *Eva*, was schooner rigged. Other examples of this type with the bugeye sail plan were the *S. A. Holland*, *Thelma Roberts*, and *Virgie G. Dean*.

Most of the skipjacks were built on the Eastern Shore in that area of the Chesapeake tidewater country ranging from Talbot County, Maryland,

down to Accomac County, Virginia. Very few were built on the Western Shore of Maryland and Virginia.

The largest skipjack on the Bay is the *Robert L. Webster* which was built at Oriole, near Deal Island, Maryland, in 1915. She is registered as being 60 feet in length and of 35 gross tons. This makes her larger than a good many of the bugeyes that were once so plentiful.

It would be well for Chesapeake yachtsmen to take the skipjack more seriously when they are thinking of building a sailing yacht. Their sailing qualities and weatherliness have been proven. Since they originated and were perfected on the Bay to meet all conditions offered by that body of water, they would seem to be the ideal sailing craft for the Chesapeake or similar waters.

The *H. A. Parks* sails over oyster dredging grounds of the Choptank River, 1948. Photo: Author

111

The Chesapeake Bay Sailing Ram

THE "RAM" was the largest of various commercial sailing types developed in the Chesapeake Bay area. Generally it was an ungainly, cumbersome looking vessel. With its bluff bow, simple lines, wall sides, centerboard, flat bottom, and three-masted baldheaded rig, it was little more than a barge with sails, but it was designed and built with a special purpose in mind and that aim was fulfilled.

Until after World War II the ram had remained in the background. Perhaps this was due to the fact that the type was never noted for its appearance or speed and, as a result, attracted little attention. When most surviving rams were converted into dude cruise ships, however, tales of " 'windjammin' on a three-master sailing schooner'' appeared in numerous magazines and newspapers.

Aside from that publicity, little had been written about them.

The design of the ram has been attributed to Clayton Moore and Jacob Smith of Bethel, Delaware. The boxlike form of these vessels was developed in order to enable them to pass through the Chesapeake and Delaware Canal with large lumber cargoes from the lower Chesapeake Bay country and the Carolinas. Prior to their introduction, "Long Johns" and canal boats were the largest vessels used in this canal traffic. "Long Johns" were long, narrow, flat-bottomed, centerboard vessels, usually two-, but sometimes three-masted. Despite the limiting width of the canal locks, the ram was developed when larger craft became a necessity.

Since the width of the Chesapeake and Delaware locks was 24 feet at that time, the rams were built

The ram *Edwin and Maud* shown as a "dude cruiser" on Chesapeake Bay, 1951.
Photo: Author

112

to conform to this width, leaving little clearance between the vessels and the sides of the lock chambers. By comparing the beams of a group of eleven rams built from 1889 to 1900, we find the average to be 23.8 feet—a close fit. Their respective beams varied but a few inches while their lengths ranged from 112.8 feet to 135.5 feet and their depths varied from 7.4 feet to 9.8 feet. For instance, the *Wm. T. Parker,* an average three-masted schooner built during the same period, had the following dimensions: 105-foot length, 28-foot beam, and 7-foot depth.

The building of rams was centered in one locality, upper Nanticoke River. In fact, they were often referred to as "Nanticoke rams." Most of them were built at Bethel, a little Delaware town situated on Broad Creek which empties into the Nanticoke. Sharptown, Maryland, also on the Nanticoke, shared the construction of these vessels with Bethel.

The *J. Dallas Marvil* was the first ram built and the smallest, measuring only 112.8 feet in length. She was built by G. K. Phillips & Co. at Bethel in 1889 for Captain William Eskridge and proved such a success that others of her type soon followed. She cost approximately $7500 to build and all the material for her planking was hauled into Bethel by mule team and sawed by hand. It is interesting to note that the top wages for ship carpenters at that time were $2.00 per day. The *Marvil* enjoyed an active career that was suddenly terminated when she was sunk by collision with the steamer *Everett* off Sandy Point, Maryland, on June 15, 1910.

"Ram" is a strange name to apply to a vessel but an explanation of its origin has been handed down that appears logical. During the era when the first ram went through the Chesapeake and Delaware Canal, much of the towage was done by horses and mules—some by towboat. There were numerous small schooners with long, projecting jib booms that required particular attention to prevent the craft from fouling each other. The ram could stand rougher treatment because it was larger, bargelike, and had no jib boom. Billy Borwick, the owner of a ship chandlery at Chesapeake City, Maryland, observed the first ram coming through the canal and exclaimed, "Look at that d—— thing butting her way through the other schooners; she's acting just like a ram."

Although the rams were built primarily for the canal, they did not confine themselves to this trade. They entered into coastwise traffic, carrying stone, coal, lumber, fertilizer, or any cargo offered. Those

built after the turn of the century were much improved in appearance over the original rams. They had a more graceful sheer and handsomer bows and sterns, but retained the other ram features. The *Edward R. Baird, Jr.* and *Edwin & Maud* were typical of the improved type.

The *Joseph P. Cooper,* built in 1905, was an improved model and was given a jib boom and foretopmast. She was engaged mainly in the West Indian trade although she had one transatlantic voyage to her credit. During World War I, the *Cooper* made a trip from New Orleans to Cadiz, Spain, with a full cargo of oak staves. The passage across required only 34 days and a good part of that time was spent getting out of the Gulf of Mexico. The return passage took 48 days with the vessel sailing light and drawing only five feet of water. Not long after this voyage, she foundered at sea, at 36°21'N, 71°41'W, on November 29, 1918.

Detail view of the forefoot and bows of the ram *Clarence A. Holland.* Photo: Author

In 1906, the four-masted ram *Judge Pennewill* was built at Bethel. She was 155 feet long and equipped with two centerboards, one forward and one aft. She was built for the coastal trade but had a comparatively short life. It is recorded that she foundered at Charleston, South Carolina on June 9, 1912.

Thirteen rams were sailing on the Bay in 1933. Most of them kept busy in the lumber and fertilizer trade, making trips from the Carolina Sounds through the Albemarle & Chesapeake Canal, up Chesapeake Bay to Philadelphia via the Chesapeake and Delaware Canal, and return. Baltimore was also a regular port of call. These vessels were the *Kinkora, Corapeake, Thos. J. Shryock, Jennie D.*

113

Bell, *Grace G. Bennett, Levin J. Marvel, Edwin & Maud, B. P. Gravenor, Mabel & Ruth, Clarence A. Holland, Agnes S. Quillin, Edward R. Baird, Jr.,* and the *Granville R. Bacon.* The latter, built at Bethel in 1911, was the last. Since she had a deeper draft than the other rams, she was forced to seek cargoes in the regular coastwise trade, entering only the lower Bay.

From 1934 to 1942, fire, foundering, and conversion to power took a heavy toll of this group. By 1945, there remained but two of these vessels in commercial use, the *Edward R. Baird, Jr.* and the *Jennie D. Bell.*

The *Levin J. Marvel* had a tragic end. As a cruise ship she was wrecked in a hurricane at North Beach, Md., on August 12, 1955, with a loss of 14 lives. The *Edwin & Maud* was renamed *Victory Chimes* in 1954 and taken to Maine to continue as a cruise ship. *The Grace G. Bennett* sank at her pier at Crumpton, Md., in October 1954 during Hurricane Hazel and was dismantled there in 1960.

The North River Bar, North Carolina, proved to be the undoing of the *Corapeake* (ex-*Ivy Blades*) and the *Thos. J. Shryock.* The former became a total loss by burning at this point on June 15, 1936; the latter was wrecked there in the fall of 1940,

Looking aft on the deck of the ram *Clarence A. Holland.* Photo: Author

Four others, the *Levin J. Marvel, Edwin & Maud, Grace G. Bennett,* and the *Mabel & Ruth,* were converted into cruise ships. This gave them a new lease on life. Although their new trade was a contrast to their former activities as cargo carriers, it kept them "in sail" and delayed their retirement to the "graveyard." The first three operated weekly and fortnightly summer cruises on the Chesapeake, visiting little tidewater ports. The venture was highly successful and profitable to the operators. The *Mabel & Ruth* was taken to Florida, renamed the *City of St. Petersburg,* and fitted out to make cruises in those waters and carried on until 1948 when she was abandoned.

towed to Elizabeth City, N. C. and abandoned.

The *Agnes S. Quillin* stranded at Smith's Point, Potomac River, on November 16, 1938, and was stricken from the register. *Granville R. Bacon* stranded at Weekapaug, Rhode Island, on January 1, 1934, and was later burned. The *B. P. Gravenor* (ex-*James H. Hargrave*) was renamed *Mayfair* and was wrecked on the North Carolina coast, November 9, 1942. *Clarence A. Holland* rests on the bottom of the harbor at Elizabeth City. During World War II, the *Kinkora* (ex-*Charles T. Strann*) was converted into a powerboat and sold to Dominican Republic interests in 1943.

After a period of idleness, the *Edward R. Baird,*

114

Jr. was sold in 1954. Her master, Captain Brewington, had died in 1953. After temporary repairs, to enable her to get from her Eastern Shore port to Baltimore for a complete refit, she set out across Tangier Sound. Heavy seas were encountered and water entered open seams in her bow, causing her to sink on September 19, 1955. She was abandoned and the Coast Guard removed the wreck.

This left the *Jennie D. Bell* to carry on as the last ram on the Chesapeake and the last commercial sail freighter on those waters. In her last days, she was employed carrying soybeans. She made her last trip in 1954 and retired to Salisbury, Maryland, where her owner and master, Captain Clarence Heath, and his wife, lived aboard. The condition of the *Bell* rapidly declined and, in October 1961, she was moved to the flats at Salisbury and abandoned. Captain Heath died in 1962.

The ram *Jennie D. Bell*, built at Bethel, Delaware in 1898 and the last commercial sailing freighter on Chesapeake Bay, lies on the mud flats at Salisbury, Maryland, in March 1962. The end of the larger commercial sailing ship on the Bay is thus symbolized.
Photo: Author

The Chesapeake Bay Pungy

"THE PONGEES, or oyster boats, and the Chesapeake Bay coast vessels, are the most elegant and yacht-like merchant vessels in the world. . . . It is remarkable that the vessels intended for the lowest and most degraded offices (such as carrying manure, oysters, and wood) are of elegant and symmetrical proportions. An English schooner from Bideford was lying among some of the worst Baltimore coasters. She looked like a hog amid a herd of antelope. . . . The true Baltimore clipper, the ideal of perfection 30 years ago, is now quite out of date. All the Baltimore shipbuilders have been gradually modifying their forms but still retaining their graceful appearance." This is an observation made in 1852 by an English naval officer, a Captain MacKinnon, R.N., and appears in a book entitled *Atlantic and Transatlantic*.

The *Amanda F. Lewis* becalmed in Chesapeake Bay, near Thomas Point. Photo: Frank A. Moorshead, Jr.

The pongees the good captain refers to are none other than the pungies, those graceful and swift sailing craft once symbolic of Chesapeake Bay, but now extinct on those waters.

Just when the pungy made its appearance on the Bay as a distinct type, separated from the Baltimore Clipper from which it was descended, is not known, but it is believed to have been in the 1840's. The derivation of the term "pungy" has never been satisfactorily explained. Some dictionaries have included the term with a rather misleading meaning: "A Chesapeake canoe, esp. one of large size."

The pungy was a keel vessel, schooner-rigged, with two tall raking masts and main topmast. Full flaring bows, raking stempost and sternpost, long lean run, deep draft aft, sharp floor, flush deck, a log rail except abaft the main rigging where an open quarter rail would be found, and a minimum of standing rigging were all characteristics of this type of craft.

In all but superficial details of construction the pungy was merely a reduced version of a Baltimore Clipper. The absence of square topsails and fore topmast on the pungy were about the only differences in the rig of the two types. In fact, the pungy resembled the old privateers so closely it is recorded that when the movie *Old Ironsides* was being filmed in California, about 1924, a fleet of a dozen pungies was purchased from the Bay to take part in the movie. They were towed to the west coast, a passage requiring about two months. After reaching their destination they were dressed up slightly to represent gunboats in battles with Tripolitan pirates.

At one time pungies were the favorite of the oyster dredgers but were gradually replaced by the handier, cheaper, shallow-draft bugeye and skipjack. When the dredging season had passed, the pungies turned to general freighting on the Bay. Here they were restricted to a certain extent, for their deep draft would not permit them to sail up the shallow rivers and creeks where the bugeyes, skipjacks, and shoal draft, centerboard schooners could sail with ease. The last of the pungies were built in the 1880's, but a few examples of these craft could be seen on the Chesapeake as long as there was work for them.

The last on the Bay rigged for sailing was the *Wave*. She had been built in Accomac County, Virginia, in 1862 and used commercially out of the Chester River until 1939 after which she was converted into a yacht. Sometime in the 1950's she was taken to the Great Lakes area and was reported abandoned there.

We can go back to 1925 and find that there were at least ten pungies active. Of these, eight were in use on the Chesapeake and two were seeing service on Delaware Bay. The oldest, the *Plan*, had been built in Accomac County, Virginia, in 1855. The youngest, the *Amanda F. Lewis,* slid down the ways in 1884.

In addition to these two, the other pungies on the Chesapeake were the *Mildred Addison, James H. Lewis, L. B. Platt, G. A. Kirwan, James A. Whiting,* and the *Wave.* The two pungies on the Delaware Bay, sailing out of Port Norris, New Jersey (both having been built in the Chesapeake region) were the *Mary and Ellen* and the *Ellen and Alice.*

One by one they started to disappear from the roster. Age had crept upon them and most were in a state that did not warrant their being reconditioned. The first of the foregoing to pass on was the *James H. Lewis,* abandoned in 1928. In rapid succession followed the *L. B. Platt* and *Plan* abandoned in 1930 and 1931, respectively. The end of the *G. A. Kirwan* and *Mary and Ellen* came in 1935. The next to go were the *James A. Whiting* and *Ellen and Alice* in 1936, and the *Mildred Addison* in 1939.

The *James A. Whiting* was typical of the pungies. She had been built in 1871 in Somerset County, Maryland, and was primarily employed in oyster fishery in her early years. The names of these smaller vessels rarely appeared in print in the past but the 1897 annual report of the United States Lifesaving Service mentions her as having lost a member of her crew in the Chesapeake while bound from Baltimore to the dredging grounds. There were twelve men in her crew at that time.

During those years she was kept in top shape. She was painted in true pungy style, "pungy pink" —flesh-color topsides, bronze-green bends, and white rail. However, by the time the ranks of the pungies had thinned out to a few survivors, the *Whiting* was in sad shape. Her last cargoes consisted of road-building materials such as rocks, gravel, and tar.

In the Northern Neck of Virginia, near where the Potomac River empties into the Bay, is the picturesque, winding Coan River. The *James A. Whiting* hailed from this area and when it came time to lay her up for good, she was taken back to her home port of Walnut Point, a former steamboat landing on the Coan. There she was pulled onto the shallows and abandoned.

By a strange coincidence, the Coan River was also the home of the last active commercial pungy on the Bay. This was the *Amanda F. Lewis*, built by Joseph W. Brooks at Madison, Maryland, for Captain M. O. Lewis. The *Lewis* could not have had a better start in life for her builder was one of the best that the Chesapeake country produced. The quality of his work was reflected in the handsome model of this pungy.

Adorning the transom of the *Lewis* was a carved decoration portraying the likeness of her namesake, the wife of Captain Lewis. She carried it during her entire life as a sailing vessel. When it was finally removed in 1939, it was presented to the Smithsonian Institution.

The *Lewis* must have been given excellent care in her early days to contribute to her longevity.

Detail of the stern and transom showing the stern decoration in position, 1939. Photo: Author

It is known for a fact that she was well cared for in her later career when she was under the guidance of Captain Gus Rice. He had been brought up in pungies and stayed in them until he left the Bay. Captain Gus lived on the Coan and when he was at home, the *Amanda F. Lewis* could be seen anchored offshore. She was kept busy freighting for E. Fallin & Brother, merchants, who maintained the steamboat wharf of Coan and operated canneries. Lumber and wheat from the Northern Neck were regular payloads to Baltimore; bagged fertilizer, coal, or empty cans could be counted on as return cargo to the country.

At an age when most larger sailing vessels on the Bay had worn themselves out, had been abandoned, or converted to power, the *Lewis* was still sound and able to keep busy. The freight trend

The *Amanda F. Lewis* on the railway at Smith's Shipyard, Baltimore, 1939. Photo: Author

on the Bay was changing, however. Lumber was being shipped by truck. After steamboats stopped operating, their landings fell into disuse and canning factories and general stores moved from the waterways to locate nearer traveled highways. Captain Rice was getting on in years, too, so he sold the *Amanda F. Lewis* to Captain Wm. J. Stanford of Colonial Beach, Virginia, in 1939.

Captain Stanford had spent his life in Chesapeake sailing craft. Prior to the *Lewis* he had owned the two-masted schooner *Federal Hill* and a little three-masted schooner named after himself that had been built in 1868 as the *John P. Connor.*

Captain Stanford took the *Lewis* to the Krentz shipyard at Harryhogan to have her converted to power. There she was stripped down to the bare hull. Bulwarks were built up from her deck and a nondescript superstructure was erected forward

to serve as a cabin and pilothouse. One of her masts was restepped abaft the pilothouse to support a crow's nest. With an engine installed, and after a complete painting, the former pungy no longer resembled her former self. Her new owner announced plans to use her in the menhaden fishery.

Not long after the *Lewis'* conversion, Captain Stanford was approached by a gentleman from Miami, Florida, with a proposition to use the vessel for transporting bananas from Cuba to Miami. This seemed like a profitable venture so her owner, after arriving at an agreement, permitted his vessel to be taken south. However, the story goes, the *Lewis* never entered the intended banana trade but merely accumulated a series of debts that finally resulted in her sale. The former pungy never did return to the Chesapeake but sought a career on the sea.

Her activities remained obscure until a small item in the newspaper indicated that on November 10, 1948, still as the *Amanda F. Lewis,* she had left Miami for Port au Prince, Haiti. The passage normally would have required three days but when she failed to reach her destination within that time, fears were felt for her safety. It was not until the 21st that the *Lewis* was found by another motor vessel 22 miles east of a section of the Haitian coast, plagued with engine trouble and leaks. She was towed to port and repairs were effected. In 1949 it was reported that she was sold to Haitian parties. No record of her activities after that period can be found. If she still exists, she is the sole remaining example of a pungy hull.

The *Amanda F. Lewis* after being converted into a powerboat. Photo: Smithsonian Institution

The Chesapeake Bay Log Canoe

SAILING CRAFT designed solely for racing have just about reached the point of perfection as far as speed is concerned. Such craft, ranging from those just large enough to accommodate the man at the tiller to schooners requiring a large crew, are common on Chesapeake Bay waters. Nevertheless, the type of boat that offers the greatest thrill in racing competition, and in many instances outsail the modern custom-built, single-hulled racing yacht, harks back to the first craft the white man encountered when he settled in the Chesapeake area, the dugout log canoe.

The log canoe of today in no way resembles the Indian dugout other than being made of the same materials. The native craft were hardly more than water troughs. But the settlers with their tools and knowledge of hull forms improved upon these by giving the blunt ends some shape.

The next change in the dugout was its method of construction—the use of more than a single tree to make up the hull. The colonists knew how to make watertight joints with their tools and found that several logs fitted together side-by-side were easier to work.

The square-sterned log canoe *Flying Cloud* built in 1932 by John B. Harrison of Tilghman Island, Maryland. Photo: The Mariners Museum

The means of propelling the early canoes varied with the users. The Indians used poles or paddles depending upon the depth of the water. The early settlers preferred oars and for years clung to them as a means of propulsion.

From records it has been determined that sail was not introduced to the canoes until the 18th century. The changes in the hulls of the canoes resulted in more shapely contours and sheer enabling the craft to cleave the water with little effort.

Most of the early log canoes were small since they were used in shoal or protected waters. But once the art of building a hull from several logs was developed the dugouts increased in size. Up to 7 logs were used in the final development of the log-built craft, the bugeye.

There were three principal centers of canoe building in the Chesapeake area. These were in the Poquoson region, York County, Virginia, and on Maryland's Eastern Shore in the Tilghman Island and Pocomoke sections. All varied somewhat in design and methods of construction and rig. But the various boats were not confined to any given area since they were sold about the Bay.

The improved sailing canoe seems to have come into existence in the 1850's. It is evident that the early boats were fitted with false keels. The centerboard seems to have appeared rather late in the canoes.

Watermen realized the sailing qualities of the canoes and when the craft were not being employed in earning a living in oystering, fishing, and crabbing, matches were held to determine the fastest boat. Racing of sailing canoes is believed to have first occurred between 1840–1860. St. Michaels, Maryland, is reported to have been the scene of the first organized race.

The races caused such rivalry that canoes designed especially for this sport were built. These were lighter craft with sides and bottom thinned down, beam reduced, and carrying a larger sailing rig. When sailing they required springboards rigged to windward on which crew members climbed as live ballast to avoid capsizing.

Up to 1885 log canoe racing on the Bay was more or less haphazard. That year the Chesapeake Bay Yacht Club, Easton, Maryland, was organized and supported the races until interest seemed to wane about the turn of the century.

From about 1880 to 1900, it is estimated that in Talbot County, Maryland, approximately 50 log canoes per year were built. The U. S. Census Records for 1880 indicate that there were 6,300 log canoes in use on the Bay and about 175 new craft were being built annually.

An effort was made in 1910, by a group of yacht clubs within the Bay area, to revive interest in log canoe racing but this failed to meet with success. Individuals, however, bestowed loving care on several of the old canoes, such as the *Mary Rider, Bay Ridge, Island Blossom, Island Bird, Magic,* and *Witch of the Waves,* to mention a few, and raced them at various events about the Bay.

The *Rider's* owner, William Howard Green, a member of the Miles River Yacht Club, continued to push the racing idea and in 1926 called on Maryland's Governor Albert C. Ritchie to explain the objectives of his club in relation to canoe racing. The Governor listened, was interested, and in 1927 sponsored the trophy known as The Governor's Cup.

Rough hollowing of a five-log canoe under construction by Clyde Smith of Poquoson, Virginia, in 1935. Photo: The Mariners Museum

In the ensuing years other trophies were provided and as interest in the sport heightened, other old canoes were restored, such as the *Togwogh, Margaret P. Hall,* and *Belle M. Crane;* new canoes, the *Mystery, Jay Dee, Flying Cloud, Noddy,* and *Oliver's Gift,* were built. The Chesapeake Bay Log Canoe Association was formed in 1933 and the sport came into its own. Under the leadership of that organization, races were held in various sections of the Bay and response to the events was very good.

Log canoe races on a smaller scale were also held in Virginia waters in relatively recent years, under the auspices of the Hampton Yacht Club. One of the outstanding canoes in that area was the *Tradition,* owned and skippered by J. Garland Miller, of Norfolk.

There are numerous log canoes still at work on the Bay but all are powered. Half a century or more in age, their stout sides and bottoms made of choice heart pine seem to go on forever.

The Drift of the
William Thomas Moore

BAY SAILING craft built for service in sheltered waters would occasionally venture far offshore and their experiences would often make the most vivid sea fiction seem dull reading.

One of the most interesting of these tales concerns a ram built at Bethel, Delaware, a town situated more than 30 miles above the mouth of the Nanticoke River. Many vessels built at this inland mid-Eastern Shore town were destined to travel far and follow varied careers.

On March 29, 1914, the *Moore,* in command of Captain Carden, left Little River, South Carolina, with a cargo of lumber for New York. Shortly after setting out on her voyage she grounded hard on the bar on the west side of Little River Inlet. For more than a week efforts were made to refloat her but to no avail.

The revenue cutter *Seminole* attempted to pull the ram into deeper water but, failing in this, she requested assistance from the crew of the Oak

The cutter *Seneca* preparing to tow the derelict ram *William Thomas Moore* in 1915 after it had drifted 1500 miles following abandonment. Photo: The Mariners Museum

One, the 134-foot vessel *Wm. Thomas Moore,* was built in 1902 by G. K. Phillips & Company. She was owned by O. V. Wooten and registered out of Seaford, Delaware. About two years of her life is revealed in this brief description. There may have been other interesting events in her career but the following will give an insight into the experiences of some of our "bay boats."

Island (N.C.) Lifesaving Station, located 30 miles up the coast from the stranding.

The lifesaving crew responded in the power lifeboat *Viking* and assisted in planting anchors, running lines, and transferring men from one vessel to the other. Through the combined efforts of the cutter and surfboat, the ram was partly afloat when a sudden storm and heavy seas brought the opera-

121

tion to a halt, causing the vessel to again ground hard and fast. On April 9 the weather moderated and the *Moore* was released from the bar at high tide. The *Seminole* then took her in tow for Cape Fear.

A year later the ram was once more in severe trouble. On April 4, 1915, she was abandoned by her crew in Latitude 36° 17′ N, Longitude 74° 1′ W, roughly off the North Carolina coast. Her cargo of lumber kept her afloat but she was nothing more than a waterlogged hulk—a menace to navigation.

On May 12 of the same year the revenue cutter *Seneca*, while on ice patrol, received a radiogram from the British steamer *Baron Polwarth* reporting a derelict in Latitude 40° 34′ N, Longitude 50° 28′ W. This placed the hulk south of the Grand Banks and directly in the path of transatlantic shipping. The cutter immediately proceeded to the reported position and came upon the derelict the following day.

Upon investigation it was discovered that the vessel was the *Wm. Thomas Moore!* In a little over five weeks the hulk had ridden the axis of the Gulf Stream almost 1500 miles. Only stumps of her three masts were standing and she was so deep in the water that seas continuously washed over her. Fortunately she had come through the most traveled section of the North Atlantic coast without running afoul of another vessel.

Due to weather conditions the *Seneca* found it impossible to run a line to the hulk until the morning of the 15th when a 10-inch hawser was made fast. Then began a long tow to a port of refuge, Halifax, Nova Scotia.

On the morning of the 21st, after towing the derelict for a distance of 665 miles at an average speed of 4.55 knots, the *Moore* was turned over to the Canadian Government steamer *Premier Lahoah* outside of Halifax harbor. The *Seneca* had been under way for 8 days and had covered 900 miles in recovering the ram, which was valued at $25,000, including cargo.

In the 1915 issue of *Merchant Vessels of the United States* is a notation that the *Moore* was sold alien. Parties in Nova Scotia probably purchased the hulk and refitted her for sea again but she was to encounter more trouble at sea and there was to be no succor this time. On November 16, 1916, this unfortunate ram foundered in Longitude 40° 05′ N, Latitude 37° 56′ W, which would place her almost in mid-Atlantic. Her crew of six was rescued.

The lives of ships may be likened to those of persons. For some the going is serene, meeting with few trials and tribulations. Others are short-lived and their few years of existence are packed with misfortunes. The *Wm. Thomas Moore,* it seems, would belong to the latter group.

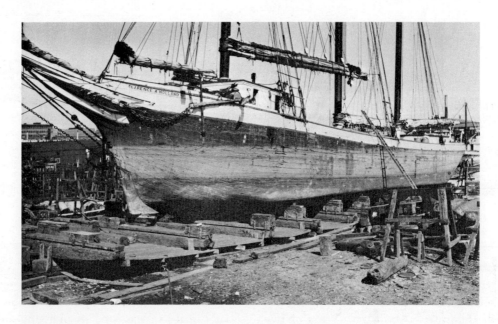

Ram *Clarence A. Holland,* built in 1893 at Bethel, Delaware, hauled out on the marine railway at Redman and Vane's shipyard, Baltimore, October 1936. The hull details of the "ram" class of ship are plainly visible: bluff bows, wall-sides, flat bottom, and little sheer. The *William Thomas Moore,* although slightly larger than the *Holland,* had these characteristics. Photo: Author

Workboat Races

THE BIGGEST BOATING event on Chesapeake Bay between 1921–1931 was the Annual Chesapeake Bay Championship Workboat Regatta. From the standpoint of interest and participation of craft from all sections of tidewater Maryland and Virginia, the workboat regattas were unique. Sometimes there would be more than 100 entrants: schooners, pungies, bugeyes, skipjacks, and Smith Island crabbing skiffs.

The late Peter C. Chambliss, one-time city editor of *The Baltimore Sun,* is credited with being the organizer of this event. Sensing the gradual decline in commercial sailing craft and hoping to revive the spirit of rivalry between the watermen and their craft, he conceived the idea of workboat races.

The idea was discussed with a number of workboat captains and many were in favor of such annual contests and agreed to support them. Only a few years previously they were compelled to race to port if they expected to beat competition and get the top dollar for their cargo. That was when sail dominated the Chesapeake and the fastest boat

The schooner *Mattie F. Dean* leads the *R. B. Haynie* around the course at the 1930 event off Piney Point, Maryland. Photo: A. Aubrey Bodine

would make the most money. Then along came the internal combustion engine and many vessels were converted into powerboats. A few die-hards clung to sail but the competitive spirit waned.

Skippers bragged about the sailing qualities of their respective boats but had never arranged a match so they welcomed the opportunity to settle the dispute of the "fastest boat on the Bay." Thus was organized the Chesapeake Bay Championship Workboat Race Association, a body of racing captains under whose auspices the races would be conducted every year for awards.

The Baltimore Sunpapers acted as sponsors of the events and offered plaques and loving cups as an incentive to race. Officers and a Board of Governors were selected from outstanding watermen and personalities in the Chesapeake country who were to plan the program for the first event. Wallace Quinn, of Crisfield, was elected the first president of the Association.

On August 4, 1921, the first of the *Sun*-sponsored workboat races was held off Claiborne, Maryland. It was estimated that more than 10,000 spectators thronged the shores to witness the races. Many more attended in their boats and anchored off the course to thrill at the sight of these commercial craft being pressed to their limit. The governors of Maryland and Virginia and many State and Government officials attended. The officers of the regatta were impressed with the response to the initial event and immediately made plans for the following year.

In 1922, on the strength of the success of the Claiborne event, the races were held off Bay Ridge, near Annapolis. The next year, Claiborne was again the site of the races. In the following years the boats met off Crisfield, Solomons, Oxford, Bay Shore, Deal Island, and Piney Point, Maryland.

The response of Bay watermen to the races was encouraging. They would strive to get their boats in top sailing trim so the craft could show their best turn of speed. A high pitch of excitement reigned around the tidewater ports as the day of the races approached.

Let us be spectators at the 10th Annual Workboat Regatta held off Piney Point, Maryland. The races had reached their peak of popularity by then and that particular event was made up of one of the largest lists of entrants thus far.

The date of the contest was Saturday, June 21, 1930. All day Friday competing boats bore down on the little southern Maryland resort town. In the afternoon the officials of the Association put out markers around the 10-mile course. A fleet of sailing vessels had arrived by dusk and their crews and guests were prepared for a gala time ashore.

On Friday evening there was a meeting of the members of the Association when officials for the coming year were elected and a site was selected for the next racing event. Preceding the meeting, Maryland's Governor Albert C. Ritchie and Baltimore's Mayor William Broening were among the honored guests at dinner in the Piney Point Hotel.

For the record let us explain how these races were staged. From the truck of the committee boat, anchored at the starting line, were flown flags of different solid colors used to designate the order in which the various races were to be run. The top flag was for the first class to start; the next flag to the top, the second to start, and so on. Flying above all of these was the blue pennant marked with the white letters RC (Race Committee).

The vessels were started over the course in classes, according to the type of boat. The schooners formed one class, the bugeyes another, then the decked skipjacks, open skipjacks, and Smith Island crabbing skiffs were the final class. The starting flags were hoisted to the truck of the committee boat at 8 A.M. and remained flying until 9:40 A.M. so that racing captains and spectators would have ample time to observe the order in which the respective classes were to race. The firing of a gun from the committee boat notified the racing captains of the breaking out of the flags.

The races started 15 minutes apart. At 9:45 A.M., 15 minutes before the start of the first race, a warning gun was fired from the committee boat and a flag was raised to denote the class of boats to engage in the first race. This allowed ample time for the boats to make sail and get under way. Ten minutes after the firing of the warning gun, the preparatory gun was fired; the starting gun for the first race was fired at 10 A.M.

Simultaneous with the firing of the starting gun, the flag for that class was lowered and the flag for the next class was hoisted. This procedure was repeated until all classes had started within 15-minute intervals. When sufficient wind to start was lacking, the International Code signal flag I was flown from the committee boat until there was a wind. In that case the powerboats, Smith Island crabbing skiffs, started first.

If the foremast of a schooner or bugeye, mainmast of a skipjack, or stem of a powerboat, crossed the starting line before the firing of the starting gun, that boat was required to make a new start.

Numerals identifying the boats were sewn on the foresails of the schooners and bugeyes, and mainsails of the skipjacks; the powerboats had numbers tacked to their sides. A program distributed by *The Sunpapers,* listing the boat's name, number, length, and captain, made it easy to follow the vessels around the course.

There were certain restrictions concerning the rigs of these craft. Only two-masted schooners could enter the schooner class and they were permitted to carry foresail, mainsail, two headsails, and one topsail. No staysail between foremast and mainmast was permitted. Sharp- or round-sterned bugeyes could enter that class and could carry foresail, mainsail, and one jib.

schooners, a gaff-rigged bugeye, and one pungy entered the schooner event. In a split-second start the big vessels made their dash across the line. The northwest winds made possible a grand sail on the first two legs of the triangular course in the Potomac River. But on the three-mile home stretch the finish line bore NW½N, right in the eyes of the wind. It was an exciting spectacle as the vessels beat up to the finish.

The *Mattie F. Dean,* skippered by Captain Mathew Bailey, crossed in first place by a narrow margin of 45 seconds ahead of the schooner-rigged bugeye *R. B. Haynie,* Captain George Ellis. The *Ella F. Cripps,* piloted by Captain Leslie Willing, was third, six minutes behind the *Dean.* The

Start of the schooner event during workboat races off Crisfield, Maryland, September 1931.
Photo: *The Baltimore Sunpapers*

Decked skipjacks could be of either dead-rise or round-bilged type, decked over from stem to stern. Their masts were to be stayed and they could carry sharp-headed mainsails and jib; open skipjacks required sharp-headed mainsails and jib. Smith Island crabbing skiffs covered motorboats of the type used around Smith Island, boats of the general type and size powered with 2-cylinder engines of not more than 6 HP.

The 1930 event had its wind made to order as it came strong out of the northwest quarter. Ten

pungy *Amanda F. Lewis,* Captain Gus Rice, placed fourth, one minute behind the *Cripps.* All four vessels sailed the 10-mile course in exceptional time, the *Dean* having crossed the finish line one hour and thirty-five minutes after the start.

But the schooners were hard pressed by the bugeyes that crossed the finish line fifteen minutes behind them. In fact, the winning bugeye closed up considerably on the *Dean,* finishing only ten minutes behind her. The winning bugeye *Nettie B. Greenwell,* sailed by Captain Winfield Mc-

Laughlin, severely beat the swift *Isaac H. Keeler,* entry of the well-known Todd family of Crisfield. This was the most startling upset of the event. The *Keeler* was almost a duplicate of the famous log bugeye *George Todd,* winner of four previous workboat races. There were about fifteen bugeyes in the race for that class.

Of the more than thirty decked skipjacks entered in the event, the *Minnie B.,* Captain Scott Bozman, placed first; second was *Myrtle,* Captain Brinkley Taylor, and *America,* Captain Leon Daniel, was third.

The open skipjacks, ranging from 24 to 31 feet in length, furnished thrills in the brisk wind resulting in victory for the *Lillian T.,* Captain Norwood Tull. *Iradell,* Captain Clifton Webster, was second and *Roland P.,* Captain Roland Parkinson, came in third.

Although sail held most of the limelight, the powerboats engaged in a lively battle between themselves and thoroughly soaked their skippers in the rough water. *Rachel Jane,* Captain Harry Evans, took top honors in this class.

At the conclusion of the big event the boats returned to their home ports, or possibly resumed a trip interrupted by participation in the races. All looked forward to next year's races to be held on Tangier Sound, off Crisfield.

September 19, 1931, saw the completion of the 11th Annual Workboat Race with the largest entry list ever posted for this event since the races were started. The veteran schooner *Maud Thomas* captured the trophy for her class. *Isaac H. Keeler* sailed away with the bugeye honors and the *Claude W. Somers* registered a decisive victory in the decked skipjack class. It seemed that with the years this regatta, strictly for commercial craft, was gaining in popularity—but this was to be the end.

The specific reason for the halting of the workboat races has never been determined but 1931 saw the last organized event of this kind on the Bay for the various sailing types. It does not seem possible that it was due to lack of enthusiasm on the part of the Bay watermen for they had previously backed the program one hundred per cent, some coming from long distances to compete. As for the vessels, many were old but they were still in good condition and could stand the stress of racing.

On Labor Day, 1933, during the Tred Avon Yacht Club's annual regatta at Oxford, Maryland, a race for bugeyes was on the program. Up to 1960, when workboat races were revived, that was probably the last contest on the Bay that had any kin to a workboat race. Actually, it was a race for four Oxford bugeyes to establish "once and for all" the championship of that little Eastern Shore port.

The day was squally but there was a good turnout for all of the sailing events—that is, except for the bugeyes. Two of the four vessels that were to compete, the *Col. R. Johnson Colton,* Captain Bob Pyne, and the *Little Jennie,* Captain James Mills, were on the prosaic mission of selling watermelons in Baltimore. The other two, the *Susie E. Parriss,* Captain Charles Pope, and *Hugh S. Orem,* Captain Isaac Elliott, were on hand. To make the race more interesting, the large cutter *Windrush* and Captain Robert Culler's replica of the famous yawl *Spray* decided to enter the race.

The 15-mile course was laid out on the Tred Avon River from off Oxford, twice down and around Choptank River Light and ending off Oxford. The wind was light after a thunder squall so there was little racing connected with the event. The winner was the *Susie E. Parriss,* not because of her great speed but because the leading boat had failed to round a course marker properly. Nor was her reward very great; cups, plaques, and purses of money had passed on with the end of the *Sun*-sponsored races. All the *Parriss* had to show as her claim to fame was "the biggest turkey on Long Farm," the prize offered to the winner.

From 1933 on, there was no hope of reviving the workboat races as the Bay had seen in the '20's. Power had too great a hold on these waters and the larger vessels were being converted. Age started to take a heavy toll and one by one they were pulled onto the shallows and abandoned.

One could run down the roster of the boats that competed in the workboat races and find a few still active on the Bay, most of these being the skipjacks used in dredging oysters. Some skippers who participated in the races are still active and occasionally, while discussing the old craft, they will display with pride the cups and plaques awarded to them for their sailing skill as revealed in the workboat races.

Within the past several years workboat races have been resumed at Cambridge, and Deal and Solomons Islands, Maryland. Only skipjacks have been represented and the turnout has not been spectacular, but it is a move in the right direction and the races may once again develop into a major boating event.

Lumber Luggers

ONE OF THE past pleasures of cruising on the Bay was the possibility of encountering commercial sailing craft under sail or at anchor in some sheltered cove. Through the 1930's it was a fairly common occurrence to meet up with these majestic old vessels and such an occasion would transport one back through the years even while at the controls of a modern cruiser. Those now sailing the Chesapeake will never witness and thrill at seeing a big two- or three-masted schooner ploughing through the clean, green waters of the Bay bound for Washington, Baltimore, or Philadelphia to discharge the lumber cargo that filled her hold and extended high above her deck.

The two-masted schooner *Maine* was one of these vessels that earned their keep by freighting Carolina and Virginia lumber up the Bay. She was not a product of the Chesapeake country but like so many of the other schooners in the Bay lumber trade, the *Lucy May, Florence A., John L. Martino, Brownstone, Robert McClintock,* and *Harriet C. Whitehead,* to mention a few, she had been built in New England and brought to these waters. Most of them had been forced out of their coastwise trades and the Bay offered a haven where they were to ply under sail for many years.

The *Maine* was a handsome vessel in her unique way. Her solid, chunky appearance differed completely from the sleeker Chesapeake-built schooner and she had a right to look that way. She had been built by shipwrights accustomed to turning out huge deepwater ships. Built for the coastwise and offshore trade, which called for a heavy, stout vessel, it is easy to understand the contrast with our smaller, local-built craft.

The New England Shipbuilding Company, Bath, Maine, started the *Maine* on her way in 1886. The ship registry shows that her first home port was Philadelphia. She was one of thousands of similar type vessels, the owners of which had but one thought in mind—that of making a dollar.

In 1913 the *Maine* first made permanent registry in Chesapeake waters, Washington, D. C. serving as her home port. At that time she still carried

fore- and main-topmasts which gave her a smart appearance, but in the latter 1920's her foretopmast was removed and her jib boom was shortened. Competition from other sailing craft was a thing of the past so the loss of speed resulting from the absence of the foretopsail and a headsail was compensated by less expense in maintenance. The only thing required of her was that she deliver her cargo and, upon discharging it, turn about and head for a loading port again. No racing was involved.

Willam B. Vane of Baltimore was listed as her new owner in 1933 and for the next ten years she

Schooner *Maine* shown light on the Bay bound south for a cargo of lumber. Photo: John S. Rowan.

127

followed the same routine she had carried out during the two previous decades. She usually sailed light down the Bay bound for a Virginia or North Carolina lumber port. On her way to Carolina she would go through the Albemarle & Chesapeake Canal and then traverse the Carolina sounds to her destination. Her return passage would follow the same route.

The author salvages the trailboards from the hulk of the *Maine*. Photo: Author

The Coulbourn Lumber Company purchased the *Maine* around 1944 and her home port was changed to Elizabeth City, North Carolina. This meant nothing to the old schooner for she still loaded lumber in Carolina for delivery in Baltimore or Philadelphia, using the Chesapeake and Delaware Canal to reach the latter port.

However, as fate would have it, she was approaching the end of her career. Sometime in 1945, while in North Carolina waters, the forward section of the schooner was damaged by fire. She had a cargo of lumber destined for Baltimore and managed to deliver it. After a survey to determine the extent of damage, it was decided that she was not worth the high cost of rebuilding. So the old schooner, then approaching her sixtieth year, was dismantled and taken to a ship's graveyard in Baltimore.

Abandoned, the *Maine* fell prey to ship wreckers intent on cutting up her frames and timbers for firewood. She gradually filled and settled to the bottom, leaving her upper works exposed. This is the picture she last presented, labeled as an eyesore to the Baltimore waterfront, until demolished completely to make way for new pier construction.

Trailer trucks have taken over the lumber trade formerly carried on by the schooners and rams. They can be loaded and unloaded by the efficient pallet system, thereby saving considerable time and labor. All of the lumber schooners are now gone from the Chesapeake. The ram *Jennie D. Bell* made the last lumber run on the Bay in 1954.

Billethead from the *Maine* in the author's collection. Photo: Wm. T. Radcliffe

The *Thomas B. Schall*, decks piled high with lumber, approaches Baltimore. Photo: John S. Rowan

Schooner *William Linthicum,* built in 1894 at Church Creek, Maryland. After a long career on the Bay, she was sold to Bermuda interests in December 1940 and taken there with a cargo of lumber. She was then converted into a hulk. Her master on that passage was Capt. Wm. M. Martino of Sharptown, Maryland. Photo: Author

The three-masted schooner *William Linthicum* discharging lumber in Baltimore in June 1936. Photo: Author

The *Maine* after being hulked at Baltimore and cut up for firewood, 1948. Photo: Author

The Ram
Edward R. Baird, Jr.

IN THE LATE 1940's Chesapeake Bay mothered the largest commercial sailing craft, active the year round, to be found in United States waters. Unfortunately, the sailing craft of our merchant marine had been reduced to such a degree that the three-masted schooner was the largest type then in service. At least two vessels of that rig were engaged

Within the bounds of the Chesapeake two three-masted vessels were kept busy throughout the year. They were the "rams" *Edward R. Baird, Jr.* and *Jennie D. Bell*. Their duties kept them within the confines of the Bay but they had known the time when coastwise trips were part of their routine. Prior to World War II they made regular trips

The *Edward R. Baird, Jr.* gets an assist from her yawl boat as she sails with a light breeze down the Chesapeake, 1939. Photo: John S. Rowan

in the cod fishing business on the West Coast. Their activity, however, was seasonal and they spent a large part of their time in idleness.

through the Albemarle & Chesapeake Canal to North Carolina, returning to Baltimore and Philadelphia with lumber via the same route.

The *Edward R. Baird, Jr.* was built in 1903 at Bethel, Delaware, by G. K. Phillips & Co., and was considered one of the handsomest of the rams built, carrying more sheer than the average and having some of the features of a regular three-masted schooner, such as the raised forecastle head and poop. Remaining true to her class, however, she was "baldheaded"; that is, she had no topmasts. Until 1924 she was registered out of Seaford, Delaware, at the headwaters of the Nanticoke River, and her managing owner was Daniel J. Fooks.

The *Baird* was rather young when she met with her first mishap at sea. On September 26, 1907, while bound from Sullivan, Maine, to New York City with a cargo of stone, she missed stays and collided with the Pollock Rip Slue Lightship at the entrance to Nantucket Sound, Massachusetts. She was seriously damaged and was beached to prevent sinking. A power lifeboat from the Monomoy Lifesaving Station went alongside the stricken ram and brought ashore her crew of six and two passengers. The two passengers were fishermen who had been picked up at sea in a dory after straying from their parent vessel. The following day a wrecking tug arrived on the scene and floated the *Baird* after making temporary repairs.

She carried on without any serious trouble for the next decade. By that time, however, the United States was at war with Germany and all shipping was a risk. About a year before the Armistice the *Edward R. Baird, Jr.* passed out of the Virginia Capes bound for New York with a cargo of lumber. When just above the Chesapeake Lightship, a German submarine surfaced nearby and ordered her captain and crew to get into the ram's yawl boat. They were informed that the vessel was to be destroyed by gunfire (torpedoes were considered too expensive to waste on small craft.) Her skipper, Captain Robert Coulbourn, complied with the order and pulled over to the submarine. He tried to convince the U-boat captain that a vessel as small as his could make little difference in the American war effort but the German was interested only in adding another vessel to his list of sinkings.

In a moment of boastfulness, the submarine skipper divulged a bit of information that later proved to be of value to the American Intelligence Corps. He stated that he had attended a show in Norfolk the previous night and produced the ticket stub as proof.

Without further loss of time, the U-boat's gun crew was given the order to fire and a shell entered

the ram's port bow. The submarine submerged, leaving the *Baird* to sink. Arriving on the scene shortly thereafter, an American destroyer covered the surrounding area with depth charges. An oily slick appeared on the surface and it is believed that the submarine was destroyed.

Because of the lumber cargo, the ram remained afloat even though filled with water. The men in the yawl boat were picked up by the destroyer and the waterlogged ram was taken in tow for Norfolk.

In the shipyard, the *Baird* was hauled out on the railway for repairs. The hole in her bow was large enough for a man to crawl through. The shell had taken up in her lumber cargo as though it had been fired into a solid block of wood. After being repaired, the *Baird* was towed to New York, both vessel and cargo finally reaching their destination.

Captain Coulbourn turned over to American authorities the information about the German having the Norfolk theater ticket in his possession. As a result, it is said that a German sabatoge ring was uncovered. A cottage near Virginia Beach had been operating as a signal station and German agents were going ashore at that point.

In 1924 C. C. Paul & Company purchased the ram and Baltimore became her home port. She was operated successfully by this firm, her main cargoes being lumber and fertilizer.

About 1946 the *Edward R. Baird, Jr.* was sold to the Worcester Fertilizer Company, Snow Hill, Maryland. She was used primarily for hauling fertilizer between Baltimore and Snow Hill, situated on the Pocomoke River 25 miles above its mouth. She continued as a sailer with no auxiliary power other than her yawl boat. On deck, however, a new hatch, 6' x 24', between the main- and mizzenmasts, replaced the two original smaller hatches to facilitate loading and unloading. Her master was Captain Ray Brewington, formerly of the ram *Levin J. Marvel* when that vessel was used in the Bay lumber trade.

The *Baird* was tied up in the early 1950's and remained idle for some time. In 1954 she was sold to two young artists. It is not known what was in store for the old vessel but, at least, it appeared as though she would see some kind of service again. Temporary repairs were made to the ship to enable her to be taken to a Baltimore shipyard for a more complete overhaul but, while crossing Tangier Sound, water entered open bow seams and she sank on September 19, 1955. She was abandoned and later destroyed by the Coast Guard.

Godfrey the Sailmaker

THE LAST sailmaker in the Chesapeake area to make sails for the deepwater sailing ships sailing out of Baltimore was William L. Godfrey. From his extensive loft on the third floor of the old brick building on the northwest corner of Frederick and Pratt Streets, in Baltimore, Mr. Godfrey produced some masterpieces in his profession.

Godfrey was a native of Elizabeth City, North Carolina, having been born there on June 18, 1886, the son of a sawmill operator. He became an apprentice sailmaker at the age of 14 and his wage during a 5-year period was $4 per week.

In September 1904 he came to Baltimore and worked with Stevenson and Magee who had a loft on Boston Street. At that time, Godfrey recalled, there were nine sailmaking establishments and about forty expert sailmakers in Baltimore.

Godfrey returned to Elizabeth City shortly thereafter and worked there and in Norfolk before returning to Baltimore in 1906. The next year he went to work for John R. Mitchell & Company. When Mitchell retired in 1923, Godfrey and Henry S. Marshall took over the business. This partnership was dissolved in 1938 and Mr. Godfrey elected to carry on the sailmaking business alone in a loft on Pratt Street.

Against a background of sailmaking gear and sailing ship prints, Godfrey sits on his bench at work on a sail, 1952. Photo: Author

The Pratt Street loft of Godfrey's was a throw-back to the days of the wind ships. There was nothing there to remind one that steamers and motor vessels were replacing sailing ships. Bolts of canvas, twine, rope, and standing fids resembled stage props. Clew irons, cringles, jack irons, and other metal fittings used in sailmaking looked like decorations but they played a very important part in the trade.

The long loft was devoid of any vertical supports so that the huge sails could be spread out and worked on. Its wooden floor was worn smooth and shiny as the result of years of dragging big sails across its surface. The only modern touches were electric sewing machines and bare electric fixtures hanging from the wooden ceiling.

Two wooden sailmaker's benches showed the wear of years of use more than anything else in the loft. Grooves one-half inch and more in depth had been cut into the edges of the benches from the miles of thread that had been drawn over them. At the ends of the benches were tools of the trade: fids, heavers, marlinspikes, seam rubbers, serving mallets, palms, beeswax, tallow and pouches, thread, needles, and needle cases.

The sailmaker freely discussed his trade and experiences with visitors to his loft. The sails of workboats and big schooners were made of heavy canvas, 22 inches wide and from bolts ranging from 100 to 105 yards in length. The canvas was cut in much the same way dressmakers cut pieces of cloth to a pattern, except not to exact measurements. Allowances had to be made for stretching along the leech and luff when the sail was in service.

In the early days, sails were sewn entirely by hand with waxed thread and needles forced through the canvas by a rawhide palm in which was embedded a lead pad. In later years, however, heavy duty sewing machines took over that arduous part of the work. Handwork was required when the sail was roped along its edges. Reef points and the metal fittings were also secured by hand.

Godfrey kept in his loft a gallery of pictures of many of the big sailing ships for which he had made sails. The walls were lined with colored calendar prints of sailing vessels and newspaper clippings. Drawings and sail plans of ships for which he had made sails were kept handy in the event a repeat job had to be done.

At one time Godfrey employed 4 or 5 assistants but when sailing vessels became scarce, he did most of the work himself. Sometimes he was assisted by his wife who operated a sewing machine.

Another old-time sailmaker, George Gardner, helped out and he was often seen repairing sails on some of the Bay sailing craft at their piers.

With the decline of sailing ships, sailmakers turned to other canvas products, such as awnings, canvas covers, and tents. Godfrey was no exception. After World War II the sailing vessels had disappeared and in 1952 he closed his Pratt Street loft and moved to a new home on Ritchie Highway in Glen Burnie, near Baltimore. He had provided for a loft in the basement of his home where he could carry on his sailmaking and canvas work. In October 1960, Godfrey determined to retire completely, sold his home, and returned to Elizabeth City. His days as a sailmaker were over and another link with the days of sail passed from the Chesapeake scene.

William L. Godfrey at work in his Pratt Street sail loft, 1952.
Photo: Author

Schooner *Bohemia*

THE BEAUTIFUL two-masted schooner *Bohemia* was built in 1884 by T. Kirby at St. Michaels, Maryland, for J. H. Steele, of Chesapeake City, and John Chelton. Chelton, who was half-owner and served as her captain, lived on the Bohemia River, Maryland, and she was named for the river. The vessel is reported to have cost $7,700. She freighted wheat, corn, and fertilizer during the early part of her career.

After Captain Chelton died, the *Bohemia* changed hands several times and was rebuilt in 1914 at Beacham's Shipyard, Baltimore. In June 1915 she was bought by Captain Edgar B. Riggin who planned to dredge oysters in Chesapeake Bay and the Potomac River. At other times she was used to carry lumber, fertilizer, wheat, coal, and canned goods.

In the middle 1920's, however, Captain Riggin discontinued dredging activities and spent his full time freighting on the Bay and its tributaries. The *Bohemia* could carry 75,000 feet of dry lumber. When Riggin commenced operation, the freight rate for 1,000 feet of lumber was $1.50 but during World War I, she loaded lumber at Aylett, 33 miles beyond West Point, Virginia, on the Mattaponi River, for delivery in Baltimore at $7 per 1,000 feet.

The manner of distributing the cargo on the schooner was unusual. If the lumber was dry, one-third of the load was stowed below deck and two-

The *Bohemia* at a Baltimore lumber dock, 1936. Photo: Author

134

thirds on deck; green lumber was stowed one-half below deck and one-half on deck. On some occasions, the lumber was so green and heavy that it was necessary to charge for freight at a flat rate rather than by the 1,000-foot rate in order to make a profit on the trip.

During her active career, the *Bohemia* was kept shipshape and Bristol-fashion, and, though not considered a "packet," she could "turn up her heels" under favorable conditions. Captain Riggin reported that the best record she made for him was on a round-trip from Baltimore to Smithfield, Virginia. She left Baltimore one evening before dark with a spanking fair wind and arrived in Smithfield the next morning. After taking on a cargo of lumber, she made a quick turnabout and was back in Baltimore 5 days after her departure.

Only once did she experience a serious grounding while under Captain Riggin. Loaded with lumber for Baltimore, the *Bohemia* came out of the Great Wicomico River before a strong southwest breeze. She hit bottom and stuck fast off Smith's Point. In an effort to tow her off with the schooner's yawl boat, the tow rope fouled the yawl's propeller and made her useless. Captain Riggin hailed a passing powerboat and arranged to transfer 25,000 feet of lumber to lighten his schooner. Relieved in this manner, she floated clear on the next high tide and put back into the Great Wicomico. She had found shelter none too soon for the wind shifted around to the northeast and blew a gale.

During the destructive storm of August 23, 1933, the *Bohemia* was bound up York River to load lumber on Mattaponi River. With no radio aboard, Captain Riggin had no advance warning of the expected severity of the storm. Riding at 2 anchors, in the lee of the land about 10 miles below West Point, she weathered the blow without mishap. Upon reaching West Point he was surprised to see a two-masted schooner cast high and dry on the beach and to hear reports of widespread damage.

When most Chesapeake sailors were turning to powerboats, Captain Riggin carried on with the *Bohemia.* Throughout World War II and up to 1947 he kept her busy. Sometime during this period her main-topmast was removed, giving her a stumpy appearance.

In September 1947 Captain Riggin decided to part with the *Bohemia.* A New Englander, Ira Cheney, purchased her and said that she was to be restored to her original rig and taken to Maine waters. However, for a year or so after she changed hands, she continued to freight lumber and scrap iron on the Bay but apparently operated at a loss. Her condition went from bad to worse. The beginning of the end came in the fall of 1948 when she was anchored off the mouth of Elizabeth River.

After a few months ashore in Baltimore, Captain Riggin became restless and decided to return to the Chesapeake. He purchased the powerboat *Honey B.,* the former two-masted schooner *Edward L. Martin,* and made several trips with her. He found it quite different from sailing, however, and soon sold her and retired permanently to his home in Baltimore.

In the latter part of 1949, the *Bohemia* was towed around to the eastern branch of Elizabeth River, Norfolk. It seemed as though interest was

Hulk of the *Bohemia* in Sarah Creek, Virginia, 1954.
Photo: Author

being renewed in the old vessel but, on the night of January 2, 1950, she settled beneath the waters, leaving only the tops of her two masts above the surface.

She lay beneath the murky waters for more than two months. On March 31, 1950, she was raised by derrick under contract with Tilton Conklin, Norfolk, and sold to Captain M. L. Tillage of Glass, Virginia. She was towed to Sarah Creek, Gloucester County, near the owner's home, and tied to a pier while Tillage contemplated the possibilities of converting her into a powerboat. She was later taken to a shipyard at Perrin and hauled out to have her bottom caulked and painted, then towed back to Sarah Creek to have her masts and bowsprit removed. Nothing was done to rebuild the vessel and, to prevent her from sinking at the pier, she was finally taken to a mud flat in the creek and abandoned. The one-time fine schooner gradually deteriorated into a crumbled hulk.

Oyster Pirates

THE FOLLOWING statement appeared in the 1887 issue of Goode's *Fishery Industries of the United States:* "Disband the force and in a few weeks the Bay would be a battle ground for tongers and dredgers." The statement referred to Maryland's oyster police force which was striving to maintain order on Chesapeake Bay and its tributaries.

Concerned with the rapid destruction of oyster beds throughout the Chesapeake area, the writer further stated: "Dredging in Maryland is simply a scramble, carried on in 700 boats manned by 5600 daring and unscrupulous men who regard neither the laws of God nor man. Some of the captains and a few of the men may be honest and upright, but it is an unfortunate fact that such form a very small minority. . . .

"It is now rarely the case that a dredger can be found who will admit that he believes there is anything wrong in disregarding the oyster laws and such a thing as being disgraced among his fellow workmen by imprisonment for violation of the laws is totally unknown. In the above facts will be found sufficient reasons why it has been impossible for the oyster police, since its first organization, to enforce the laws. Seven hundred well-manned, fast sailing boats, scattered over such a large area as the Chesapeake Bay, are rather difficult to watch, and especially at night.

"All blame for violating laws does not, however, attach to the boat owners as some of the men are prominent gentlemen of the most upright character. It is the misfortune of such men that their captains have often been trained by less honest

Maryland State Fisheries' patrol boat in an engagement with oyster pirates in 1886.
Harper's Weekly—The Mariners Museum

employers and having once acquired a love of ill-gotten gain it is difficult to keep them from continuing in the same course. As he usually has a share in the profits, it is of course to his interest to make his trips as quickly as possible; and while the boat owner may be opposed to breaking any laws his captain may think and act otherwise.

"The unscrupulousness of the captain is well assisted by the character of his men. These men, taken as a class, form one of the most depraved bodies of workmen to be found in the country. They are gathered from jails, penitentiaries, workhouses, and the lowest and vilest dens of the city. They are principally whites, many of whom are foreigners (almost every European country being represented) unable to speak more than a few words of English.

"When a crew, which usually consists of about 8 men, is wanted the vessel owner or captain applies to a shipping agent, who then gathers these men wherever they may be found, drunk or sober. As one large boat owner expressed it, 'We don't care where he gets them, whether they are drunk or sober, clothed or naked, just so they can be made to work at turning a windlass.' The shipping agent having placed a crew aboard is then paid $2 for each man furnished. With such a crew as this, who neither know nor care for laws, the captain is able to work wherever he desires to.

"As may be supposed, the life led by these men on board of the vessels is of the roughest kind. When sleeping, surrounded by vermin of all kinds; when working, poorly clad and with every garment stiff with ice, while the wind dashes the fast freezing spray over them, hour after hour winding away at the oyster dredging windlass, pulling a heavy dredge, or else stooping, with backs nearly broken, culling oysters. Returning from a trip, the men take their little pay and soon spend it in debauchery, amid the lowest groggeries and dens of infamy to be found in certain portions of Baltimore. It is a gratifying fact, though, that even amid such surroundings as these there are some few who are respectable and honorable men. This is more especially the case on the boats owned in the lower counties of Maryland."

Under those conditions, is there any wonder that so much trouble existed on the Bay? In 1868 Maryland commissioned an oyster police force and furnished a steamer and several fast sloops and schooners, each carrying cannon and small arms. The police boats were constantly cruising in search of violators of oyster laws. When apprehended, they were required to appear before a magistrate for trial. Battles with well-armed illegal dredgers were common.

The January 1886 issue of *Harper's Weekly* commented on oyster wars: "A more peaceful and unexciting occupation than the pursuit of the dumb and unresisting oyster can hardly be imagined . . . yet there is engaged in this quiet walk of life a class of as blood-thirsty pirates as ever drew cutlass or hoisted the black flag. Oysters are shovelled up in the Chesapeake like coal from a well-filled bin, and as they are always a marketable commodity it is not to be wondered at that they attract piratical river men in large numbers. To thwart the work of these oyster poachers the State of Maryland keeps in service a fleet of police war ships which cruise among the islands below Annapolis and frequently come into contact with the thieves. The first affair of the present season occurred a night or two before Christmas, when a police steamer swept down upon a fleet of the oyster pirates and was received with plenty of cold lead from the poachers."

Harper's continues, "Last year there were several serious battles, and the outlook is said to be bright for several fierce engagements in the near future. Trouble appears to be brewing all around the Bay. The police steamer *Kent* a few nights ago met a flotilla of determined dredgers making for Fishing Bay bent upon recapturing an oyster boat that had been taken by the authorities. A general fusillade was opened upon both sides and continued until the small boats of the pirates succeeded in escaping in the fog. The routing of the oyster pirates is rendered difficult by the fact that they spring up from all points on the Bay taking advantage of the removal of the police boats to any one threatened point by hurriedly working forbidden beds in other localities. They also, reversing the order of making hay while the sun shines, are quick to take advantage of the frequent and heavy fogs which hang over the Bay. Although a police sloop is kept continually on patrol at ground reserved for oyster tongers near the mouth of the Wicomico and Nanticoke rivers, the piratical dredgers, by bold sorties, have already this year (1886) succeeded in taking hundreds of bushels of oysters from the forbidden ground. It should be explained that the State law forbids dredging, while permitting oysters to be fished for with tongs, in many portions of the Bay. As a consequence of this law there are innumerable conflicts between the dredgers and the tongers, in addition to the battles between the dredgers and the police."

The January 1894 issue of *Harper's Weekly* further discussed oyster pirates, It reported: "The Chesapeake Bay, with its thousands of square miles of surface, and its hundreds of miles of tributaries, has more than 600,000 acres of oyster bottom which have for years supported nearly 50,000 people. The supply was so magnificent that exhaustion was thought to be impossible. And so when the State found it necessary to pass and enforce certain regulations, the bolder of the fishermen looked upon the action as an interference with the laws of Providence which was not to be tolerated. To many of them the taking of oysters where the State said they should be let alone was not a crime and they were ready to fight for what they believed to be their rights. This resulted in serious differences of opinion which were emphasized by powder and shot, and embittered by bloodshed.

The former Maryland State Fisheries' patrol boat *Governor R. M. McLane* after conversion to Diesel power and in use as a towboat at Baltimore, 1950. Photo: Author

". . . The oyster navy has a history. In its early stages Captain Hunter Davidson commanded it. With a single steamer in those days he kept the violators in a state of supreme fear and constant anxiety. . . . In two counties the piratical dredgers preyed on the tonging territory so outrageously that the tongers established batteries on the land and bombarded their enemies. It was a merry war and several were killed. The pirates ended it by going ashore at night and stealing the cannon.

"For 12 years the navy fired only one shot and that was to bring a fleeing pirate to terms. . . . A new state of affairs has come about in the past 4 years. It was mainly due to Captain Thomas Howard, a man of sturdy and courageous qualities, who violated the precedents of years by daring to think that it was his duty to enforce the laws. The pirates looked upon Captain Howard as well meaning, but somewhat unorthodox in his views, and they began to work with renewed vigor. In Dorchester County a lot of them boldly captured a police sloop, drove her crew ashore, threw her arms overboard, and dismantled her. In the upper Chesapeake another band made bold to fire on a passenger steamer on which the United States mail was carried. They afterwards regretted this in the isolation of prison cells. The lesson that the pirates were to teach Captain Howard for his impertinence took place in the Chester River. The Captain called upon a fleet of violators to surrender. It was at night. They refused and opened fire. Unlike some of his predecessors Captain Howard did not retreat. He used the cannon with good effect until he could not work it well at close range, and then he put on full steam, ran the nose of his boat into the enemy, and sent several of them to the bottom. The next day the Chestertown jail was filled with dredgers.

"Since that time the navy has been in better repute, but there have been a few fights, and last winter a dredger was killed by a shot from the Anne Arundel police sloop.

"Virginia has had several experiences. Her navy consists mainly of one steamer, a very slow one, and her engagements have not been particularly brilliant. Two years ago she sent a sloop to the bottom in the Potomac, and last winter she had a battle royal, and wasted a great deal of powder and shell with satisfactory results to the majesty of the law. The only man injured was a valiant pirate, who was overtaken by a bullet as he was retreating into the cabin.

"As a rule, in these oyster wars, there has been a use of ammunition on both sides entirely out of proportion to the results. They have fired abundantly, but not accurately, and enough lead has been wasted to supply sinkers for all the fishing lines along the Atlantic Coast. In the 30 years of oyster wars only about 50 men have been killed, and the wounded would not reach 50 more.

"Politics is the bane of the oyster in the Chesapeake. The bad oystermen as well as the good oystermen have votes, and therefore political protection. Neither Maryland nor Virginia gets enough from its oyster revenue to pay for the maintenance of its oyster navy. There is a story of one of the deputy commanders that illustrates the political phase of this organization. The commander was a good party man, who, failing to get higher office, accepted the captaincy of one of the sloops, because it was an easy berth, and the pay was sure. His duties consisted in sailing over his district and avoiding pirates. For a while, all went well, but one fateful day he fell in with a lot of depradators, and before he could get away they were impolite enough to fire at his boat. He was not a man of indecision, and acting quickly, he put on all his canvas, and sailed shoreward with all possible speed. When he reached the harbor he went promptly to the telegraph office, and sent his resignation to Annapolis. A week later Commander Seth met him and asked him why he had resigned. 'General Seth,' he replied, 'during the war I paid three hundred for a substitute, and at my time of life I have too much self respect to allow myself to be shot by an oyster pirate.'

"The oyster navy is better now since General Seth has reorganized it, and the oyster pirates do their stealing more modestly. There is less of it to do, because the oyster supply is growing less, and the greatest oyster beds in the world will be exhausted by the end of this century unless the universal depletion is checked by the policy of oyster culture, which is being tried nearly everywhere except in the Chesapeake."

Since the gay '90's oyster wars and bloodshed have continued. Oysters became scarcer and dredge boats fewer, but violations occurred and shots continued to be exchanged. Outmoded oyster navies were modernized; the old steam patrol boats were replaced by faster internal combustion engine craft and planes were acquired to check on poaching and other violations. Then the "pirates" (particularly those on the Potomac River) resorted to speedboats capable of outrunning the patrol boats.

The problem is likely to remain unsolved so long as healthy oysters continue to grow in Chesapeake waters and the philosophy of some watermen remains unchanged.

The steamer *Corsica*. The oyster war of 1888 is said to have been precipitated as a result of a group of oyster pirates in Chester River firing upon the Baltimore-Chestertown passenger steamboat *Corsica*, which was carrying the U.S. mails. Governor Lloyd Lowndes sent the patrol steamer *Governor R. M. McLane* and schooner *Helen M. Baughman* with orders to clear out the pirates. Two days of maneuvering put the State vessels in a favorable position and their gunfire brought the oystermen into submission. It is reported that many oystermen were given secret burials along the Bay shores to avoid embarrassment of explaining to the coroner the causes of death. Photo: The Mariners Museum

Maryland's Oyster Dredging Fleet

THE LAST all-sail fleet of commercial craft operating in North American waters can be found in Maryland's portion of Chesapeake Bay. No modern metal-hulled vessels are these, with auxiliary engines tucked away beneath their decks. Instead, they are the clipper-bowed wooden craft decorated with carved trailboards and figureheads, and the shrouds of their masts are drawn taut with lanyards reeved through deadeyes.

"It shall be unlawful to use any powerboat or vessel of any kind in the taking or catching of oysters by dredge, and the captain or master of any dredge boat shall not have on his boat any equipment or motor of any kind, whether attached to said boat or not, which is adapted to or can be used in the propulsion of said boat; provided, however, that a separate boat may be used in towing, pushing or pulling any dredge boat to or from an

Portion of the dredging fleet tied up at Deal Island, Maryland, 1958. Photo: Author

Some may wonder why this solitary fleet can carry on under sail while other wind-driven commercial vessels have virtually ceased to exist in American waters. This is explained in a booklet entitled, *Maryland Laws Relating to the Tidewater Fisheries,* as follows:

oyster bar when such dredge boat is not engaged in taking or catching oysters."

This line has not been drawn as a matter of sentiment but rather as a means of trying to preserve the oyster beds. If power-driven craft were permitted to dredge, the oysters would soon be

140

depleted. As long as Maryland retains its law barring powerboats as dredgers, commercial sail will continue to flourish on Chesapeake Bay.

The most common type of craft now used as a dredger in this fleet is the skipjack. This is a beamy centerboard vessel with a raking mast, jib and leg-of-mutton mainsail, dead-rise or V-shaped bottom, and of shallow draft. The skipjacks are supplemented by a few bugeyes and a sloop.

The average skipjack, about 45 feet in length, is manned by six men. The captain, who is usually the owner of the boat, steers and tends the mainsheet. He also orders when to lower the dredges over the side and when to haul them in. Four men tend the dredges, handle the sails, operate the winding engine, and cull the oysters. The cook also helps out on deck when he is not looking after the pots and pans.

No fair-weather sailors man these craft. The dredging season runs from November 1 to March 15—just when the Chesapeake presents its worst side. Cold means nothing to the men. In fact, in mid-season, the vessels often have to break through ice on the creeks in order to reach the dredging grounds. The stronger the winds blow, the better the crews like it. This means more speed for the craft that will, in turn, enable them to make more "licks" over the oyster beds.

Oyster dredging may be carried out in season, between sunrise and sunset, over oyster beds designated by the State of Maryland. The boats get under weigh before the break of dawn so that they can be over the oyster grounds as the sun comes over the horizon. If the wind is reasonably fair, sail is used to and from the anchorage and the oyster beds. If there is no wind, or if it is ahead, the power yawl boat is lowered from the stern davits and its bow is nudged up against the larger vessel's stern to push her along. Upon reaching the oyster bar, the powerboat is hoisted into its davits and the winds are the sole source of power thereafter.

To assure adherence to this rule, motor police boats of Maryland's Department of Tidewater Fisheries are usually first on the dredging grounds. They also see that the dredgers stay within the areas allotted for dredging and do not trespass on the more fruitful tonging grounds.

Two dredges (triangular iron frames with sharp teeth on the lower edge and a rope net supported between the frame to hold the oysters) are dragged simultaneously over the bottom from the port and starboard sides of the dredging vessel. The dredges are attached to long steel cables reeled around the drums of a winder engine situated on deck amidships. When the captain thinks that he is over a good bed of oysters, he gives the signal for the dredges to be thrown over the side. The length of the cable released is determined by the depth of the water. To lessen friction, the cables are run over rollers mounted on top of the log rails opposite the winder.

As the dredges drag along the bottom scooping up oysters, the forward motion of the vessel is cut considerably. When the captain "feels" that the dredges have a good catch, he signals the men tending the winder to start reeling in the cables. As the heavy dredges are wound in, they act as anchors and the vessel is actually pulled astern at times, even though her sails are full.

Skipjack *Lottie Bell* dredging in the Choptank River, 1959.
Photo: Author

Before the dredges are brought on deck, they are repeatedly dipped over the side, by clutching the winder engine, and thoroughly rinsed. This cleans the mud and sand off the oysters. When the dredges are on deck, they are dumped and the men start to "cull." This is the process of separating the legal-size oysters (3 inches or more in length) from small oysters, crabs, and empty shells.

The good oysters are thrown into four piles on deck, two forward and two aft. This keeps the craft in trim and working space clear. All the refuse and empty shells are shoveled over the side and the crew await the signal to lower the dredges over the side for another lick. The number of licks made on one tack depends upon the size of the bar. When the edge of the bar has been reached, the dredger comes about and sails parallel to its last course. This same routine continues throughout the day. At the end of the day, the dredging craft go alongside a power buy-boat to sell their catches after which they either return to their home ports

by the swift, shallow-draft bugeye shortly after the end of the Civil War. Toward the end of the nineteenth century, the skipjack gained favor. They were cheap to build and maintain, handy, and simple in rig.

In the old days, oyster dredging on the Chesapeake was a hard school. Murder, shanghaiing, piracy, and wars were not uncommon. Before the turn of the century when dredges were hauled in by means of hand-winders, the low wages attracted

After a long career, the skipjack *Esther W.* is abandoned along the shore of Deal Island to serve as a breakwater. Photo: Author

or anchor in a sheltered creek near the dredging grounds.

Dredge boats are operated on a share basis and this may vary in the different fleets on the Bay. Thirty cents out of every dollar are taken out for the boat. This is to take care of all gear, overhaul, and maintenance. Then the captain and crew each receives 11½ cents out of the balance of the dollar. With six men in the crew, this easily takes care of the dollar. All hands chip in for food and gasoline.

Sloops, schooners, and pungies were the favorite type of craft for dredging oysters in the Chesapeake at one time. They were superseded in popularity

few men. As a result, crews were shanghaied around the Baltimore waterfront and forced to serve through a season. It is said that many were slain at the end of the season so that they could not reveal the identity of their abductors. Others met their fate in this manner in lieu of receiving wages. Many perished from exposure and in attempts to escape from their imprisonment on board the vessels.

Pirates roamed the Chesapeake long after others of that "profession" had been swept from the Golden Main, but Chesapeake pirates were of the oyster variety. Maryland had, and still has, laws

142

that prohibit dredging oysters at night, limit the season to cold-weather months, and mark off certain areas for tongers.

No more do we read of the turmoil which used to prevail in the oyster dredging business. Today's smaller oyster dredging fleets make it easier for police boats to keep them under surveillance and enforce the laws of the State. Small planes are used as spotters to see that yawl boats are not lowered during calm spells to enable the craft to pull their dredges over the bottom. If a vessel is spotted violating the law, photographs of the transgressor are taken as proof and the skipper runs the risk of a heavy fine or even loss of his craft. Dredging vessels are identified by huge numerals painted on canvas and sewn to the mainsail.

At the end of the dredging season, the vessels are stripped of their gear and hauled out on marine railways to have their bottoms painted. Everything topsides is painted to ward off the ravages of weather and some skippers remove the trailboards to preserve gilt and colors. After everything is shipshape, the craft are tied up in the tidewater Maryland ports of Tilghman Island, Oxford, Cambridge, Fishing Bay, Deal Island, Smith Island, Annapolis, or some other anchorage, to await the reopening of the dredging season.

At one time the vessels could find employment during the warm-weather months by carrying produce to city markets. This trade, however, has been taken over by trucks and powerboats.

Though our last sailing fleet is one of a seasonal nature, it is still a throwback to the days of cordage and canvas, an extreme contrast to the gasoline and Diesel-driven vessels that have replaced their rakish, archaic wind-driven sisters.

A hurricane casts the skipjack *Ida Mae* against the Deal Island bridge, 1954.
Photo: Author

143

Skipjack Builders

THE CHESAPEAKE BAY region is the only place in the country where sailing craft are still built for commercial use. Here, sailing vessels without auxiliary engines still find a job to do in American fisheries.

Notable mid-twentieth-century additions to America's meager merchant sailing fleet were the skipjacks *Martha Lewis* and *Rosie Parks*. The former was built for Captain James M. Lewis, of Wingate; the latter for Captain Orville Parks, of Cambridge. Launched in the fall of 1955, they were soon over the oyster grounds bringing payloads of oysters aboard.

The builder of these skipjacks was Bronza M. Parks, of Wingate, Dorchester County, Maryland. Parks had worked as an oyster dredger and knew the requirements of a boat in that grueling trade. His father and grandfather had been watermen and his maternal grandfather had been a boat-

builder. No doubt, this combination of backgrounds had some influence on his choice of occupation.

He began dredging at sixteen and soon decided that the vessel on which he worked was a dull sailer, vowing that some day he would design and build the ideal dredging skipjack.

At twenty-three Parks abandoned dredging and started his own oyster and crab packing plant. His capital was limited and soon a series of bad checks put him out of business.

The next oyster season found him back on the water as half-owner of the skipjack *Nodie North* which he dredged for several years. When the price of oysters dropped so low that he could not make wages, he laid up the *North* and planned to "do some crabbing."

A skiff was required for crabbing so Parks drew up plans and built one in his back yard. Before

The *Martha Lewis,* at left, built by Bronza Parks, shown at the Krentz Shipyard for annual overhaul. Photo: Author

the crabbing season started, a neighbor bought his new skiff for a price that gave him a profit. This started Parks in the boatbuilding business.

The boats he built were "good and able" ones and found a ready market. Skiffs and powerboats for pleasure and commercial uses were his specialty.

In 1936 he drew up plans for the skipjack *Joy Parks* which was built in Parksley, Virginia, for his brother. His reputation as a designer and builder was becoming known up and down the Bay

Bronza Parks and the bow of a skipjack he had under construction in 1955. Photo: Author

and he was kept busy building workboats and pleasure craft. In 1940 he designed and built his first skipjack, the 46-foot *Wilma Lee;* after twenty-three years, she is still dredging oysters in Dorchester County waters.

Mr. Parks had great faith in the continuing use of the skipjack in the oyster dredging business and, in 1954, decided to build three vessels from new plans that he had been working on for many months. They were to be 51 feet long and built of the best material available.

Old-growth yellow pine was the best boat timber growing on the Shore, so Parks set out to explore the native stands of pine for keel logs and planking. The trees selected for keel logs must be large enough and tall enough to saw out a keel approxi-

mately 12 inches x 14 inches x 52 feet long.

The trees for planking would generally be 24–36 inches on the stump and produce a log about 52 feet long. The trees are felled in the fall after the sap goes into the roots. The planking logs are sawn into flitches and stuck up on edge, under cover, to season; some builders apply pine oil during the seasoning process. The keel logs are squared up and sawn to size and shape. The frames are sawn from the best quality oak and great care is exercised to be sure that no knotty ones are used.

Parks' boatyard was next to his home and consisted of a large shed building, where the boats were built, and adjacent storage sheds. In the spring of 1955 keels for the three boats were laid simultaneously and a back-yard assembly line was started. All units were "gotten out" in "threes" and fabricating progress was steady. By October, two of the boats were ready for launching.

Parks' boatyard was a quarter of a mile from a launching site so house-moving equipment, consisting of long steel beams and four pairs of heavy steel wheels with wide tread, was used to move the skipjacks from the yard to the water. Each boat was secured to a timber cradle and at the launch-

The *Rosie Parks* during workboat race at Deal Island, 1960. She won the race. Photo: Author

145

ing site trucks and jacks were used to slide the cradle off the steel beams and into the water. An entire day was required for launching each boat.

The *Rosie Parks*, with her 65-foot mast and boom lashed to her deck, was towed to Cambridge where a derrick would step her mast and she would be outfitted for dredging.

The *Martha Lewis* was placed between two other skipjacks and her mast was stepped with the aid of their blocks and tackle.

Bronza was certain that his improved design would sail and handle better than most skipjacks in the dredging fleet. He relaxed a bit after the rugged summer's work and waited for the verdict.

Captain Orville Parks dredged the *Rosie Parks* for eight years and found that she measured up to her builder's prediction. In the 1962 workboat races off Solomons Island, Captain Parks sailed his *Rosie* to victory.

The third Parks skipjack, the *Lady Katie,* is now owned by George Powley, of Wingate.

Bronza Parks was fatally shot at his yard in 1958 during an argument with a Silver Spring

man for whom he was building a pleasure boat.

Another skipjack builder was Herman M. Krentz & Son, of Harryhogan, on the Yeocomico River. The elder Mr. Krentz had established a yard in 1911 on the Little Wicomico at the mouth of the Potomac. His yard boasted three railways and he developed a flourishing repair business with the oyster and fishing industry and at one period Krentz built an 85-foot power freighter.

Skipjack *Herman M. Krentz* under construction at the Krentz Shipyard in 1955. Photo: Author

With the passing years the mouth of the Little Wicomico shoaled, which prevented larger boats from using his railways. This condition cut his business so much that he moved to the Yeocomico River location in 1932. Here he continued his repair work, on wooden boats, drawing customers from both sides of the Bay. A visitor to the Krentz yard would be impressed by the tall, raking masts of the skipjacks in for repair.

About the same time Bronza Parks was ranging the pine forests of lower Dorchester County in search of keel logs and planking timber, Herman Krentz was searching out the best available material to build a 45-foot skipjack in his yard on the Yeocomico in Virginia.

Krentz did not expend the time and energy to draw up a set of plans; instead, he took off measurements from one of the better designed skipjacks in the Maryland fleet, the *Fannie L. Daugherty,* and used them as a basis for his new boat.

Mr. Krentz went to Baltimore for Georgia pine planking and fir timber for the keel. The best white oak was secured for frames and the 63-foot mast was once a tall pine on Maryland's Eastern Shore.

When the Krentz skipjack (named after its

Herman M. Krentz standing under the transom of the skipjack named after him, which he constructed in 1955. Photo: Author

builder) was ready for launching in 1955, it was moved from its building stocks to the marine railway alongside to be eased into the water. It became the second boat on Chesapeake Bay to bear the name *Herman M. Krentz;* the other was a 52.9-foot freighter built at Kayan, Virginia in 1928.

A Bay custom dictates that the sponsor, or the person whose name a vessel bears, must present the vessel with a suitable item of equipment or decoration. Mr. Krentz chose a beautifully carved pair of trailboards executed by his son as an appropriate gift. They were secured to the longhead under the bowsprit.

This was the only skipjack Mr. Krentz built for the Maryland oyster fleet but his yard was kept busy repairing and rebuilding. In the case of some of the older boats, repairs over a three-year period would represent, from a practical viewpoint, a rebuilt vessel.

The Northern Neck of Virginia has also contributed several other skipjacks to the Maryland oyster dredging fleet in recent years. In 1949 the *City of Crisfield* and *Somerset* were constructed at Reedville and the *Caleb W. Jones* in 1953.

The oyster crop has been on the decline for a number of years and ice has been heavy in the rivers and over the dredging grounds. These conditions have cut down dredging activity and the demand for new skipjacks. None have been built since 1955, but if the demand should come, men with skills and know-how are still around and they will be built.

The *Herman M. Krentz* at work dredging oysters on the Choptank River, Maryland, 1962.
Photo: Author

The Bay's Artist

AN ARTIST equally adept at painting lions and log canoes is a most unusual one. Louis J. Feuchter, a Baltimorean, was a specialist in these widely diversified fields. Drawings of his animal studies were acquired by Mrs. Harry Payne Whitney, founder of the Whitney Museum of American Art, New York City, and his portraits of Chesapeake Bay craft hang in The Mariners Museum, Newport News, Virginia.

When the marine museum, the largest of its kind in America, contemplated a series of paintings of the types of sailing craft developed or employed on the Bay, a number of Feuchter's marine works were examined. Museum officials were impressed with

his attention to detail in portrayal of the vessels, as to rigging, sails and hull forms, and commissioned him. Ten beautiful canvasses were the result: one each of a log canoe, crabbing skiffs, bugeye, pungy, skipjack, sloop and ram, two of schooners and a scene of watermelon-laden craft at Long Dock, Pratt Street, Baltimore.

Except for crabbing skiffs, all vessels in the paintings can be identified, including the seven which appear in the watermelon scene. Most of the vessels featured were no longer in service when the paintings were executed, but Feuchter's files contained numerous sketches he had made along the Baltimore waterfront and in tidewater towns, when the

Louis J. Feuchter doing a watercolor of a pungy in 1953. Photo: Hans Marx

craft were still sailing the Chesapeake. Little additional research was required, although sometimes a background would need checking to ensure accuracy in surroundings. Feuchter took sketchbook and pencil to the location for these details.

He insisted on the proper color schemes and details peculiar to each vessel, such as its trailboard, even though it would be minute in size in the painting. Future generations can view Feuchter's paintings and observe the vessels as they were in real life.

The artist was first attracted to the picturesque smaller craft of the Chesapeake in the early 1900's while on vacations at boarding houses at Neavitt and Wade's Point, on Maryland's Eastern Shore. He saw the log canoe, bugeye, and sloop in their natural surroundings and detected unique beauty in their sculpturesque hull forms. With sketchbook and water and oil paints, he recorded some of his first impressions of the Bay craft.

Through the years he added to his collection pictorial records of the larger craft, by making sketches of them when they visited Baltimore with cargoes or for overhaul in local shipyards. Here he was introduced to the rakish pungy, a type of sailing craft now extinct on the Bay. The pungy was the outgrowth of privateers and Baltimore Clippers and their simplicity of rig and mode of painting in pink and green attracted his artistic eye.

He had a boat built at Wittman, in Talbot County, to enable him to reach out-of-the-way tidewater creeks. It was built from his own design and followed the pattern of a skipjack. He rigged it himself for singlehanded sailing, which made it possible for him to sketch many scenes utilized in his marine paintings.

Ships were not always his chief interest. His first love was wild animals. After completing a scene of skipjacks dredging oysters, he could place a clean sheet of paper on his easel and produce a striking scene of a lion and his mate reclining on some imaginative African plateau.

A look into the artist's background will reveal even more striking contrasts in his array of artistic talents. Feuchter was born in East Baltimore in 1885, and first attended primary school #25 on South Bond Street. Teachers recognized his artistic ability when he was 7 years old.

One day while the school commissioner was attending his class, the teacher called upon young Feuchter to draw on the blackboard. He selected as his subject the interior of a blacksmith shop and drew it entirely from memory. The commissioner

was impressed and gave the young artist a small reward for a copy of his drawing on paper.

His drawing skill came naturally, and as a lad he learned the body structure of animals by studying picture books. His teachers encouraged his art and had him prepare a series of animal drawings which they sent to the World's Columbian Exposition in Chicago as an example of the work of a Baltimore public school student.

When Feuchter progressed to school #2 at Bank Street and Broadway, Baltimore, he was called upon frequently to make drawings on the blackboard, especially during the holiday seasons. Through the efforts of a teacher and a school commissioner, he was granted a four-year scholarship to the Maryland Institute when he was 12 years old. He was unable to take advantage of the day course but attended classes on Saturday for two years. He then started the full-day course, but had to discontinue his art studies and seek employment to supplement the family income, due to the unstable condition of his father's pottery business.

Fortunately, he obtained a job in which he was able to express his artistic talents. He joined the firm of the Baltimore silversmiths, Samuel Kirk and Sons, as an apprentice in chasing silver. He completed his apprenticeship in half the normal time and, although he was only 16 years old, Kirk's recognized his ability and developed a designing department to utilize his unusual talents.

In 1905 the silversmiths were commissioned to prepare a silver service to be presented by Maryland citizens to the new United States battleship *Maryland*. This was a high point in the career of the 19-year-old youth. To determine the character and significance of each piece, he worked with H. C. Kirk, Jr. and Colonel William Love, as one of a committee assigned to do research in connection with the designs. Feuchter made the drawings, designed the scenes, made models in wax from which some of the cast parts were made, and scribed on the silver as a guide for embossing by the chasers.

The service consisted of 46 pieces and related the history of Maryland and its 23 counties in silver. Months were required to complete the set and, at times, as many as 35 skilled silversmiths worked on it. May 31, 1906, was selected as the presentation date. Feuchter, with representatives of Kirk's, boarded the steamer *F. C. Latrobe* in Baltimore for the trip to the port of Annapolis where the *Maryland* was anchored. It was his responsibility to place the service in its proper position on the wardroom table aboard the battleship prior to the presentation ceremonies. The silver service remained on the ship until she was decommissioned and is now in the collection of the Maryland Historical Society.

Feuchter continued designing at Kirk's and attended night classes at the Charcoal Club, winning honors in many of their contests. His interest in wild animals never waned. A series of his drawings on animal life, on display at the Maryland Institute, was noticed by an outstanding contemporary artist who arranged for them to be placed in the collection of Mrs. Harry Payne Whitney, sculptor and art fancier.

Zoos and circuses around Baltimore were frequented by Feuchter as he sought real-life studies of the animals but his secret ambition was to observe wild life in its natural habitat. He realized such plans were beyond his scope and directed his attention to an entirely different subject closer to Baltimore—the sailing craft of Chesapeake Bay.

After 25 years with Kirk's, Feuchter entered the interior decorating business which he followed until the depression of the 1930's. Thereafter, he concentrated on sketching and drawing various types of Bay sailing craft. Marine historians consider it a fortunate circumstance that the artist was unable to pursue his study of wild animals in far-off places, for his detailed artistic works portraying scenes of Chesapeake craft are unparalleled.

Louis Feuchter died on January 11, 1957. He left behind a pictorial record of Chesapeake Bay sailing craft which serves as a fitting monument to this outstanding artist.

A Feuchter watercolor of a pungy on a marine railway. Author's Collection

Watermelon Time at Long Dock

IF ONE SHOULD visit Long Dock, Pratt Street, Baltimore, during August and September in recent years, he may see an occasional powerboat loaded with watermelons. It would be a rare scene compared to the activity there during the melon season through the 1930's.

The melon market was lively. Boat operators and commission merchants' agents hawked the fruit from the decks of sailing craft used to transport the fruit from tidewater farms. Long Dock was congested with pedestrians and trucks; horses and wagons were backed up to the boats to take on melons for sale around the streets of Baltimore.

Missed most of all would be the forest of masts of the Bay sailing craft that once made up the greater part of the fleet in the watermelon trade.

Long Dock usually presented a carnival-like scene in the old days. Vendors of ice cream, snowballs, and hot dogs made their stand there to profit from the crowds attracted either through business or curiosity. All ages sat on the pier's curb and ate melons purchased from the boats for a pittance.

Water surrounding the area was almost covered with whole melons, rinds and spoiled rejects. Whole ones were the targets of boys trying to salvage them with home-made spears.

Oil painting of Long Dock, Baltimore, during watermelon season, by Louis J. Feuchter.
Photo: The Mariners Museum

151

Entire families could be seen aboard the melon boats, having come up from tidewater areas for a brief stay in town while the melons were sold. The crews often found their way to entertainment spots a few blocks from the dock.

A few melons still come to Baltimore by way of the Chesapeake. Powerboats are now used exclusively in the trade, and the total volume brought by boat is negligible compared with other years. Most of the luscious fruit reaches the city by trucks that congregate only a block from Long Dock—at Market Place and Lombard Street. The large trailer trucks can carry almost as many melons and offer faster delivery. Bearing license plates of North or South Carolina and Virginia, the huge trucks line up to unload their melons on the waiting trucks of produce merchants. Large horse and wagon rigs of hucksters have been replaced by pony wagons.

Much of the activity once prevalent at Long Dock now goes on along a two-block stretch fronting the market. The boys are there, still trying to salvage a dropped melon, and traffic policemen struggle with the maze of vehicles. It's all very different from the days of the sailing crafts' traffic in watermelons, and much less colorful.

When Bay boats controlled the melon trade, both sides of Pier 4, which makes up Long Dock, were occupied by the craft, some so deeply laden that their decks were awash. All pier space was taken and they were tied up three or four abreast waiting for a berth. The majority of the vessels were sailing craft—schooners, bugeyes, and skipjacks—so characteristic of Chesapeake Bay.

The melon boats would first appear in the harbor about the first week in August and make repeated visits to port as long as the fruit was in season, often well into September.

Oyster dredging craft, idle in the summer, would join the fleet of watermelon carriers. Two-masted schooners, normally occupied in freighting lumber or canned goods, also helped to bring melons to market.

This commercial scene of other days, with its sailing craft and allied congestion, was so colorful and typical of the trades in which the Bay's craft were engaged, that The Mariners Museum, of Newport News, Virginia, felt it worthy as a subject for a painting to be added to its pictorial collection. The Baltimore artist, Louis Feuchter, was commissioned to do the work and the painting is shown in the accompanying illustration.

In the foreground of the painting is the bugeye *Gorman C.* just arriving with a cargo of melons. To maneuver into the narrow slip, her sails have been lowered and she is being pushed by her yawl boat. Melons are piled high on her deck and slats have been erected to keep the cargo inboard.

To port of the *Gorman C.* is the pungy-schooner *John Martin;* backed up to the *Martin* is a huckster's wagon preparing to take on a load of melons. At the end of the pier is the bugeye *Nettie B. Greenwell,* noted for her speed in the Baltimore *Sun*-sponsored workboat races. One wagon has been loaded from this vessel and another is waiting to relieve the boat of more melons. The skipjacks *E. C. Collier* and *Mary M. Clark* lie at the far side of the pier.

The *Clark* is making sail, preparing to beat down Baltimore harbor against an easterly wind. Already under way is the schooner *J. A. Chelton,* bound for Maryland's Eastern Shore for another cargo of melons. The *Clark* is evidently waiting for the tug *Esther Phillips* and its tow to pass, before casting off. Federal Hill forms a backdrop in the distance.

Of the vessels portrayed in the Feuchter painting, only one still exists as a sailing vessel. The skipjack *E. C. Collier* continues to operate during the winter months as an oyster dredger. The bugeye *Gorman C.* left the Chesapeake to dredge oysters on North Carolina's Pamlico Sound. She is now a hulk in a salt marsh at Belhaven, N. C.

Bugeye *Nettie B. Greenwell* was converted to power in the late 1930's and eleven years later was sunk in the lower James River after being rammed by a steamer. The schooner *J. A. Chelton* "broke her back" in the 1930's and was abandoned soon afterward in Jones Creek, near Sparrows Point. The *John Martin,* first of the group in the painting to be shorn of her sails, was converted to power in the early 1930's and is still active as an oyster buy-boat in the lower Bay.

The skipjack *Mary M. Clark,* after almost a half century of dredging oysters, was abandoned at Deal Island several years ago. The tug *Esther Phillips* has been broken up.

Little remains of the watermelon scene depicted in the painting. Buildings have been erected on that portion of Pier 4 shown in the picture; they serve as a Coast Guard base of operations.

In keeping pace with the times, the watermelon trade shifted from the waterways to the highways and, in the process, Baltimore lost one of its most colorful waterfront activities.

Dredging Oysters the Hard Way

IN 1954 Captain Ivy B. McNamara of Cambridge, Maryland, recalled previous hard winters and the resourcefulness of Bay watermen in their attempt to make a living.

"I have heard some people remark that there are indications this winter will be a severe one. If true, that means a hard life for the oysterman. Since that has been my work all my life, perhaps the outlook for the next few months isn't too bright. But I don't think the weather could be any more severe than some winters I have experienced in the past.

"Whenever there's talk of a hard winter, I can't help but recall that of 1917–18. That was when the battleship *Ohio* was called on to break a ship channel in the Chesapeake because the ice was too thick for Baltimore icebreakers. I don't think I've seen it any worse than that season and I've been around these waters for almost three-quarters of a century. The rivers and creeks were a solid sheet of ice and dredging and tonging craft were locked in.

"I was born on James Island in 1880. At the time of the "big freeze" I owned and skippered the skipjack *Lena S. Mills.* I was sailing out of Cambridge, my home for the past fifty-two years. When I became aware that my boat was to be frozen in for an indefinite period, I put in with a group of idle dredgers who were determined to get oysters by one means or another.

"Ice on the Choptank River was about fourteen inches thick, strong enough to hold a team of horses. Five of us: Ed Vickers, Allie Vickers, Tom Vickers, Charles Ross, and myself, all of Cambridge, made a rough sort of sleigh and piled on dredges, lines, shovels, axes, and tubs. This we pulled out over the Choptank. When we felt we were about over Trim Pines Shoal, we unloaded our gear and cut a hole through the ice large enough to lower the dredge to the bottom of the river.

"Then we cut a slot through the ice three-hundred or more feet long, wide enough to permit a line to pass along it. At the other end of the slot we cut another hole through which we could pull up the dredge.

"With the holes cut, we all grabbed a hold onto the line and started pulling along the slot, the dredge dragging over the bottom picking up the oysters. At the end of the slot, we pulled up the dredge and emptied the oysters. Then we cut another passage for the line so we wouldn't pull the dredge over the same bottom, enlarging the two holes at the same time. There were other groups out on the ice doing the same thing—usually five men to a team. Tongers also worked through the ice but the dredges brought up more oysters. There were almost as many spectators as workmen.

"Other oyster grounds over which we worked on the Choptank were Back Sandy Hill and Loon Hill. Dragging those heavy dredges over the river bottom was cold, hard work. Filled dredges had to be pulled to the surface, lifted onto the ice, and the oysters culled. Then at the end of the day we had to pull the sleigh full of oysters and our dredging gear back to shore. As I recall, that situation lasted for more than two weeks before we were able to use our dredging craft.

"Since there was a shortage of oysters because of the freeze-up, one might think we got a good price for the oysters but they sold for only one dollar a bushel. No, I wouldn't like to see another winter as bad as that of 1917–18. However, we had a big freeze in 1936 and had to dredge through the ice in a similar manner.

"I've been oystering since I was nine years old and I'm still at it on my bugeye *Edna E. Lockwood,* one of about five such craft in Maryland's oyster dredging fleet. It is still a rugged life but half a century ago it was something to talk about. Then we usually picked up a crew in Baltimore and paid each man fifteen dollars a month and his keep. Out of that amount would be deducted six dollars for their outfit, clothing, and foul-weather gear. It was work in those days with hand-winders; no engines on deck to pull in those heavy dredges.

"The first time I went out as captain was on the skipjack *Dunnock*, around the turn of the century. I've dredged on Chesapeake waters from November to March practically all of my working life. I also oystered on the Delaware Bay for seed oysters in May and June. When I was younger, I served as quartermaster on steamers of the Merchants & Miners during the summer months.

"I owned the skipjack *Lena S. Mills* for about ten years. I also skippered the schooner *Samuel E. Egerton,* sloop *Daisy M. Tall,* and sloop *Henry W. Ruark*. I've owned the *Edna E. Lockwood* for about seven years and she is an old one—a log-bottomed bugeye, built in 1889 on Tilghman Island. She's out on the Choptank again this year and I'm at her wheel. I'd like to think our season won't be interrupted by another freeze-up."

Oystermen on the frozen Choptank River dredging through a slot cut into the ice.
Author's Collection

Yankee Skiffs

ONE YANKEE that came to the Chesapeake in the mid-nineteenth century and was whole-heartedly accepted may still be found in the lower reaches of the Bay. This is a small boat from New York that was adapted to the oyster industry on the York and James Rivers. Referred to in those waters as "Yankee skiffs," or "Staten Island skiffs," the surviving ones are used on the York River as oyster tong boats.

The "Yankee skiff" is unlike any small craft constructed around Chesapeake Bay. Twenty-three feet in length and with a six-foot beam, the boats are lap-strake or clinker built; that is, their side planks are placed so that one edge of each overlaps the edge of the plank under it like clapboards on a house.

Lightly built of white cedar over oak frames, with heart-shaped stern transom, spoon bow, and flat-bottomed or plank keel, the skiffs are easily

A Yankee skiff at Capahosic, York River, Virginia, after a day on the oyster grounds. Photo: Author

rowed by one man who sits forward with oars between thole pins. They are the most handsome of any small boat employed in Chesapeake fisheries today. Except for the flat bottom and transom, their hulls are made up of a series of graceful curves.

One may wonder how these boats migrated to the Chesapeake where an ample variety of locally developed small boats existed. The men who own the few examples still in service heard their ancestors tell of northern oystermen who came to the lower Bay for cargoes of oysters to replace those depleted on their home oyster grounds. Schooners, with these skiffs on deck, came through the Virginia Capes in great numbers.

The 1887 issue of Goode's *Fishing Industries of the United States* records: "In the lower part of New York Bay immense plantations of southern oysters have been carried on since 1825. The central place is Prince's Bay, Staten Island. . . .

". . . Rappahannock and York River stocks seem to have been preferred always in this district and a large number of sloops and schooners run each spring to and from those rivers. The crews of those vessels are not only Jerseymen or Staten Islanders but often Chesapeake men who come up for a brief season's work and then return to their homes."

Some of the northern schooners would dredge their own oysters or buy them. Many of the boats, however, brought their skiffs and hired local oystermen to tong for them.

One Staten Island oyster packer, Peter Van Name, took a liking to the York River area and its abundance of oysters and settled there near West Point. His schooner, the *William H. Van Name,* built by David Carll, City Island, New York in 1872, was one of the faster vessels to run between New York and the Chesapeake. She showed her seaworthiness and ability as a working vessel during the 20 years she operated in the trade for which she was built—up and down the coast in winter, coming down light without ballast and returning with oysters loaded almost to the plank-sheer.

Captain John M. Clayton, first oyster packer on Hooper Island, Maryland, owned and operated the *William H. Van Name* from 1895 to 1902. He used her to freight pineapples from the Bahamas during the summer season. The schooner's last owner was Captain Al Simmons who bought her in 1902. She was loaded with coal when she was lost in Hampton Roads on March 31, 1906, after striking the submerged barge *Oak*.

The builder's model of this two-masted schooner now hangs in the office of J. M. Clayton Co., Cambridge oyster packers. Partners in the company are Ellison R. Clayton and Clayton Brooks, son and

The shapely hull of a Yankee skiff is evident in this view.
Photo: Author

grandson, respectively, of the company's founder. Mr. Brooks' paternal grandfather was the well-known boatbuilder of the late 1800's, Joseph W. Brooks, Madison, Maryland.

Van Name was largely responsible for placing "Staten Island skiffs" among York River oystermen where they once existed in great numbers. There are six skiffs still in service on the York River. They are found in no other waters of the Chesapeake. Two of these are privately owned by oyster tongers; the other four are owned by the York River Oyster Corporation, located at the mouth of Foxes Creek, Gloucester County.

That firm holds the leases on York River bottom from Indian Field Creek, near Yorktown, to West Point. Except for a few isolated tracts, it owns all the oystering rights between these points.

With a number of outboard-powered boats in addition to the skiffs, the company allows its boats to be used by oystermen who do "piecework"; that is, the men tong oysters on the firm's grounds and are paid so much per bushel caught. When the weather is favorable and oysters are plentiful, the skiffs are usually busy. In recent years about a dozen skiffs have been placed in retirement in a marsh near the plant. Contributing factors to their decline have been the scarcity of oysters and the younger oystermen's dislike of the manual labor required to row the boats.

Little is known about the background of the "Yankee skiff" before it came to the Chesapeake. Until now the type has not come under the scrutiny of marine historians.

Some authorities link the "Yankee skiff" to the New Jersey beach skiff which is similar in build and appearance. Others believe it stems from the New England wherry, which was very common in Colonial times and the early 19th century but has virtually disappeared. It is interesting to note that during a recent filming at Williamsburg, one of the York River skiffs was used in a scene as being representative of a boat of the Colonial period.

Farmers
Plant Seed Oysters

To THE AVERAGE farmer springtime means planting of crops to be reaped the following summer and fall. Some Virginia tidewater farmers, however, plant oyster crops.

The Virginia farmers living on waterfront sites took to the briny rivers and creeks when prices for oysters soared during World War II. One section particularly affected was the Northern Neck, a long peninsula between the Rappahannock and Potomac Rivers. On a number of waterways in that area oyster-shucking houses sprang up virtually overnight.

To ensure a profitable crop of oysters farmers soon realized it would be necessary to use top-grade seeds and none surpass those found in the James River. They sent buy-boats down to Deep Creek, situated on the James just above Newport News, to purchase thousands of bushels for planting on their state-leased bottoms.

A typical buy-boat employed in this trade was the *Yeocomico,* which for several years had been coming to the James River from the Northern Neck to fill her hold and deck with the lucrative bivalve. To obtain a first-hand view of the seed-oyster trade from the time the oysters were tonged from the James until they were transplanted in other waters, the author boarded the *Yeocomico* at her Deep Creek anchorage in 1953.

The vessel was taking on 2,200 bushels consigned to the Coan River, a scenic waterway making off the Potomac River, about 13 miles above Smith's Point. She had been in harbor about six days picking up her cargo from the tongers. Her extended stay was caused by several days of bad weather that had kept tong boats in port.

The day the *Yeocomico* planned to sail for the Coan, tongers began coming into Deep Creek with their catches around 3:30 P.M. Fifteen buy-boats were anchored, waiting to receive the oysters; a few were anchored in the James River near the tonging grounds. Usually, there were sufficient oysters for all. A number of buy-boats were operated or chartered by large Norfolk seafood packing houses who purchased the seed for their own oyster beds in Hampton Roads or the Mobjack Bay area.

Independent buy-boats, such as the *Yeocomico,* paid slightly higher prices per bushel than the company-operated buy-boats. To announce this fact, they displayed the American ensign on their forestays—certainly a breach of flag etiquette afloat and a novel use for "Old Glory."

As a tonger's boat sidled up to a buy-boat, it was assigned a number to aid in tallying the number of bushels it placed on the buy-boat. With as many as four or more tonging boats discharging oysters at the same time, that was the best way to keep an accurate account. The oysters were unloaded in bushel tubs operated from gear on the buy-boats and a tallier kept the record on a clean board in multiples of five bushels. As the oysters came aboard, the tonger announced the number assigned to his boat and the number of bushels he had discharged—such as 1:4—meaning that his boat was number 1 and he had discharged 4 bushels. When he had discharged 5 bushels, he yelled "Tally," and the process was repeated. The tallier verbally repeated the figures and everything ran smoothly despite the number of boats unloading at the same time. When a tonger had discharged his oysters, he climbed aboard the buy-boat, the figures on the tally board were totaled, and he was paid in cash. On that occasion the price being paid was 85 cents per bushel and most of the tongers averaged between 50 and 70 bushels per day. The buy-boat then sold them to the consignee at $1.05 per bushel; this included the freightage.

By 7 P.M. the *Yeocomico* was loaded, and since she had arranged with the consignee to be in Coan River the next morning, she weighed anchor and passed out into the James River just as the last tonger was making his way into Deep Creek.

The *Yeocomico* was a typical Chesapeake Bay power freighter, built at Ruark, Virginia, in 1931. She was 64 feet, 10 inches long. Regulations required vessels over 65 feet long to be operated by licensed officers. Her owner and skipper, Captain Arthur Richardson Eubank, need feel no concern about a license. In the *Yeocomico's* pilothouse was displayed her master's license, good for "all oceans and all tonnages" and "1st-class pilot on Chesapeake Bay." This was a rare combination on a smaller Bay freighter.

Captain Eubank, a native of Lewisetta, Virginia, a little town overlooking the Potomac at the mouth of Coan River, started his seagoing experience when he was 18. He first sailed out of Baltimore on excursion steamers and then on the *President Warfield* of the Old Bay Line. This deck-hand detail was followed by service on Merchants and Miners steamers, first as cadet, later as quartermaster and third mate. He sailed with the Standard Oil Company as mate and in 1942 was on the tanker *E. M. Clark* when she was torpedoed off Cape Hatteras. He and 14 crew members drifted in a lifeboat for two days and were finally picked up and brought into Norfolk by the tanker *Rhode Island*.

His next ship was the tanker *E. J. Sadler* on a passage to the Gulf. At Galveston, his decision to leave the ship proved to be a fortunate one, for the *Sadler* was lost with all hands after leaving port. Eubank returned to Baltimore and obtained his master's license, thereby becoming one of the youngest captains in the American merchant marine, at 26 years of age. He was given command of the Liberty ship *Nathaniel Alexander* soon after she was launched from the yard of the North Carolina Shipbuilding Corporation, Wilmington, North Carolina. He skippered that ship for five years, sailing to Murmansk, Great Britain, Africa, Italy, Egypt, India, South Pacific, and American ports. Hampton Roads was a familiar port of call for him, bringing in prisoners of war and taking out troops.

Buy-boat *Yeocomico* with a deckload of seed oysters for planting in the Coan River, Virginia, 1953. Photo: Author

When he left the *Alexander* at New York in 1948, he decided to give up deep-sea ships primarily because of unions and crew difficulties. He readily admitted that he could think of nothing more gratifying than being master of a seaworthy ship manned by a good crew.

Because this ideal combination was difficult to find after World War II, he took up freighting on the Chesapeake, first as part owner and skipper of the *Yeocomico* and later as full owner of the vessel. He had no crew trouble for he played the role of captain, engineer, and cook. He usually carried one or two deck hands to assist in steering and handling lines and cargo, but he could handle the vessel easily himself because her engine was controlled from the pilothouse. He made solo trips from the Coan to Baltimore several times.

Captain Eubank may have felt out of his element by confining his activities to the Chesapeake but he had no difficulty in navigating the numerous unmarked tributaries or in obtaining freights. He usually tied up his boat in the Coan during the summer months and served as pilot on menhaden steamers active along the coast and in the Bay.

On this particular trip as the *Yeocomico* left the James River astern, Captain Eubank steered his vessel into the Newport News Boat Harbor in order to phone his consignee and advise him that he was bound up the Bay. Before leaving again there was the usual chat with other buy-boat skippers about market prices and weather.

Threading her way past anchored naval ships in Hampton Roads, the *Yeocomico* met the swells of the Chesapeake as she passed Old Point. Coming up from astern, the collier *Charlestown* gave two blasts on her whistle to signify that she was passing to port of the deeply laden buy-boat. Captain Eubank acknowledged the signal and pulled over as the towering steamer glided by bound for the Virginia Capes.

Coan River was reached at 8:30 the next morning after a calm, uneventful trip up the Bay. As the *Yeocomico* entered the river, her arrival was witnessed by the captain's wife from the living room window of their home which overlooked the channel. There was little time for greeting because men were waiting to discharge the powerboat's cargo up an arm of the Coan, known as The Glebe.

The *Yeocomico* came to anchor offshore from a point of the 300-acre farm operated by Homer Downing. Mr. Downing was considered a successful farmer but talk of high oyster prices led him to investigate the possibilities of becoming part-

time tonger. His farm was bounded by water on three sides; sandy bottom and a depth of 8 feet of water close to shore made this an ideal site for planting oysters.

Leasing the bottom from the state of Virginia at $1 per acre per year, Downing decided to invest in 1,100 bushels of seed oysters, an investment that should have more than doubled its original outlay. From every bushel of seed oysters he expected to get almost three of marketable oysters. He hoped to start tonging that fall since some of the seeds were large enough to have matured by the time the season opened.

The *Yeocomico* anchored close to shore and then transferred its deck load to three small boats from which the oysters were scattered over the water with shovels. Within five hours the James River seeds had been placed in their new home to grow and develop in the clean waters of the Coan.

Seed oysters being planted in the Coan River from a small boat with zero-freeboard. Photo: Author

The 100 bushels in the hold had been ordered by a Mr. Fisher who had leased a section of bottom in the main branch of the Coan. The Coan River is deep for its size and until 1932 steamers, 192 feet in length, made stops at six landings along its course as they plied between Baltimore and Washington. Because of this depth, the *Yeocomico* could anchor directly over Fisher's oyster bottom where once again the cargo was discharged into smaller boats and scattered over the water with shovels. Nature took over from that point.

Along with the discussion of farm crops and politics, seed oysters have found a place in general store conversations throughout the Virginia tidewater area.

Menhaden Purse-Net Profits

On THE EXTREME end of Virginia's Northern Neck (the peninsula between the Potomac and Rappahannock Rivers) is the little town of Reedville. When approached by the highway, it resembles any other tidewater country town, but if one travels by water and enters the Great Wicomico River from the Bay, tall stacks and numerous factories come into view to belie its quiet landward atmosphere.

The sizable industry apparent to the water-borne traveler has been a source of fame to Reedville, once considered one of the richest towns per capita in the United States, in an area chiefly devoted to farming and with no rail transportation. The reason for this prosperity is found in Chesapeake Bay and the Atlantic Ocean in the form of a fish that has great commercial value, though considered unfit for human consumption.

American Indians called the fish "munnawhateaug" (fertilizer). The Narragansett tribes recognized the value of decomposed fish as nourishment for their crops and the "munnawhateaug" was the fish most commonly used for this purpose because it was so abundant.

The fish has many local names—"pogy," "alewife," "bunker," "mossbunker," "menhaden," among others. The menhaden, the name by which it is known to Chesapeake watermen, is a member of the herring family. Most abundant of all ocean fish, it ranges along the entire Atlantic and Gulf coasts and as far inland as brackish water extends.

Menhaden are of little value as food because their flesh is too oily and mealy. The oil extracted from them, however, and the residue from this process, are the reasons this lowly fish is the foundation of an important industry.

Menhaden vessel *William S. Brusstar* races to Reedville to discharge her catch of fish, 1948. Photo: Author

Fish oil is used in the manufacture of soap, stains, varnishes, linoleum, certain heat-resisting paints, and waterproofing compounds. The residue, or fish meal, once of prime importance as fertilizer, is now used as feed for fowl and stock. It contains nitrogen and calcium phosphate, vital for bone building in stock and egg production in chickens.

An early method used to extract oil from the menhaden was to place the fish in casks, cover them with water, and press them with weighted boards. As the fish decayed, oil rose to the surface and was skimmed. As their value became better known, more efficient methods of processing were developed and utilized.

The first steam-processing factory was established in Rhode Island. Others followed in New York, Connecticut, and Maine. In 1886 a floating factory, the steamer *Ranger,* came to Virginia, where the fish were found in large numbers in the lower Bay and off the Virginia Capes. Three years later,

Reedville's first factory was built and the town has become the most important fish oil and meal center on the coast.

Menhaden are a migratory fish and the location for catching them varies with different seasons. In coastal areas the vessels fish from the last week in May until the first week in July. During July, August, and September the fish move into the Bay, with the vessels after them. Since Maryland has a law forbidding the use of purse seines (the method employed to catch menhaden), the vessels never venture above Smith's Point, at the mouth of the Potomac River. The fish go out to sea again in October and Reedville vessels pursue them until around the first of November, when the season ends.

Most of the menhaden vessels were especially designed for the fishing business. Originally they were steam-propelled but have now been converted to Diesel. They are 125 to 150 feet long and are quite deep and narrow. One Reedville company

Using the dip net to transfer menhaden from the purse net to the larger vessel.
Photo: Author

161

purchased a former landing craft and fitted her out for fishing.

The menhaden factories are busiest at night when the vessels put in with their catches. Between 9 and 10 P.M. a procession of these craft enter Cockrell's Creek, where the factories are located. Three blasts are given on their horns as they approach their respective docks.

Before the vessels' arrival the only sign of activity around a plant is a watchman making his rounds of the various buildings and docks with a lantern. By the time a vessel's mooring lines are fast, the fireman, who has been near his boilers, has steam up to operate the equipment for unloading and processing the fish. Lights begin to glow throughout the factory as the men who have been resting nearby, but out of sight, take up their stations. Smoke pours out of the tall stacks and the clatter of machinery disturbs the quiet of the waterfront.

As a vessel glides up to the pier, her bow cuts across a ray of light and her nameboard identifies her as the *Margaret*. She is a stoutly built wooden boat, 128 feet in length. Her white coat is rust-streaked and scarred from rough usage. She is inactive during the fishing season only in the event of urgent repairs, heavy weather, and Sundays in port. Within two hours she will be unloaded, washed down, and on her way back to the fishing grounds.

Amidships is the hold into which the fish are dumped when caught. Several deckhands climb into the hold and hoses are passed to them as the preliminary steps to removing the fish. Water pressure is applied as the nozzles are forced down through the fish. In the bottom of the hold are eight metal plates, each about one foot in diameter. Attached to the top of each plate are chains which lead up to the deck level. By means of these chains, the plates are pulled out of place and the water from the hoses washes the menhaden through the openings into a channel under the ceiling (the inner planking).

Powerful pumps suck the fish from the channel through hoses and deposit them in hoppers at the factory. A full hopper holds approximately 1,000 fish, with an average weight of 667 pounds; the fish are counted in this manner. Officers of the vessel are paid by shares; deck hands receive a wage and percentage of share.

When a hopper is filled it is tripped and another falls into place. The fish fall into a conveyor which carries them to the cooker or to the "raw box" to be stored for later cooking. The cooking process which breaks up the fat cells usually begins as soon as the unloading starts.

The fish go to the press from the cooker, where intense pressure is applied to extract the oil and water which is conducted through a trough into a settling tank. The oil and water then pass through a series of tanks and gradually are separated. The oil is again cooked and stored in uncovered tanks where it is bleached and washed by sun and water. Six or seven gallons of oil are obtained from 1,000 fish.

The residue, or press scrap, is discharged at the opposite end of the press and is sent through driers to remove all moisture, then to the coolers and storage. The scrap is bagged the next day to be sold to feed mills.

After the hold has been cleaned and the vessel washed down, she casts off. Backing away from the pier, the *Margaret* heads out to the Bay with her course set for Cape Henry.

Thirty-two men make up the crew of this vessel, including the pilot, captain, mate, two engineers, cook and helper, and deck hands. The pilot takes the vessel in and out of port and assumes command when the captain and mate are in the purse boats on the fishing grounds. Each engineer stands a six-hour watch in the engine room and tends the winch; each deck hand stands a one-hour trick at the wheel in addition to handling the nets and doing routine ship's work.

The vessel requires about four hours to reach the Virginia Capes from Reedville. The day begins at 5 A.M. when the cook sounds the alarm for breakfast. Food is placed on long tables in large quantities to provide the excessive energy required to handle the huge nets later in the day. The menu may be salt cod, boiled potatoes and raw onions, cereal, hot biscuits, black molasses, and coffee. Pancakes and eggs are served in turn, to vary the morning meal. Although the men see, talk, and smell fish the whole season, they never tire of eating it. The officers eat in their mess forward of the galley but the fare is the same.

After breakfast, the captain, mate, and a deck hand take up their positions in the crow's nest, a platform atop the mast, to begin the day's search for schools of menhaden.

The vessels usually work in groups and, on this occasion, there are six fanned out to cover a wide area as they head south along the Virginia coast below Cape Henry. They are equipped with two-way radio communication and captains discuss the prospects of fish in the immediate area and on the grounds ahead. After going as far south as False

Cape, Virginia, without having spotted a single school, they decide there is little chance for a catch in that section, so the vessels turn about and head for the fishing grounds near Cape Charles Lightship. Steering instructions are relayed by the captain to the helmsman over a phone in the crow's nest connected with a speaker in the pilothouse.

Dinner is served at 10 A.M. The deck hands busy themselves about the deck or gather in their quarters or the galley to while away the time between "sets." This is the term used to designate the operation of setting out the purse net after the menhaden have been sighted, and the return to the vessel with the fish. When the fish are plentiful the crew is kept busy; when the "sets" are few they have little to do.

Up in the crow's nest the lookouts keep constant vigil for telltale signs of menhaden. This fish is pelagic, which means it swims and feeds on the surface. The signs may be either small flurries of foam kicked up by the fish, or a reddish hue in the water reflecting from the fishes' bodies as they swim in large schools. When a school is sighted, the cry "Boats away" is given and the three lookouts quickly descend to the deck. Those hands assigned places in the purse boats go quickly to their stations.

The *W. B. Rowe* on the marine railway at Humphrey's Shipyard, Weems, Virginia, 1959. Photo: Author

The two purse boats, each 33 feet long, are carried on davits on the port and starboard quarters. They are lowered by a winch and tied to the stern of the fishing vessel where the crew members climb into them, the captain in charge of one boat and the mate the other. The first boat away, however, is the "striker," a small round-bottomed rowboat that is quickly lowered over the side. The deck hand, who has been in the crow's nest serving as a lookout, climbs into the boat and rows to where the fish have been sighted. He tracks them and, with an oar, signals to the captain the direction in which they are moving.

The two purse boats, both powered, put off from the vessel. They are lashed together but when the captain judges that they are in a proper position to lower the nets, they separate to encircle the "striker" and fish. The purse net is about 1,000 feet long, 60 feet deep, and has a one-inch mesh. One-half of this is stowed in each purse boat and is thrown out by the "seine setters" as the boats separate to meet again after the fish have been encircled.

Along the bottom edge of the net are lead weights to keep it hanging down in the water. A number of brass rings are fastened to the underwater end of the net. A purse line passes through these rings, with ends remaining in the purse boats. On the top line of the net are hundreds of round cork floats which support the entire net.

When the two boats meet, they are lashed together and the "tom," a piece of lead weighing about 400 pounds, is dropped overboard from the captain's boat. Attached to this weight are two snatch blocks through which pass the ends of the purse lines. The "tom" serves to hold the ends of the net together and acts as a fulcrum as the purse lines are taken in and the end of the net is pursed, or closed. The purse lines are taken in by a winch mounted on top of the engine housing in the captain's boat.

The ends of the net, with the floats, are hauled into the boats as the net is being pursed and arranged in an orderly manner so as to be in readiness for the next "set." In the meantime, the "striker" boat takes in the cork floats on the arc of the circle opposite the purse boats. This prevents the fish from escaping if the net tends to submerge when the fish are in its bunt.

After the "tom" has been taken up, the bows of the purse boats are lashed to each other, allowing enough space for the bunt of the net, with the haul of fish, to be suspended between them. Throughout the entire operation teamwork reigns supreme. Every man has a job to do and does it smoothly and willingly. The prevailing attitude of coöperation is of paramount importance since the work calls for split-second maneuvering and the slightest delay or mistake may mean a loss of thousands of dollars in gear and fish.

While the "set" is being made, the fishing vessel stands by until the captain signals her to come alongside and take on the catch. The bunt of the net is made fast to the vessel's port gunwale and the purse boats are held in position with the net between them.

A bailing net, about 4 feet wide and 4 feet deep, is used to dip the fish out of the purse net into the hold of the vessel. This net is suspended from a boom hung to the mast directly over the hold and is maneuvered by the winch. Attached to the net is a long wooden handle which is controlled by a deck hand on the vessel and directs the bailing net in the purse net. When the bailing net has a load of fish to be dumped into the hold, it is released by pulling a line on the bottom of the net.

After the purse net has been emptied, the purse boats and "striker" boat are taken astern of the large vessel to be towed. The lookouts once more ascend to the crow's nest and the vessel moves on to resume the search.

Sometimes a "set" is made and the net is found to be empty. This is referred to as a "stab." If the fish disappear before the net is entirely out, this is called a "pull-back." If the captain exclaims, "They are showing color," as the net is being taken in, it signifies that the fish have been trapped and a payload is assured.

Supper is served at 3 P.M. or at a convenient time between "sets." Fishing operations usually cease at sunset but some "sets" have been made by moonlight. At the end of the day's work the purse boats and "striker" boat are hoisted in place and the ship is washed down.

The law requires that menhaden vessels must throw overboard any food fish caught in their nets. This refers to large quantities—if a stray hardhead or trout becomes enmeshed, the crew members may prepare them on the spot.

Food fish trawlers and menhaden vessels have a friendly agreement. If the trawlers spot a school of menhaden, the word is passed over the two-way communication to the menhaden vessels and they, in turn, reciprocate when quantities of food fish are observed.

The *Margaret* had finished a day's fishing but lacked a sufficient quantity of fish to warrant a trip back to Reedville to unload, so plans were made to anchor at Lynnhaven Roads, just inside Cape Henry. As she passed a trawler on the way in, the captain developed a yen for fried fresh trout. One of the deck hands was sent over to the trawler in the "striker" boat to see if some fresh fish could be purchased. He returned in a short time with a peach basket filled with trout—gratis. After the vessel had anchored these were cleaned, fried, and served with rolls and coffee.

When the season ends in the Chesapeake Bay region, some of the Reedville menhaden vessels go to Beaufort and Morehead City, North Carolina. One company has branch factories all along the Atlantic and Gulf coasts, and their vessels follow the fish. Many Reedville vessels, however, remain idle until the next spring.

One captain was asked how the crew members spend the slack period and replied, "Some of them work in the lumber mills or help to fish the pound nets. Me—I'm going hunting."

The preceding description of the menhaden industry was observed in 1948. Since then numerous innovations have been adopted in the spotting, taking, and processing of menhaden. Airplanes are used to spot schools of fish and radio their location to the vessel. Aluminum purse boats have replaced the wooden models, the "power block," a new method of pursing the net, is in use, and a more efficient pump system to take the fish out of the net and hold of the ship has been developed.

At the end of the season, the menhaden vessels tie up at Reedville and Fleeton, Virginia, unless they move south in search of the fish.
Photo: Author

Wooden Steamers of World War I

THE CONSTRUCTION of big wooden freight steamers enveloped this country during the height of World War I and for a short period after the Armistice. Their rotting remains lie in many ports along America's east and west coasts. The hulking frames of some loom above the waterfront as glaring examples of what has been termed "one of the most absurd and disastrous enterprises ever foisted upon the American public—the wooden shipbuilding program that cost the country five hundred million dollars."

We must go back to 1917 to see just how this project was introduced. At that time the Germans were sinking ships faster than at any other period of the war and, for a few weeks, ships were going down at the rate of fifteen million deadweight tons a year. According to contemporary statistics, barely twenty million tons of shipping were available in the entire world for Allied war needs. It was essential to build any kind of ship that could get across the Atlantic or release other ships for that purpose.

Shortly after this country entered the war in the spring of 1917, the first chairman of the newly formed United States Shipping Board introduced the program for building wooden steamships and launched it in the press with all the power of the government behind it.

It was known that the wooden steamship was a mere temporary war expedient and the chairman of the Board was aware that such a vessel would be of little value in maritime commerce three years after the end of the war. However, wooden ships seemed to be the answer to the shipping shortage at the moment. If submarines sank them, the loss would be comparatively small and others could be built easily to take their place. The emergency made it necessary to turn to the forests and unorganized forces of woodworking labor, smaller machine shops, and boiler factories not serving the steel shipbuilding plants.

Plans provided for the building of wooden vessels with about 3,500 tons deadweight carrying capacity and a speed of ten knots. Propelling machinery of about 1,500 horsepower was required for each vessel. It was considered possible to produce a fleet of 800 to 1,000 ships of this type within about 18 months. This, combined with the output of steel merchant ships built in that time, would exceed or keep pace with the highest rate of submarine destruction, thus making the German submarine blockade ineffectual.

So the wooden shipbuilding program got under full swing. Huge timber orders were placed with the Southern Pine Association in July 1917, sufficient for hundreds of wooden hulls. For several months thereafter the material was piling up in new shipyards erected all along the Atlantic and Gulf coasts. It was all the lighter timbers for upper frames and deck planking—no ships could be started because there were no heavy materials for keels or floor timbers.

It was November 1917 when the purchasing department of the Shipping Board discovered this fact, made inquiries, and was advised by the Southern Pine Association that they would be unable to furnish the heavy timbers because they were inaccessible within its cutting regions.

Efforts were made to change the designs of the ships by cutting down on the size of the lower timbers. One member of the Shipping Board suggested ordering the heavy lumber from Oregon so 90 million feet of Oregon spruce was ordered for the Atlantic and Gulf shipyards and priority was demanded for through trains over the transcontinental railroad lines. A "river of wood" was to flow across the nation.

Overland shipment of this timber in the winter

of 1917–1918 contributed immeasurably toward the transportation breakdown of that winter. This, in turn, induced the coal shortage and slowed up war preparation.

The prediction of ships within six months after the program started failed to materialize. In fact, the first wooden steamer was delivered late in May 1918, more than a year after the United States entered the war. Relatively few were completed in time to be of use before the war was over. Not one of the wooden steamers crossed the Atlantic before the signing of the Armistice.

The vessels were all kept in coastwise trade or on the Honolulu route until March 1919 when the government decided to try them out across the Atlantic. Some carried sulphur from Texas to the munition plants in Delaware; others carried coal and cotton to New England, coal to naval bases, and raw sugar from Hawaii to San Francisco.

Approximately 115 of the 703 wooden steamers contracted for were completed and in service by April 1, 1919. Of 264 ships delivered prior to September 1, 1919, 195 made the transatlantic trip once and less than 40 were sent across twice. But

Wooden steamer *Dover* as a barge and abandoned in Curtis Creek, Baltimore, 1954. Photo: Author

by confining their activities to the coastwise trade, they were releasing steel tonnage for the run across the Atlantic.

The building of wooden steamers might have been an immensely valuable wartime program if the war had lasted longer—it should have proved worth-while before the war did end. It is felt that the project was grossly mismanaged and was not pushed because few of those connected with it had any faith in the vessels.

There were at least five distinct designs built. These were the Ferris, Hough, Ballin, Daugherty, and Grays Harbor types. Detailed plans were not ready to guide inexperienced builders at the beginning. It is said that wherever there was an estab-

lished wood shipbuilding plant they refused to construct vessels according to the designs of the Shipping Board but developed plans of their own.

The Ferris type was most widely used of the Shipping Board plans. There were varying opinions of the merits of all types. They were said to have possessed structural defects which precluded the possibility of their being profitably utilized for commercial purposes. The green timber used in their construction is said to have shrunk on the maiden voyage of some of the steamers. One irate skipper, in referring to the materials in his ship, remarked, "They sent out oak shoots in April and provided pine cones for our Christmas mess."

There were many complaints from the operators of the wooden ships who said that the chief trouble was due to faulty workmanship. They were not properly caulked and the rudders could not stand the strain because they were not suitably bolted. Chips left in the bilges of the vessels were drawn into the pipes and choked the pumps.

Two outstanding ship operators of that period expressed their opinions in the maritime publication, *Nautical Gazette*. A. H. Bull said, "A wooden steamship of over 3,000 deadweight tons would prove herself a burden to owners. It would need continual repairs. Wooden steamers cannot stand the constant jar and vibration of machinery and at the same time stem the currents, heavy seas, and wind. A wooden freighter steamship is something that ought never to exist, and when built will not exist very long."

Robert Dollar said, "The wooden steamers were too small for long voyages in normal times. Cost of operating one of the vessels after the war would be more than the cost to operate an up-to-date modern, steel 10,000-ton foreign steamer . . . no current solution of what will be done to save the ships from the scrap heap."

The Chesapeake Bay area contributed to the wooden shipbuilding program as several shipyards devoted to this type of construction were located in the Baltimore area and in Virginia.

While Newport News, Virginia, was involved in producing and repairing steel ships during World War I, another Virginia peninsula community was playing a part in the wooden shipbuilding program. On the banks of Sunset Creek at Hampton was erected the plant of the Newcomb Shipbuilding and Dry Dock Company. From that location emerged two large wooden steamer hulls which helped swell the ranks of the fleet.

A poster issued by the firm carried the notation, "15 months old and still growing—employs 830 men—occupies 39 buildings—weekly payroll $25,-000—building and outfitting 24 Ferris type cargo carriers for the United States Shipping Board."

Before the two vessels ever reached the launching stage, the company was taken over by the C. H. Tenney & Company, of Boston, on August 20, 1918.

Those who know Sunset Creek today find it difficult to envision two 3,500-ton ships towering over the narrow waterway poised for launching but on January 21, 1919, the first of the two hulls, the *Luray*, was ready to wet her bottom. The creek had been dredged to a depth of 18 feet to receive the big vessels and all was in readiness for what had been termed "a new era for Hampton." The shipyard was open to the public and prominent officials of the Emergency Fleet Corporation and the Shipping Board were present.

Shortly after 10:30 A.M. the signal was given to send the *Luray* down the ways. Mrs. John West, wife of the former resident manager of the shipyard, christened the ship with a bottle of champagne. Amid the cheers of spectators and whistles of small boats the *Luray* took to the waters "with the grace and ease of a swan." Several small boats were almost swamped by the wash of the ship and people were drenched as waves came over the low retaining walls of the creek but the launch was successful.

On May 15, 1919, the other vessel, the *Kahoka*, was ready to slide down the ways. This time the launching was a private affair and no one was admitted without a special pass but the local newspapers carried an announcement of the launching and spectators lined the shores of Sunset Creek to witness the launching of such a large wooden ship in restricted waters.

At 10:40 A.M. the *Kahoka* was successfully launched. Since she was only about 75 per cent completed, she was towed to the headquarters of the Shipping Board at Baltimore to be completed as the *Luray* had been.

One of the first wartime programs to be curtailed when the war ended was that of building wooden steamers. In June 1919 about 20 hulls of the Ferris, Hough, and other types of wooden steamers in various stages of construction at Puget Sound shipyards, were advertised by the Shipping Board to be dismantled on the stocks. Nearly two years after the inception of the program, 462 hulls remained unlaunched. Over 150 of the hulls launched were not to be completed as steamers.

It was the fate of Hampton's products, the *Luray* and *Kahoka*, not to become steamers but they shared a kinder fate than hundreds of their kind. The two hulls were purchased in 1921 by Anthony O'Boyle Inc., of New York, operators of a fleet of barges and steamers. The *Kahoka* was renamed *Jerry E. O'Boyle* and the *Luray* became *Francis O'Boyle*. They were employed as barges in the coal trade between Hampton Roads and New England with a capacity of 4,000 tons each.

On January 16, 1924, the *Francis O'Boyle* was bound to Boston with a cargo of Hampton Roads coal in tow of the tug *Underwriter*. Off Ocean City, Maryland, the tow encountered a storm and, since the tug could not hold the heavily laden barge, the *O'Boyle* anchored. The anchors dragged, however, and the vessel fetched up on the beach and became a total loss.

The *Jerry O'Boyle* was destined to have a comparatively long life. The O'Boyle firm operated her until 1942 when she was sold to Bowater's Newfoundland Pulp and Paper Mills Limited. The company immediately renamed the barge *Pine Lake* and she was employed in carrying sulphite and pulpwood for three years.

The *Pine Lake* was finally laid up at Robert's Arm, Notre Dame Bay, Newfoundland, with two anchors out and mooring cables out from her stern to suitable fastenings ashore. During a gale in early September 1948, her stern lines parted and her starboard anchor chain carried away. One anchor held and after the storm an examination disclosed that her decks and all of her upper structure were in poor condition. A new boiler and new gasoline engine to operate her windlass were required. Her holds showed an advanced stage of rot in many places so pumps and other usable materials were salvaged from the hull.

To prevent her from becoming an obstruction to navigation should her remaining anchor carry away, she was beached on November 20, 1948, on the eastern side of Robert's Arm. In February 1949, she burned to the water's edge from a fire of unknown origin. So the Hampton-built *Kahoka* came to the end of her career at the ripe old age of thirty years. She lasted almost as long as any of the wooden steamers built during the World War I program. What may have been the last to visit Hampton Roads was the *Frederick*, a coal barge that was dismantled in 1952.

At the end of the wooden ship program, most of the wooden steamers and hulls were placed in idle fleets at Staten Island, Delaware River, James River, New London, off Long Island, and in the Potomac River. The big hulls were not suitable as barges, for they were too heavy to tow in bad weather, too deep to enter many coastwise harbors, and too large for general demand. Some of the west coast steamer hulls were utilized as sailing ships. Three of them were converted into six-masted schooners and seven followed the sea lanes for a short time as five-masted barkentines, but their period of activity was short-lived.

In September 1925, 200 of the wooden steamers were burned in the Potomac River near Quantico, Virginia, each having cost about one million dollars to build and, in the end, yielding only about 300 tons of scrap metal apiece. The same destruction took place on the west coast. In Baltimore, 15 of the hulls were used to form a breakwater.

In the Curtis Creek ship graveyard, Baltimore, are the hulls of the *Dover, Ashland,* and *Fort Scott.* They were acquired by the Davison Chemical Company, Baltimore, about 1919 and used as barges to transport pyrite ore from Cienfugos, Cuba, until 1923.

In 1922 the Southern Shipyard, Newport News, at the Boat Harbor, dismantled the wooden steamers *Harish* and *Agria* and a few of their timbers still protrude above water. The *Caponka,* aground in the Rappahannock since 1923, burned near Tappahannock, Virginia, in September 1949. Within recent years the *Mayo* was a breakwater at the Kiptopeke ferry landing. These remnants served as monuments to one of the most unsuccessful types of ship ever to slide down a launching ways.

Wooden steamer hulls *Dover, Ashland,* and *Fort Scott,* with other hulks in Curtis Creek, Baltimore, 1954. Photo: Author

The Old Ships

SOME SHIPS, like persons, carry the years well and their figures belie their age. For more than a half century some of the oldest vessels on Chesapeake Bay have retained the contours with which they started their careers.

The chief reason the Chesapeake has acquired the honor of mothering what is probably America's greatest number of ancient craft in one group is Maryland's law which permits only sailing vessels to dredge its oysters. Many of the boats in this fleet were built in the early 1880's and '90's, but these sail-propelled vessels are not the oldest on the Bay. The honor of being the senior craft belongs to a powerboat operating out of Weems, Virginia. This vessel, the *Major Henry Brewerton* has passed her century mark of service.

The oldest active vessel on the Bay, the powerboat *Major Henry Brewerton,* built as the steam tug of that name in 1857. Photo: Author

Although it has been many years since the *Brewerton* was registered out of Baltimore, where she was built, that name is familiar to most watermen and all Bay pilots who sail in and out of Baltimore. All deep-draft vessels must negotiate the Patapsco River via the Brewerton channel, named after the same individual who gave his name to the Chesapeake's oldest craft.

The ship and the channel came into being about the same time. In 1819 a chart was drawn up by Lewis Brantz pointing out the need for a 25-foot channel running the entire length of the Patapsco from Baltimore to Chesapeake Bay. It was not until 1851, however, that the need for a new channel was officially recognized.

In 1852 Captain Henry Brewerton was constructing defenses for Baltimore harbor, so he took over the supervision in the development of the channel. The following year Captain Brewerton commenced the formation of the channel by dredging it 150 feet wide and 22 feet deep at low tide.

Congress appropriated $100,000 for this work in 1856 and operations were conducted at the joint cost of the City of Baltimore and the United States Government. In 1857 the firm of Murray and Hazelhurst, Baltimore, built an 85-foot iron-hulled tug. Owner of the vessel was listed as "Board of Commission of Baltimore for Improving the Ship Channel of the Patapsco River." For the important part our good engineering officer played in this work (he had achieved the rank of Major) the tug was named after him.

The duties of the tug were not recorded but she probably handled the dredges and scows, in addition to transporting dignitaries to witness the progress being made on the channel. Major Brewerton's work was confined to the lower division of the channel until the depth was equal to that in the upper division between Fort McHenry and Fort Carroll.

Dredging work was suspended in the early 1860's as Civil War clouds gathered, and Major Brewerton looked after the construction of defenses at

Point Lookout and Hampton Roads. In 1862 the tug was rebuilt and emerged as a beamier vessel but somewhat shorter and with less tonnage.

In 1863 the *Brewerton* was transferred to the Pennsylvania Towing and Transportation Company, in Philadelphia. The Baltimore and Ohio Railroad purchased the vessel on October 5, 1872 and she began a career that was to last for 66 years under that ownership. She towed carfloats, barges, and scows handling company freight in Philadelphia harbor.

In October 1906 the tug was used as a ferry between Alexandria, Virginia, and the District of Columbia, in joint service with the Southern Railway. That routine was short-lived, and in December of that year the vessel went back to Philadelphia. A Baltimore shipyard rebuilt the aging tug in 1912 and she carried on for many more years.

The *Brewerton* left Philadelphia in 1938 when the Baltimore and Ohio sold her to H. R. Humphreys, Sr., of Weems, Virginia. She was stripped, dieselized and converted into a freight boat. Her appearance was completely transformed above deck but the stout iron hull remained the same. Since her conversion, the *Brewerton* has been employed in hauling fish scrap from a Virginia menhaden plant.

The powerboat *Betty I. Conway,* built at Stony Point, New York in 1866, is the second oldest vessel on the Bay. She started her career as the two-masted schooner *George S. Allison* and first made her permanent registry at Baltimore around 1921. Owned by the Conway family of Cambridge, Maryland, who operated a large fleet of sailing vessels about the Bay, the vessel was converted into a powerboat in the late 1920's after having been given her present name in 1924.

Until 1954, the third oldest vessel on the Bay was also built at Stony Point, New York, on the Hudson River. She was the powerboat *Normandic,* built in 1867 as the two-masted schooner *Daniel Tompkins.* Her sponsor was engaged in the brick business, so she was used to haul bricks out of New York and New Jersey ports.

In the late 1920's the *Tompkins* was transferred to Philadelphia, converted into a powerboat, and renamed *Normandic.* The craft visited the Chesapeake many times but was not registered out of a Bay port until 1941. Unlike the *Betty I. Conway,* the *Normandic* lacked the fine lines of a former sailing vessel and her deck looked as spacious as a field. The *Normandic* burned at Deal Island, Maryland, January 9, 1954.

Until 1959 the City of Baltimore owned and operated two ancient vessels, the paddle-wheel ice-breakers *F. C. Latrobe* and *Annapolis.* These iron-hulled steamers were built in 1879 and 1889, respectively, and although they had a rigorous life, they succeeded in keeping open the ice-clogged channels leading to Baltimore. Every winter, in later years, city politicians clamored for more modern type boats; they claimed the two veterans were outmoded and obsolete. They finally won their point and in 1959 the two boats were sold to a Baltimore scrap dealer and dismantled.

As late as 1952 many older vessels were also operating in the lower end of Chesapeake Bay. The oldest, the wooden-hulled tug *William Stewart,* was built at Chester, Pennsylvania, in 1869 as the

Powerboat *Betty I. Conway,* built as the schooner *George S. Allison,* is the second oldest vessel on the Chesapeake. Photo: Author

John Taxis. Although first registered out of Philadelphia, the *Stewart* spent most of her career on the Chesapeake. Baltimore was her home port from 1874 to 1898, then she came to the lower Bay and hailed out of Norfolk, Richmond, and Newport News. In the early 1920's the 52-foot-long tug was given her present name. She was dieselized in 1945 while owned by the Virginia Electric and Power Company which firm used her as a towboat handling coal-laden scows for their generating plant on Sunset Creek, Hampton, Virginia. The *Stewart* was sold to the Norfolk Shipbuilding and Dry Dock Company in the late 1950's.

The oldest passenger steamboat on Chesapeake waters in 1952 was the *Elisha Lee,* serving on the route between Norfolk, Old Point, and Cape Charles. She was built as the *Richard Peck* at Wilmington, Delaware, in 1892 and spent most of her career on Long Island Sound. The United States Navy bought the *Peck* in 1943 for use as a barracks ship in Newfoundland. She was released from her naval duties that same year and was chartered by the Pennsylvania Railroad to assist on their Norfolk-Cape Charles route as a ferry. Renamed *Elisha Lee,* this boat served admirably and her trim appearance belied her 60 years of service. She was sold to the Patapsco Scrap Metals Corporation, in Baltimore, in 1953 and broken up.

Notable among the older vessels on the Bay are the barges that were hulls of former steamboats. The Chesapeake Corporation of Virginia, a paper pulp mill at West Point, Virginia, on the York River, operated a number of these barges. In their fleet were six built prior to 1900 and one built shortly after the turn of the century.

The oldest is the *Tolchester,* built as the *St. Johns* at Wilmington, Delaware in 1878. After serving on many passenger routes on the east coast, she was overhauled and rebuilt at New York in 1927, and renamed *Bombay.* She came to Baltimore in 1933, was renamed *Tolchester,* and served as an excursion steamer to the Maryland resort of Tolchester. She burned to the main deck at Baltimore on May 15, 1941, and her hull was converted into a barge. In this role she carried pine logs from various sections of Chesapeake Bay to the West Point mill. She is still active and now carries the finished paper products to Hampton Roads ports for transshipment.

Her running mate since 1950 is the former Hudson River steamer *Albany,* built in 1880. A three-funneled side-wheeler, she was taken to Washington, D. C. in the early 1930's, renamed *Potomac,* and placed in the Potomac River excursion trade. After being dismantled in Baltimore, she joined the West Point fleet as the barge *Ware River.*

After burning on the Bay in 1924, the hull of the *Three Rivers* was converted into the barge *Richmond Cedar Works No. 6.* Hollerith Collection

Other former steamers converted into barges for the pulp mill, but disposed of since 1954, were the former New York-Coney Island excursion side-wheelers *Pegasus* and *Sirius,* built in 1881, and renamed respectively, *Mattaponi River* and *Pamunkey River.*

The barge *York River* was built as the *Robert Garrett* in 1888 for service as a New York ferry. She was renamed *Stapleton,* and later *Express.* As the *Express* she operated out of Baltimore as an excursion steamer to Tolchester Park. The Chesapeake Corporation also owned the former Baltimore-Rappahannock River steamboat *Potomac,* built at Philadelphia in 1894. They acquired her in 1937 and retained her original name. Both of these barges were scrapped at Baltimore in 1954.

The Cape Charles-Norfolk ferry *Elisha Lee,* originally the Long Island Sound steamer *Richard Peck,* for a period was the oldest passenger vessel on the Bay. Photo: Author

In 1962 the Chesapeake Corporation sold their barge *James River,* built as the *Rensselaer* in 1909, to the Norfolk Ship Salvage Company for scrapping. Their fleet, in addition to the *Tolchester* and *Ware River,* is now composed of barges especially designed to facilitate the handling of pine logs.

A tug used to tow these barges around the Bay is aptly named *Chesapeake,* built as the *William P. Congdon* in 1889. She is assisted by a more modern Diesel tug.

Another fleet of old-timers in the lower Bay was a group of barges once operated by Richmond Cedar Works, a lumber mill situated near Norfolk. The *Richmond Cedar Works No. 1* was the former side-wheeler *Tivoli,* built at Sparrows Point, Maryland, in 1894. She burned off Kent Island, Maryland, in 1915 with a loss of five lives, and was converted into a barge.

Richmond Cedar Works No. 2 was the former

Chesapeake Bay steamboat *Virginia,* built at Sparrows Point in 1903. She was dismantled at Baltimore in 1936 for use as a barge by the cedar mill. She sank in the Pasquotank River, North Carolina, in December 1953.

The ferry *City of Portsmouth,* built at Wilmington, Delaware in 1888 and employed on the Norfolk-Portsmouth route, eventually became the barge *Richmond Cedar Works No. 3.* Perhaps the most famous of these barges was *Richmond Cedar Works No. 4,* which started her career as the U. S. Navy gunboat *Nashville* at the Newport News shipyard in 1897. She is noted for having been the vessel that was credited with firing the first shot in the Spanish-American War.

After the Chesapeake Bay side-wheeler *Old Point Comfort* ended her career as a passenger and freight steamboat, she became the barge *S. W. Burgess.* She was taken over by the mill and renamed *Richmond Cedar Works No. 5,* but was abandoned in 1936, ending a useful life that started in 1894 when she was built at Sparrows Point.

Richmond Cedar Works No. 6 was originally the Baltimore-Washington steamboat *Three Rivers* that burned in 1924. She was dismantled in 1958. The Coast Guard cutter *Onondaga,* built in 1898 at Cleveland, Ohio, eventually became the barge *Richmond Cedar Works No. 7.* This vessel, with barges *No. 1* and *No. 3* sank at Gilmerton, Virginia, in 1955, during a hurricane.

The *Express,* that operated between Baltimore and Tolchester Beach from 1925 to about 1933, eventually became the barge *York River,* and was dismantled in 1954. Photo: C. C. Knobeloch—Author's Collection

The *Emma Giles*

THE VETERAN side-wheel excursion steamer *Emma Giles* rounded out her last summer season in 1936 carrying throngs to Tolchester Beach. In that year of her operation her forward deck had been cut off to enable her to ferry high trailer trucks and cars across the Bay from Baltimore to Tolchester. When the *Emma Giles* and her running mate *Express* were sold in September 1936, her active career as a steamboat ended.

In 1938 the old steamer was taken to the former William E. Woodall shipyard, Locust Point, Baltimore, where she had been built in 1887, to be dismantled and converted to a barge. Her engine was removed and scrapped, the superstructure was cut down to the freight deck, and her pilothouse was moved aft. After alterations she spent 10 years freighting lumber to Baltimore from North Caro-

lina points. Her owner, Captain George F. Curlett, operated several other converted Bay steamboats and boasted her shallow draft allowed the *Emma Giles* to carry more lumber than any other barge working the inland waterway.

When she had outlived her usefulness in this trade, she was acquired by a Baltimore ship wrecker at Leading Point, near Quarantine, Curtis Bay, Baltimore, and pulled onto the mud flats.

The metal in her construction was difficult to reach. On the surface she appeared to be a wooden-hulled vessel but she was of composite construction —wooden planking and decking over iron frames and beams.

The ship wrecker opened a yard at Hawkins Point and towed the hull of the popular *Emma Giles* there to be used as a bulkhead.

Her decks crowded with picnickers, the *Emma Giles* heads for Tolchester Beach, 1935.
Photo: Author

173

In the 1950's that site was required for a new ore pier so all the hulks, including the land-bound *Emma Giles,* had to be moved. She was towed to the wrecker's new yard up Curtis Creek, beyond the Pennington Avenue bridge, and pulled close to shore. In an effort to reduce the hulk to salable scrap, the wood deck and planking were burned. Today, only a portion of the stern section of the former handsome side-wheeler remains.

The *Emma Giles* had an unusual paddle-box decoration—undoubtedly the only design of its kind to be found on a steamboat. In the center of each paddle box she carried a rural scene of a beehive with bees hovering over flowering plants. Generally, carved spread eagles decorated steamboat paddle boxes. In gold leaf and full color, they were beautiful examples of the ship carver's art.

It is reported that at one time in her career a painted legend beneath the carving read, "She Was Busy As the Bee." This proud statement aptly describes her at the apex of her service when she carried passengers and freight between Baltimore and the upper Bay, Tolchester, Annapolis, West River, Little Choptank River, and many other tributaries of the Chesapeake. (A laurel sprig from residents of the Cambridge area!)

The *Emma Giles* at Hudson Wharf, Dorchester County, Maryland, in the early 1900's. Photo: Mrs. Wm. G. Linthicum

Unusual carved wooden paddle-box decoration of the *Emma Giles.* Photo: Author

Remains of the *Emma Giles* in Curtis Creek, Baltimore, 1961. Photo: Author

174

The *Chase* Comes to the Bay to Die

WHILE READYING a yacht for the 1950 season in a little shipyard at Hampton, Virginia, the author observed remains of a wooden ship piled on the flats in Sunset Creek, an arm of Hampton Creek. The timbers and size of her metal fittings indicated that the vessel was larger than the type native to Chesapeake Bay.

Conversation with a Mr. Davis, a local resident, revealed that the wreck was the Revenue Service training bark *Salmon P. Chase*. He related some of the latter-day history of the vessel, which stimulated research to learn more of her early history. It was known that the *Chase*, as she was commonly called, had contributed much to the development

The *Salmon P. Chase* in all her glory as a training ship. Photo: U. S. Coast Guard

of the Revenue Service and the present United States Coast Guard Academy but how such a splendid vessel ever became abandoned in the backwaters of a Virginia creek was a mystery.

Small for a square-rigged vessel, the *Chase* was originally only 106 feet, 3 inches, on deck but handsome and extremely fast. She was designed by Captain J. H. Merryman, United States Revenue Marine, to replace the topsail schooner *J. C. Dobbin* which had been used as a training ship by the Revenue Service. The *Dobbin* had proved inadequate so the *Chase* was ordered built by Thomas Brown and Sons, Philadelphia, in 1877–78. Her builders met with financial difficulties and the government completed her at a cost of approximately $20,300.

Of wooden construction, the *Chase* had a round stern, sharp lines, and a beautiful clipper bow graced by a carved, spread eagle.

In 1878 the *Chase* began her service as the cruising and winter home of the Revenue Service cadets. From 1878 to 1890 she was stationed at New Bedford and made practice cruises to Europe each summer.

Between 1890–94 the expansion of the United States Navy was at a virtual standstill. This meant a surplus of Naval Academy graduates for which no posts could be found in that service. As a result this overflow went to the Revenue Service. Since these men were adequately trained, there was no need for the *Chase* so she was decommissioned. But Captain Leonard G. Shepard, Chief of the Division of the Revenue Marine Service, disagreed with this policy of procuring officer material. He felt that the Navy would designate its overflow from the bottom of the graduating classes and that the Revenue cutters would not receive top personnel.

When expansion of the Navy picked up rapidly in 1894, the Naval Academy overflow ceased. Shepard welcomed the opportunity to recommission the *Chase* and a new class of cadets was appointed to train on her. In 1895 she was extensively repaired and lengthened 40 feet to accommodate more cadets.

The *Chase* had several accidents during her career. One was on May 6, 1897, while on a cruise, when she collided with the three-masted schooner *Richard F. C. Hartley* about 50 miles east of Charleston Bar and was completely disabled. She was towed into Charleston and later brought to Baltimore for repairs.

That same year, on October 16, the *Chase* stranded at night on a shoal three and one-half miles southwest of Sullivan's Island Lifesaving Station, South Carolina. A beach patrolman saw her running into danger and burned a Coston signal that was answered by a rocket from the vessel. A surfboat was launched and the lifesaving crew pulled out to the stranded bark. The captain of the *Chase* requested the station-keeper to report his plight. The surfman proceeded to Charleston and notified the officers of the side-wheel Revenue cutter *Colfax* which freed the bark from the bar undamaged, and towed her into port.

In 1900, when the *Chase* moved to her usual winter quarters at Arundel Cove, near Baltimore, a move was started to provide a permanent Academy. When the School for Instruction for the Revenue Cutter Service was later established, instruction was given in buildings ashore for the first time but the cadets continued to be quartered aboard the *Chase*.

The *Chase* continued to act as the Service's practice ship until 1907 when she was replaced by the *Itasca*, a former Naval Academy training ship propelled by both sail and steam. In July of that year the *Chase* was decommissioned.

On June 15, 1912, the bark was delivered from New London to Surgeon General Hugh S. Cummings of the U. S. Public Health and Marine Hospital Service for use as a station ship at Fort Monroe, Virginia. Her duties were to house the employees of the Service at that point and to act as a store ship for quarantine supplies. She was anchored in Hampton Roads and, although her rigging had been removed, leaving only stump masts, she retained her fine appearance.

During the severe winter of 1918, ice floes in the Roads caused her to part her moorings a number of times so she was brought into Fort Monroe and tied up at a pier. This was her permanent position until 1930 when she was replaced by a barge named *Argus*, a former concrete hull steamer built during World War I. The Public Health Service sold the hull of the *Chase* for a nominal sum to John S. Mertens of Newport News. Mertens operated a small boatyard on Sunset Creek and the *Chase* was towed to a dock on his property. His only object in purchasing the vessel was to salvage any usable fittings as he had little use for the hull.

Although Sunset Creek is narrow, it carried considerable traffic in sand and coal barges. In May 1930, while one of these barges was negotiating the narrow channel, it swerved and rammed a hole in the *Chase,* causing her to sink.

Considering her a menace to navigation and of no further value, Mertens abandoned the hulk to the United States Government on September 3, 1930. The task of removing the wreck fell upon the U. S. Army Engineers, Norfolk, and they literally blew her to pieces with explosives. Portions of the hull were salvaged for firewood and other sections were placed among numerous old pilings that had been the site of a World War I shipbuilding plant.

In 1950, as the flats were bared at each low tide, the remains of the *Chase* appeared to be stout but the only recognizable portions were the rudder, and the deadeyes and chainplates attached to the timbers.

In an attempt to identify the remains in Sunset Creek, contacts were made with the Public Health Service, Washington; U. S. Coast Guard Headquarters, Washington; and the U. S. Coast Guard Academy, New London, Connecticut. None of these sources could shed any light on the final disposition of the *Chase.* It remained for the U. S. Army Engineers to prove that the remains were definitely those of the *Chase.* Their files contained complete data concerning her sinking and removal and the actual location of the hulk was indicated on a portion of the U.S.C. & G.S. Chart No. 400.

Though her fate was not a fitting one for a vessel with such an illustrious past, an interesting relic from the old bark has been preserved. Her eagle figurehead is displayed at the U. S. Coast Guard Academy, New London, Connecticut.

Remains of the *Chase* in Sunset Creek, Hampton, Virginia, in 1950. Photo: Author

They Penned
a Bay Classic

COUNTLESS ARTICLES and a number of books have been written extolling the merits of Chesapeake Bay as a cruising ground for small boats. They have become more numerous as pleasure boating increased in popularity and favorable comments appearing in these stories tend to bring more boatmen to the area. Many of these boatmen discover what they have read is true and, in turn, try their hand at telling the story to others.

In 1909 the book, *Cruises, Mainly in the Bay of the Chesapeake,* was published. This was one of the first cruise books to be written dealing with Chesapeake pleasure boating and was destined to become a classic in that field. It is believed to be the first cruise book to reach the third edition in this country.

That edition was recently published by one of the surviving co-authors of the book, George Bar-

rie, Jr., a resident of Ardmore, Pennsylvania. George and Robert Barrie wrote the book after their many cruises on the Chesapeake. Some of the articles originally appeared in boating magazines in this country and in Europe, around the turn of the century. They were later compiled to form *Cruises.*

This is not a continuous story with a plot but the book comprises 14 complete articles, each dealing with a particular subject. Such headings as *A Cruise to the Chesapeake, The Chesapeake Again, Haunts of the Bugeye* and *Two on the Chesapeake,* reveal the extreme interest of the authors in this body of water. *Loafing* and *An April Dash* describe the mode of cruising and the season.

If one wants to grasp the spirit of the tidewater country at the turn of the century, the slow, easygoing way of life that has been supplanted by

Tug and tow of schooners in the Chesapeake and Delaware Canal, about 1900.
Photo: George Barrie, Jr.

178

speed and progress, a few hours spent in reading *Cruises* will be rewarding. The authors described the towns, the natives, and general stores and landings they encountered. Many photographs of historic buildings and other scenes accompany the text.

George Barrie, younger of the co-author brothers, was born in Philadelphia in 1879. He comments, "At the age of six I learned the rudiments of boat-handling by going to leeward with an umbrella in the bow of a skiff and to windward with oars." Through the years he graduated from various sailing craft of different rigs and even tried his hand at one of the early gasoline launches.

The brothers were introduced to the Chesapeake in 1896 by a relative who had made a cruise to the headwaters of the Bay and had aroused the curiosity and the roving spirit of the Barries. In July of 1897 Robert had his 42-foot cutter *Mona* hastily rigged and, with George and a paid hand who knew the Chesapeake, set out on his initial cruise of these waters.

George reminisces, "To me it turned out to be such a paradise that every year thereafter I have sailed, cruised, or lived on the shores of this inland sea. Yachts on the Bay in those days were almost as scarce as hen's teeth. On our first cruise, which extended from Chesapeake City to Norfolk and return, we saw but one yacht, the *Panola,* owned by William O'Sullivan Dimphel, one of the founders of the Chesapeake Bay Yacht Club. It was many years before we met more than a few yachts when we made a cruise on the Chesapeake."

The Barries were members of the Corinthian Yacht Club of Philadelphia and their cruises originated from that city, necessitating passage through the Chesapeake and Delaware Canal. In those days the waterway was narrow and was comprised of locks. A single tug would take a great number of boats in tow, principally commercial sailing craft, and release them at the Chesapeake end where they would await a favorable wind to carry them on their way.

In the early 1900's, George became the owner of the 38-foot cutter *Irex* which he converted into a yawl and used in cruising on the Bay for about five years. In 1905 he conceived the idea of having a yacht constructed along the lines of the shallow-draft skipjack, a Chesapeake type then gaining a strong foothold in the Bay's commercial sailing fleet. All other boats in which he had cruised the Bay were of deep draft; this had limited his exploration of many interesting creeks.

He visited the Kirby Shipyard at St. Michaels to discuss the building of such a yacht and to examine a skipjack. For the actual construction, however, he went to Shadyside, on the West River, to see Captain Charles E. Leatherbury. Starting from Annapolis, he rode 14 miles to Galesville on a bicycle over sandy roads, and from there, obtained a boat and rowed over to Shadyside. He engaged Captain Leatherbury to build a 40-foot skipjack, bare hull and spars, with only the best materials, for the sum of $500. On completion, it was named *Omoo* and is believed to be the first of the skipjacks built for yachting purposes.

George Barrie was an avid camera fan, interested primarily in the historical attractions of the Chesapeake. Old houses, churches, and landmarks were photographed and described in *Cruises*. His chief interest, however, was in the picturesque native craft of the Bay and the colorful shipyards where the vessels congregated.

Heller's old yard in Annapolis must have been a focal point for the Bay watermen, judging from the vast numbers of boats of all types appearing in Barrie's views of that yard. St. Michaels and Oxford were the home ports of many of the craft and were on the cruise itinerary of the Barries. The sleek pungies were his favorite subjects both under sail and anchored in port.

By 1918 George had become so intrigued with the Chesapeake area he purchased Hackett's Point, near Annapolis, with an exposure of the Bay and Whitehall Creek. This was to serve as a base for future Chesapeake cruises, but business curtailed the extensive cruising he once enjoyed, so he sold the *Omoo* and bought a smaller craft for day sailing in the creek and nearby Bay.

Thoughts of past visits to the tidewater towns and rivers eventually caused George to dispose of Hackett's Point in 1928 and have *Omoo II* built at Seaford, Delaware. The depression of the 1930's made cruising prohibitive, so *Omoo II* was sold.

Since that time George has continued to sail the Chesapeake, mostly in small day sailers with friends on the Eastern Shore. At every opportunity he visits Bay shipyards to renew acquaintances with the oyster dredging fleets that are the remnants of the once great fleet of Chesapeake sailing craft he encountered on his early cruises.

"No more will one see, as I have, forty-one Bay sailing vessels anchored in refuge under Drum Point," recalls George Barrie. "Come a southerly breeze one would see throughout the day a continuous stream of bugeyes and schooners bound up the Bay, with always one or two in sight at a time. And with a northerly breeze there would be a like number bound the other way."

In recent years he visited a shipyard at Galesville, Maryland, on the West River, to look at a sailing yacht under construction. He also had occasion to look at some of the town and found it quite different than a half-century ago. The countryside he remembered had been subdivided and developed into urban areas. The same is true, of course, for most of the places he once visited.

"About the only thing that has not changed," he says, "is the waters of the Chesapeake. Yachts are now profuse. The channels are all well-buoyed and lighted, and the shorelines are all dotted with summer cottages and permanent homes. But it's still the best boating area in this country."

When not pursuing his maritime interests around the Chesapeake, George Barrie devotes his time to the restoration of antiques, which has become his vocation. In his little shop at Bryn Mawr, near Philadelphia, he lovingly puts new life in the neglected treasures of other days. He never hesitates, however, to put his work aside when a customer wants to talk about the Chesapeake Bay country. That is his favorite subject and few have such wide knowledge of the Chesapeake area of half a century ago.

Shipyard at Solomons Island, Maryland, about 1901. The Barries photographed many similar scenes. Photo: George Barrie, Jr.

Yachts of Other Days

THE ARRIVAL of spring causes a sudden upsurge in yacht club attendance. Just as some birds herald the approach of warm weather, the feverish activity of preparing pleasure craft for another season indicates that summer is drawing near.

There were many boat clubs in Baltimore waters in the 1890's but probably the first large and successful yacht club in that area was organized in 1891 and named the Baltimore Yacht Club. Social facilities for owners of the larger yachts had been lacking, so in January 1890 George W. Coale, owner of the sloop yacht *Lagonda*, contacted several prominent yachtsmen to enlist their support in organizing a yacht club. Those approached in-cluded Alexander Brown, Edward L. Bartlett, S. C. Townsend, J. J. George, E. Bradley Jones, and F. W. McCallister. A committee was appointed to draft a constitution and bylaws; these were accepted August 6, 1891.

The membership increased slowly because there was no clubhouse, and several committees were appointed to seek appropriate locations. A site was finally selected on the shores of Curtis Bay, and a comfortable structure was erected.

The boats on the club's roster included some of the largest yachts in Baltimore at that time. Heading the list in size was the steam yacht *Bally-mena*, 143 feet in length. She was owned by Alex-

The side-wheel steam yacht *Comfort*. Photo: The Mariners Museum

ander Brown, head of the famous local banking firm bearing his name, who had been appointed Commodore of the club. Next in size was the steam yacht *Comfort* owned by Edward L. Bartlett, O. L. Bartlett, and J. Hayward, of Bartlett, Hayward and Company. The fleet also included schooners, yawls, sloops, and launches.

Steam yachts were in vogue in the 1890's. They attended the major regattas and were the center of the club's social life afloat. These vessels were usually clipper-bowed, fine-lined, and bore rakish masts and stacks. One of the steam yachts in the Baltimore Yacht Club, however, was a complete departure from such a design. The steam yacht *Comfort* was designed purely for the purpose of insuring the comfort of her owners afloat. With an iron hull and paddle wheels, she resembled a typical Chesapeake Bay steamboat.

Designed by Frederick Mayer, the *Comfort* was built in 1887 at the shops of Bartlett, Hayward and Company, Baltimore. When completed, all the parts were taken to William E. Woodall's shipyard, Locust Point, Baltimore, and assembled. Shortly after she was launched the owners decided the yacht was too small, so she was cut in half and an additional section was constructed in their shops and placed between the forward and after sections. This brought her length to 110 feet overall. Two engines that worked independently of each other were installed.

The *Comfort* was the only pleasure boat of her kind in local waters. She presented quite a picture as she steamed down the Patapsco River, trailing a wide frothy wake astern. Paddle wheels were probably installed in order to obtain a shallow draft (4 feet, 6 inches). This was necessary because the yacht was used on the Susquehanna Flats during the ducking season.

Many Baltimoreans enjoyed the hospitality offered aboard the *Comfort*. It would tax the imagination to conceive of a vessel better suited for entertaining. She was finished throughout with mahogany. In the dining room was a horseshoe-shaped table with a seating capacity of 16 persons. The after cabin was arranged as a sitting or reading room. There was also a large sleeping compartment containing 8 double berths. Furniture covering was of Morocco and the interior decks were carpeted with rich Axminster rugs; the owner's stateroom was finished in ivory and gold. She had every convenience of the times for both guests and members of the crew and there was a headroom of 8 feet throughout the vessel.

The *Comfort's* 10-knot speed was slower than that of other steam yachts of comparable size, but her beam (25 feet, 6 inches over the paddle boxes) made her comfortable in a seaway.

This luxurious yacht was a feature around Baltimore harbor for almost 20 years. In 1906 she was advertised for sale in a leading yachting magazine. Styles in yachts had changed since her construction and there were no buyers.

In the spring of 1908 she was dismantled at the foot of Charles Street, Baltimore, and her remains were taken to the Scott Street plant of Bartlett, Hayward & Company. This ended the career of one of the most distinctive steam yachts registered out of Baltimore.

Gradually steam yachts in the area became obsolete and were replaced by smaller gasoline and Diesel powered craft. The original Baltimore Yacht Club succumbed to progress as the Curtis Bay section became industrialized. The name was later adopted by the club situated at Sue's Island but there was no connection between the two organizations.

Broadway-Locust Point Steam Ferry

ONE OF BALTIMORE'S most prosperous organizations in the late nineteenth century was the Broadway-Locust Point ferry. Street-cars had not yet penetrated Locust Point and the ferry was the most convenient and quickest method of transportation "uptown."

The exact date the ferry was established is not known, but some records indicate the year was 1813. It may have started earlier, since oar-propelled craft probably initiated the route. The distance between the two points was small and such craft could easily handle the traffic.

In 1868, however, the Broadway-Locust Point Steam Ferry Company was incorporated. As indicated, steam vessels were used, but this did not end the oar-propelled boats on the route. In fact, competition between the ferry and the smaller boats became so serious that the ferry company owners submitted an amendment to the Legislature of Maryland seeking protection.

They stated that on clear, calm days swarms of rowboats would gather at the foot of Broadway to carry passengers across the harbor. Only heavy wagons and drays remained to be carried on the ferry, with little profit. They declared that the ferry, if it were to survive, must have protection from the rowboats. It was proposed in the amendment that oar-propelled craft be kept at a distance of 200 yards on either side of the ferry slips. The Legislature evidently responded, for the company continued operations.

The ferry was a great convenience for workers who lived in East Baltimore and were employed in Locust Point industries. Housewives from Locust Point used the ferry for their shopping trips to Broadway. Immigrants brought to Pier 9, Locust Point on steamers of the North German Lloyd Line crossed on the ferries to settle in various sections of Baltimore. Vehicles also preferred the water route instead of the long ride on rough roads around the head of the harbor.

The first blow dealt the ferry system was a streetcar line extension to Locust Point. Then the Baltimore and Ohio Railroad moved its coal piers to Curtis Bay. These changes eliminated many ferry customers.

The side-wheel steam ferries S. W. Smith and Samuel W. Tagart operated on this route. Both were built by the Baltimore firm of Stevenson & Newman, in 1877 and 1878, respectively, and both were rebuilt in 1901. For a period, two boats were run continuously and a spare was kept for emergency, but by the turn of the century, only one vessel was operating while another was held in reserve.

In the early 1900's the ferry company started losing money. Automobiles and paved streets were partly to blame as the company's receipts dipped sharply below operating costs. World War I, however, gave the ferries a boost, since large numbers of industrial workers used them to reach their jobs at Locust Point.

The company experienced another slump at the end of the war. The Samuel W. Tagart was sold to the Davison Chemical Company, renamed The Davco and used to transport workers from the Curtis Bay street-car loop across Curtis Creek to the Davison plant. She was abandoned in 1930.

In 1921 the veteran S. W. Smith broke down and service was suspended until the city took over the company's rights and equipment. Operation continued at a substantial deficit, but the route was considered a vital link that could not be abandoned.

Plans for a new vessel to replace the Smith were drawn which called for another side-wheel ferry, a type considered obsolete by many marine experts.

The new vessel, named the Howard W. Jackson, was built by the Maryland Dry Dock Company at Fairfield at a cost of $136,000 and sailed on her maiden voyage August 4, 1925. The *S. W. Smith* was given to the Boy Scouts and taken to the Magothy River.

Hopes for the survival of the ferry system were growing dimmer. In 1923 the street-car fare was raised from five cents to ten cents. The ferry likewise raised its fare but later reduced it to seven cents. Many thought this too much for the 4 to 4½-minute trip across the harbor, covering 5/16th of a mile.

The *Jackson* plied her route until May 23, 1936, after which she was idle for 16 months while repairs were made, using WPA and city funds. She was virtually rebuilt, with main deck renewed, sprinkler system installed, and engine overhauled.

She resumed service August 23, 1937 and the first week of operation ended with a daily passenger average of 115 and few automobiles. After eight months, operating costs amounted to $19,964 and collections totaled $3,273; it was decided to abandon the route.

The service was halted January 1, 1939 and the *Jackson* was tied up until February 1940, when authority was given to sell the vessel. She was purchased by B. B. Wills, operator of the Tolchester Line, for $13,000, and the final chapter in the history of the Broadway-Locust Point ferry was closed.

The *Jackson* lay at Pier 5, Pratt Street, Baltimore for a number of years, being slowly dismantled and was eventually broken up for scrap.

The *Howard W. Jackson* crossing Baltimore harbor. Photo: Thomas D. Conn

Veteran Battlers of Chesapeake Ice

TWO UNUSUAL STEAMERS were operated out of the port of Baltimore every winter for a period of 70 to 80 years. When winter covered upper Chesapeake Bay with a solid sheet of ice, these veterans went into action. Their task was to cut lanes through the ice for steamships many times their size and younger by scores of years.

In the late 1950's the *F. C. Latrobe* and the *Annapolis* enjoyed the distinction of being Baltimore's oldest steamers, the last side-wheel vessels in the Chesapeake region, and the southernmost ice-breakers in the United States.

The *F. C. Latrobe,* whose hull was made of puddled wrought iron, was built in 1879 at the Canton shipyard of Malster & Renney, Baltimore. The *Annapolis,* also an iron-hulled, 200-foot vessel, was built in 1889 by the Columbian Iron Works & Dry Dock Company, at Locust Point, Baltimore. This firm was reorganized in 1884 from Malster & Renney.

The *Latrobe* was named after her sponsor, Ferdinand C. Latrobe, seven times mayor of Baltimore. As the launching ceremony was about to begin, it was discovered that the traditional bottle of champagne had been "misplaced." A nearby saloon supplied a bottle of brandy to be used as a substi-

The *F. C. Latrobe* in the ice-clogged channel approaches to Baltimore, 1936.
Photo: Author

tute. During the launch, the snubbing lines parted and the big hull went out of control and rammed and sank a schooner anchored in the harbor. She atoned for that misdeed, however, by rendering assistance to thousands of ice-bound vessels during her career.

The City of Baltimore and the State of Maryland shared the expense of operation and maintenance of the *Latrobe* and *Annapolis*. Their main field of operation was the ice-choked Chesapeake between the Patapsco and Elk Rivers. They could cut a 65-foot-wide swath through the ice for vessels using the Chesapeake & Delaware Canal.

Each steamer was powered by two coal-fired horizontal single-cylinder steam engines. Each paddle wheel was operated by its own engine, providing great maneuverability.

The individually-powered paddle wheels, permitting full-speed-ahead on one and full-speed-

their weight. They would then back off and repeat the process.

In later years, it became increasingly more difficult to keep steady crews for these coal-fired steamers. Oil-fired boilers had replaced most coal-burners and the turnover of engineers and firemen was heavy.

One of the last skippers was Captain Benjamin McCready who, with a crew of 38, kept one of the vessels in service while the other was laid up for repairs.

The *Latrobe* was a roomier vessel and could accommodate crowds better than the *Annapolis*. Her decks and lower housing were built almost flush with the paddle boxes while the paddle boxes on the *Annapolis* extended outward from her sides, as on British side-wheelers.

The *Latrobe* was the better known of the two vessels because she was used in the summertime to

Gigantic wooden paddle wheel of the ice-breaker *Annapolis*. Photo: Author

Her powerful spoon-bow enabled the *Annapolis* to ride up on the ice and break it with her weight. Photo: Author

astern on the other, made it possible for the vessels to turn in their own length. This maneuverability enabled them to extricate themselves from ice jams. Their coal capacities were sufficient for five or six days' operation.

The bucket system on the *Latrobe's* paddle wheels was more efficient as a driving force than the radial wheels on the *Annapolis,* but was more vulnerable to damage.

After each season of ice-breaking, both vessels were laid up for repairs. At the end of a season's battle with the ice, some of the white oak timber arms on the radial wheels were worn to half their original thickness from the chafing action.

These vessels were called ice-breakers, or ice-crushers. Their spoon bows permitted them to ride up on the ice for some distance and crack it with

take conventions and other groups on sightseeing tours in Baltimore harbor. She also served as an excursion steamer for the Free Summer Excursion Society of Baltimore, transporting thousands of underprivileged children and their families to Chesterwood, on Bear Creek, just below Baltimore.

During periods of inactivity, the veteran steamers were tied up at their piers with a skeleton crew aboard near the point where Jones Falls empties into Baltimore harbor. In September or October they were taken to a shipyard to be readied for winter service.

In 1959, while these two ice-breakers were under the control of the Maryland Port Authority, they were sold to the Scrap Corporation of North America and were dismantled at Montford Yard on Baltimore's waterfront.

The *F. C. Latrobe* and *Annapolis* end their long careers together at Montford Yard, Baltimore, as shipbreakers dismantle them for their content in 1959-60. Their wooden superstructures were torn apart and their iron hulls were cut up. Some items were salvaged and distributed among museums at opposite ends of the Chesapeake. The Maryland Historical Society, Baltimore, has in its collection a pilothouse nameboard from each of the two steamers. That organization also has the builder's and rebuilder's plate, steam gauges, lights, and life preservers from the *Latrobe*. The *Annapolis* is also represented in the Baltimore institution by its builder's plate, engine plate, and life ring. In The Mariners Museum, Newport News, Virginia, are a pilothouse nameboard from each of the two vessels and the rebuilder's plate of the *Annapolis*. These veterans of the Bay will not be easily forgotten. Photo: Author

Adams' Floating Theatre

SHOWBOATS usually are associated with the Mississippi and other western rivers, but Chesapeake Bay played host to one for a quarter of a century.

The James Adams Floating Theatre was long advertised as the only floating theatre on the Atlantic Coast. The official name of the huge barge-like craft was *Playhouse*. She was listed under that name in the register of American merchant vessels, and her name and home port, Baltimore, were painted on the stern.

The floating theatre came to Baltimore for the last time in December 1939. She was moored at Long Dock, Pratt Street, and presented to the big city her repertoire of "tear-jerking" drama and light comedy reminiscent of a vanishing era.

James Adams and his wife were former circus performers and carnival operators. After visiting a showboat at Huntington, West Virginia, the idea occurred to him that a similar craft might be a successful venture on Chesapeake Bay and the Carolina Sounds.

Adams' showboat was built at Washington, North Carolina, in 1914, from timbers he had selected standing in the forests of South Carolina. She measured 128 feet in length, 34 feet in beam, and drew only 14 inches of water. Unlike the western showboats, the *Playhouse* was extremely plain, and sturdily built to withstand the more exposed waters of Chesapeake Bay.

The showboat could seat 700 people in the auditorium, boxes, and balcony. There were 8 bed-dressing rooms behind the 19-foot-wide stage; additional rooms, including a dining room, were located forward.

Adams' Floating Theatre was towed around her maritime circuit by the powerboats *Elk* and *Trouper*. The big craft normally wintered at Elizabeth City, North Carolina, and the year's premiére was held there the last week in February or the first week in March. Then she would be taken in tow for stops at towns in the North Carolina Sound area before traversing the Inland Waterway to Chesapeake Bay. Here she would work up one side

James Adams Floating Theatre at Bundicks, Coan River, Virginia, 1928. Photo: Author

of the Bay and down the other, stopping at towns or landings that consistently furnished large audiences. When the fall season arrived she would move to Norfolk for a showing, then proceed to Elizabeth City for the winter lay-up.

On western showboats one of the most important pieces of equipment was the steam calliope. It was played to announce the showboat's arrival at river towns. The *Playhouse* did not have a calliope, and it has been reported that the vessel's orchestra often boarded one of the towboats upon arrival at a tidewater town and made the rounds of the numerous creeks and inlets, blaring forth their own style of music. In later years a small announcement in a country newspaper, listing the week's program, was used as a means of advertising.

Normally, the showboat would spend a week at each of its stops, with a show every night except Sunday; sometimes a Saturday matinee would be included. Only the plays producing the highest box office receipts were repeated, and there was a different show each night. The main show would start at 8:15 P.M. Admission was thirty-five or forty cents. At 10:15 P.M. there was a concert or vaudeville show, which cost an additional ten or fifteen cents. A typical week's program included: "Big Shot," "Breakfast for One," "Tempest and Sunshine," "Frisco' Jennie," "Man's Will, Woman's Way," and "Shooting Gold."

During the showboat's career on Chesapeake Bay, Charles Hunter was the director and leading man. His wife Beulah, James Adams' youngest sister, was leading lady for many years and has been referred to as "Mary Pickford of the Chesapeake."

In 1924 Edna Ferber spent a week on Adams' Floating Theatre collecting material for her immortal novel *Show Boat*. After the book was published and won popular acclaim, the owners of the showboat felt they would benefit from some of the publicity given the novel. Her sign was removed and "The Original Floating Theatre" was painted on either side of the vessel, in letters 3 feet high.

The novel was later made into a movie, and when the showboat visited Baltimore in 1939, that movie was featured at the local Times Theatre.

In 1930 Adams sold the boat to Mrs. Nina Howard of St. Michaels, Maryland, who continued to operate it around the Chesapeake's circuit. Times were changing, and movies and radio were becoming popular in the tidewater area. Country folk no longer patronized the showboat. Steamboats had discontinued their visits to the Chesapeake landings and piers fell into disuse. This left the craft without moorings near tidewater towns.

In the summer of 1941 *Billboard Magazine* carried an item to the effect that the showboat was to be converted into a movie theatre and permanently moored to a pier in the Chesapeake Bay area. Evidently this plan failed to materialize, for she was taken south later that year, possibly to resume her role as a true showboat. She was totally destroyed by fire in the Savannah River, Georgia, November 14, 1941. This rang down the curtain on the Bay's showboat.

Sailing the Family Tree

CAPTAIN SID COVINGTON, noted boat-builder of Tilghman Island, Maryland, plunged his adz into a prime timber to sculpture another of his famous log canoes of the Island B group. The year was 1882 and the finished craft was named *Island Bird*.

Had the good captain been gifted with a bit of clairvoyance, he would have been proud and happy to know that his great-grandson, John C. North, II,

would one day—68 years later, in 1950—help sail the *Island Bird* to victory for the coveted Chesapeake Bay Racing Log Canoe Trophy, the Governor's Cup.

During a racing event on the Miles River, Maryland, in 1948, the *Island Bird* capsized and was abandoned because of heavy weather. She was recovered the next day, found only slightly damaged, and offered for sale.

The *Island Blossom* heels and the crew clambers out on the springboards to keep her erect. Photo: Robert V. George

John C. North, an Easton, Maryland, lawyer and Covington's grandson, was anxious to preserve the craft as an example of his forebear's work so he purchased it for his son.

The *Island Bird* had not raced for a number of years prior to the 1948 Miles River Yacht Club Regatta, and when the Norths began her restoration, they found her in need of major repair. Two large areas in the hull had to be replaced and this required the services of a log canoe builder, a trade virtually extinct. George North, uncle of the new owner, had helped Captain Sid build several log canoes and was the logical expert to make these strategic repairs.

Paint, 15 coats deep in some spots, was burned from the craft. George North then took over with mallet and chisel to remove all bad wood in the hull. Fir blocks were fitted into the holes and doweled with half-inch galvanized rods.

The next step required the skillful use of the log canoe builder's most important tool—the adz. It is reported that George North, at age 76, could split a pencil line with every stroke of his adz in full swing.

The repair job was done so expertly that it was almost impossible to distinguish the new wood from the old after the paint was applied. After a few minor repairs in other areas, the canoe was again in racing condition. The hollow, oval masts, sprits, and bowsprit were sound. Her Egyptian duck sails, though used, were in good condition.

The Norths completed their sanding, painting, and varnishing in time to enter the *Bird* in two Bay regattas featuring log canoe races. After launching the canoe they experienced a mishap, more disconcerting than serious. While getting the feel of the rejuvenated craft, the crew received a dunking as the canoe capsized. Later, at the Tred Avon Yacht Club Regatta, the veteran sailed into first place to capture the Commodore's Bowl.

In 1950 the *Island Bird* proved her ability when she won the Governor's Cup and the Covington Memorial Trophy. By odd coincidence, John North had donated the trophy to the Miles River Yacht Club in 1934 as a perpetual award in memory of his grandfather. At that time the donor had no idea that he or his son would actively participate in races for this trophy, especially in a canoe built by the man it memorialized.

While the *Island Bird* had long been recognized as an unusually fast log canoe, her big sister *Island Blossom* was more renowned. Built by Captain Sid in 1892, her tremendous rig (41-foot foremast and 37-foot mainmast on a 32-foot hull) would turn over under bare poles in dead calm water unless her crew stood alongside in the shallows to steady her. The 2,000 square feet in her seven racing sails made her extremely sensitive.

During the summer of 1950, the Norths learned that the *Blossom* was still in existence up on the Bohemia River, Maryland, and that she was for sale. They were anxious to restore another of Captain Covington's canoes, particularly the *Island Blossom*.

The canoe was found on shore, protected by a shelter. Except for a small area under her forefoot, the hull was as sound as the day she was built. Before each race, during her years as a champion racer, the *Island Blossom* had her hull thoroughly dried, sanded, and greased with a block of country butter to reduce her resistance in the water.

The Norths purchased the *Blossom* and she was towed to the Miles River and restored to racing trim. New spars, sails, rudder, and springboards completed her racing equipment. She won the Governor's Cup in 1951 to perpetuate her legend of superior performance.

More skill is required to sail racing log canoes than any other type of sailing craft on Chesapeake Bay. Because of their shallow hulls and towering rigs they capsize easily. To counteract this, the canoes carry springboards, with one end placed under the lee washboards and the other extended over the weather side. The crew clamber on the springboards when ballast is needed. The *Island Bird* usually carries only two springboards but the *Island Blossom* often uses as many as five or six to prevent her capsizing in heavy winds. Sometimes a sudden flaw will catch the crew out on the springboards and before they can transfer their weight back into the canoe, the craft overturns. Canoes temporarily knocked out of a race in this manner, however, have been known to cross the finish line in first place after being righted and rerigged.

Log canoe racing has been given new impetus by enthusiasts like the Norths and Captain Bill Green, Life Honorary Commodore of the Chesapeake Bay Log Canoe Association, who owned the famous log canoe *Mary Rider* for many years.

The Island canoes are usually skippered by experienced sailors, including Captain Clarence Dobson, whose father once skippered the *Island Bird*. John B. Harrison, Jr., another grandson of the canoe's builder, serves as skipper for the *Island Blossom*. Her crew usually consists of 9 to 11 men, a number of them also descendants of Captain Covington. The jib-tender is a nephew; 2 board-men are grand-nephews; one board-man is a grandson; another board-man is the husband of a great-granddaughter. They keep the sport, as well as the canoe, in the family.

Other canoes of the Island B group built by Captain Covington were *Island Belle, Island Bride,* and *Island Beauty*. Considerable effort has been made by the Norths to locate these canoes, but so far they have been unsuccessful. If these craft are eventually found, the fleet of Island B canoes may be increased. The veteran craft could not fall into better hands.

The *Island Bird*, built by William Sidney Covington of Tilghman Island in 1882, after reconditioning in 1958. Photo: R. H. Hollyday for John C. North

A Whale
in the Harbor

A WHALE once came to Baltimore and surfaced in the harbor off Canton Hollow, to the amazement of all who witnessed its appearance. The beginning of the events which led to its presence must have been rather disconcerting to the big fish, too.

On March 9, 1940, the oil tanker *New Orleans* arrived in Baltimore deeply loaded. The vessel docked at her Canton pier and prepared to discharge her cargo. As oil was pumped from the ship's tanks her hull rose higher and higher. Casually, someone checked the depth marks on the stem of the ship, and in shocked surprise noted a huge blubbery form draped across the prow. Closer scrutiny revealed the body of a forty-foot whale bent into a modified horseshoe shape. This was probably the largest sea creature that had ever entered the confines of Baltimore's upper harbor.

Moored to a pier on Boston Street, Baltimore, is the whale brought to that port on March 9, 1940, after being impaled on the stem of the oil tanker *New Orleans* off Cape Hatteras. Photo: *The Baltimore Sunpapers*

Discovery of the whale on the tanker's stem answered several questions that had puzzled the crew of the *New Orleans*. While the tanker was proceeding up the east coast, off Cape Hatteras, North Carolina, a sudden shudder was felt throughout the ship. During the remainder of the passage to Baltimore the speed of the ship was diminished, without any apparent cause. The explanation was now much in evidence. After the tanker rammed the whale in its mid-section, the mammal was unable to free itself, and pressure of the ship's forward motion kept it pinned against the sharp stem. At the same time, the mass acted as a drag on the ship and slowed her down.

The carcass was dislodged from the ship's stem and allowed to float away. The owners of the *New Orleans* felt no responsibility for the presence of the whale and no obligation to remove it. Operators of small craft protested to the Coast Guard that the bulk was a menace to navigation. Coast Guard officials held the position that the whale was the problem of the U. S. Army Engineer Corps or the Harbor Board. The Army Engineers disclaimed any responsibility in the matter and the dead whale drifted around the harbor at the mercy of wind, current, and the wash of passing ships.

Finally, the carcass was towed by the police boat *Robert D. Carter* to the bulkhead of the Pennsylvania Railroad, off Boston and Clinton Streets. Grappling hooks were embedded in the mass and it was moored to the bulkhead by two-inch hawsers.

Crowds swarmed to the location to get their first glimpse of a whale. They reached such proportions that the railroad company employed special police to prevent delays to their switching engines.

John G. Miller, operator of a local rendering business, volunteered to get rid of the carcass if it could be deposited on a trailer or flat car and delivered to his plant. He planned to convert the remains to ingredients used in soap. A large fertilizer company offered to accept the whale if it were floated to its nearby Curtis Bay plant. The Harbor Board considered that their best offer and accepted it with much relief.

The deep waters of the seas are the natural habitat of the whale and they seldom stray far afield. On occasion, however, they have entered the Chesapeake of their own free will. It was not uncommon to see them in the Bay before whaling became an industry. In 1698 Virginia forbade the killing of whales in Chesapeake Bay since it "poysoned" great quantities of fish and made the rivers "noisome and offensive." Records show that in 1746 a 54-foot whale entered the James River, in Virginia, and was sighted by the crew of a ship. The men pursued the mammal in the ship's longboat, drove it ashore, and killed it.

Whalebones are occasionally brought to the surface of the lower Bay by commercial fishermen. This suggests that whales may enter the shallower waters of the Chesapeake to escape foes, or to die. Porpoises, their smaller counterparts, are common in all sections of the Bay and many of its tributaries. They are often mistaken for whales.

Other strange looking fish from the waters around Baltimore may have attracted the attention of the public, but it is doubtful that any of these commanded the attention and publicity received by the 40-foot whale that rode up Chesapeake Bay on the tanker *New Orleans*.

Artistry in Wood

WILLIAM W. GEGGIE, of Newport News, Virginia, follows a career that went out of style many years ago, yet he is a surprisingly busy man. Now in his 83rd year, this former figurehead carver still works at his trade.

Although there are no new figureheads to carve for ships today, Geggie is called upon to restore the carvings of that nature in the collection of The Mariners Museum. Having traveled around the world's sea lanes for approximately half a century, most of the figureheads are in bad condition. He replaces their limbs, facial features, and flowing garments with the same deft touch used by their original carvers.

Geggie also designs and carves new work. Some of these carvings are more massive than many figureheads. Geggie executed one expressly for The Mariners Museum, as a decorative motif to supplement the figureheads of King Neptune and a mermaid, mounted at the museum's entrance.

William W. Geggie, Virginia woodcarver, at work on a huge carving of a seahorse.
Photo: Wm. T. Radcliffe

The carver was shown the space reserved for the proposed carvings and advised of the theme the museum wanted to express—that of rampant seahorses, usually associated with the motive power for Neptune's chariot. He was to prepare the sketches and scale drawings for approval of the directors.

The drawing measured 10 feet in length, and 4 feet in height. A template of the drawing was placed on the wall and the size and design were approved.

Geggie's first task was to obtain suitable wood; well-seasoned Idaho white pine was chosen. Each carving was made up of seven planks 10 feet long, 8 inches wide, and 4 inches thick. These were glued and doweled, and the drawing traced upon the surface of each built-up section. Excess wood in certain areas was roughed away.

The carver then began work with his mallet and chisel. With a sureness displayed only by experienced craftsmen, he boldly cut away the wood to obtain the general shape. Each carving was made in two sections, for greater ease in handling.

Bushels of fragrant pine chips fell to the floor before the desired shape and thickness were achieved. The carver then set to work cutting in the details—the innumerable scales on the bodies of the seahorses, feathers in the wings, features in the faces, and ornamental flourishes. His early training as a figurehead carver was easily detected in the work.

Geggie worked 40 hours a week and completed the carvings within four months. A combination of a sea serpent and horse was depicted with the sea curling beneath. An appearance of motion was gained by the skillful manipulation of the carver's tools. In bold relief the horses give the impression of riding the crests of the sea.

No sandpaper was used on the carving. The marks of chisels and gouges furnish a quality found only in hand-tooled work. The crispness in the cuts could not be duplicated by a machine.

The carvings were brought to the museum and painted with gold leaf and a color scheme suggested by Geggie. Secured to the wall of the museum's foyer, they make an indelible impression on visitors.

Wood carvers rarely produce large pieces like these in this era. By virtue of his training and background, however, Mr. Geggie is well qualified to undertake such as assignment. He was born in Scotland in 1880 and studied ornamental design at the Glasgow Technical College and Glasgow School of Art. His five-year course included both study and apprentice work in wood-carving, partly under the guidance of a figurehead carver. After working at his trade in a shipyard in Scotland, he came to America in 1903. He worked for a time in Boston and Chicago, and later came to the Virginia peninsula on a vacation. In 1907 he decided to settle in Newport News, Virginia, and was employed by the Newport News Shipbuilding and Dry Dock Company as a wood carver. It was the vogue at that time to embellish ships with wood-carvings and Mr. Geggie worked on the interior decorations of steamers.

While in the Virginia shipyard he had the opportunity to carve two figureheads. One was for the Italian bark *Doris,* which put into the shipyard for repairs during World War I. She had been in collision off the coast and had sustained considerable damage to her bow, including the loss of her figurehead. The bark's captain was superstitious and would not put to sea after repairs were completed until another figurehead graced her bow.

Within seven days the carver had completed the figure of a female. It was painted and secured to the ship's stem, and the ship sailed out to resume her wartime trading. The captain's faith in the carving as a good-luck charm was in vain as the *Doris* was torpedoed shortly afterwards.

Another vessel for which Mr. Geggie carved a figurehead was the big steam yacht *Viking,* built at the Newport News Shipyard in 1929. The carving was a three-quarter length figure of a Viking, done in teak. It was completed in about five weeks, gold-leafed, and bolted to the sleek yacht's stem. It was a handsome thing and gave the perfect touch to her graceful clipper bow.

Most wood carvers of today limit their services to reproductions of antique furniture and, after leaving the Newport News Shipyard in the early 1930's, Mr. Geggie occupied part of his time in this manner. Many tidewater Virginia homes contain examples of his work in the form of chairs, four-poster beds, sofas, stair rails, and newel posts. When famous Gunston Hall, near Alexandria, Virginia, was restored, he replaced some of the missing carved work.

Carter's Grove, near Williamsburg, contains some of his handiwork; also the Methodist Church in Colonial Williamsburg. Other religious buildings are similarly adorned with his carvings. A Lynchburg home boasts of a stairway carved by Mr. Geggie that was copied from one in the Metropolitan Museum of Art, New York City.

Mounted on the doors of the courtrooms on all floors of the Newport News Courthouse are the likenesses of six famous Virginia judges: Monroe, Henry, Wythe, Marshall, Madison, and Jefferson. These profiles were carved in walnut by Mr. Geggie and bear striking resemblance to their portraits.

Mr. Geggie's shop, located in the back yard of his Newport News home, is that of a typical figure-head carver's. Usually, a ship's figurehead, eight or more feet in length, undergoing repairs, is laid out on wooden horses. Numerous carving tools, mallets, and slip and whetstones are on the bench. Patterns, models in plasteline, and photographs of previous carvings hang on the walls. Often the shop's floor is deep in shavings of pine, mahogany, teak, or oak. Each chip marks a step towards a masterpiece in wood. As long as fine wood-carving is appreciated, Mr. Geggie's tools will never be idle.

Steam yacht *Viking* in dry dock at the Newport News Shipbuilding and Dry Dock Co., April 1929. The teak figurehead of a Viking was carved by William W. Geggie. Photo: The Mariners Museum

A Seagoing Pullman Car

A SHIP under construction in a Baltimore shipyard in 1890 was aptly described, "Like a razor blade on edge" and "Sharp as a knife." Her designer, Robert M. Freyer, hoped she would be able to cross the Atlantic in three-fifths of the time required by contemporary liners.

The eyes of the shipping world were on the *Howard Cassard,* named after a Baltimorean who had amassed a fortune in the lard business.

The *Howard Cassard* was built at Ramsey's Shipyard, Locust Point, under the title of the Monumental Construction Company. The designer claimed that a vessel built according to his plans would be safe, fast, cheap to construct and maintain, and virtually indestructible.

The method of her construction was even more unique than her design. The yard in which she was built was not arranged for the purpose of shipbuilding. Except for the riveters, none of the workmen had been employed previously in ship construction.

The *Cassard* was to be an experimental vessel 222 feet in length, with a 16-foot beam. If she proved successful, a ship 555 feet in length, with a beam of 40 feet, was to be built on the same plans. Her unorthodox length-beam ratio of 14 to 1 caused wags to nickname her "razorback."

Freyer planned to apply the Pullman car idea to ocean travel. Adjustable upper and lower berths were to be concealed during the day and each "section" supplied with handsomely upholstered seats. Meals were to be served on small tables from a galley in the hold. The seats in the sections could be transformed into beds, upper berths let down, and each section screened from the aisle by drapes.

Her services were to be confined to passengers, mail, and express packages. She had a main deck, cabin deck, and hold. The engine and coal occupied the hold; the cabin deck was made up of cabins with a narrow aisle running down the center of the ship; the main deck was a promenade.

On such a narrow ship the sharp prow would cut

The *Howard Cassard* presents a strange appearance with her narrow beam.
Photo: The Mariners Museum

the water like a knife. Its equilibrium was to be maintained by a heavy keel, whose depth was 15 inches at the bow, 4 feet at the stern, with a thickness of 5 inches and built up of bars and plates having a total weight of 68,000 pounds. Her machinery weighed 80,000 pounds and, with her normal supply of 200,000 pounds of coal, this total weight added to her stability. Even with her narrow beam, the *Cassard's* center of gravity was said to have been 6½ inches lower than the average transatlantic steamer of the time.

Construction on the vessel had started on May 1, 1890, and she was ready for launching in Baltimore harbor the following November 6. The Bay Ridge steamer *Columbia* was chartered to carry 2,000 persons to witness the event; five thousand more had gathered on the shore. No previous Baltimore launching had received such acclaim. The Great Southern Band, under the leadership of Professor Chambers, was on the wharf ready to play the *Howard Cassard March,* composed by the leader.

At the appointed hour the tripping blocks were hammered away and Miss Alice Freyer, 11-year-old daughter of the designer, broke a bottle of champagne across the vessel's stem. Tugs were waiting in the harbor to take the ship in tow when she became waterborne. With the tripping blocks removed the ship should have started her slide down the ways but she remained stationary. The tug *Parole* tried to start the *Cassard* down the ways but her tow line parted and no further attempt to launch that day was made. It was decided that tallow hardened on the timbers held the sliding boards fast to the ways. Launching would be attempted the next day. The ship was shored up, the tripping hammer was replaced, and the ways were regreased and wedged up again.

At 2:25 P.M. on November 7 the *Cassard* was ready for launching but when the tripping hammer was released, the ship again failed to move. The tug *Britannia* passed a line to the *Cassard* and pulled. The vessel started down the ways but careened to starboard when the launching ways spread before she reached the water. As she continued on her way, the *Cassard's* mast struck the tug *Baltimore* and carried away her stack and flagstaff. The *Cassard* lost two of her masts in the con-

fusion and glided out into the harbor with an extreme list caused by shifting of the coal. This unfortunate showing did not discourage her designer—he regarded it as a true test of the vessel's strength and buoyancy.

After the launching the *Cassard* was towed to a dock where the coal was shifted to normal position, putting the ship back on even keel. Later she was placed in the dry dock of Wm. E. Woodall & Company for installation of her tail shaft.

In running condition, the steamer was prepared for a trial trip down the Patapsco with a number of special guests aboard. It has been recorded that the trial was rather unsuccessful for the *Cassard* developed a decided list. Some reports said that a number of frightened passengers disembarked and returned to Baltimore by train.

For several years the *Cassard's* name appeared in local maritime notes or maritime magazines in reference to work being done on her engine and hull. She was becoming a landmark in Baltimore harbor and all but the designer had lost faith in the future of such a design. Constant reference was made to projected trial trips but results of these have failed to come to light. In an 1895 issue of *Harper's Weekly* appeared a picture of the vessel lying at a pier in Alexandria, Virginia, and a note telling of another projected trial trip.

The February 13, 1902 issue of *The Nautical Gazette* contained an item stating that the *Howard Cassard,* after having been tied up at Essington, Pennsylvania, for some years, had been sold on November 12, 1901 by the United States Marshal for $1775 to Mason and Lavin, Philadelphia scrap dealers.

The ship evidently was never recognized as a United States merchant vessel for there is no indication in the shipping registers that an official number was ever assigned to her and the National Archives in Washington had no information concerning her. For what was probably the most unusual ocean vessel ever constructed in this country, very few pertinent facts have been preserved.

The author contacted a grandson of Howard Cassard, of Baltimore, seeking vital information about the ship. All he could say was: "Grandfather lost his shirt on the vessel which was renowned for its lack of success."

The Chesapeake Marches On

THROUGH THE COMBINED action of currents, tides and waves, the land area around the Chesapeake is shrinking annually and the Bay is becoming more expansive. Melting glaciers in the south pole regions raise the level of the oceans and bays. It is recorded that in a 30-year period the level of the Chesapeake has risen six inches. During a 100-year period, from 1923 to 2023, it will have risen one and one-half feet.

Islands once prominent on charts less than half a century ago have vanished completely. Points have been scoured away and shorelines eroded until the general contour of the Maryland and Virginia mainlands has been altered.

A striking example of the erosive power of the Bay is the gradual disappearance of Sharps Island, situated in the Chesapeake off the mouth of the Choptank River. It has been reported that in the middle of the last century the island measured about 600 acres and was the site of several prosperous farms. By 1900 it had dwindled in size so that its value as farm land was negligible. A Baltimorean purchased it and built a hotel on the remnants. Steamboats brought patrons from Baltimore and, for a while, the resort was successful but the waters did not cease their eroding tactics and the hotel owner found it unprofitable to continue his battle against the Bay.

By 1914 the island had been reduced to about 100 acres. Thirty years later, when the U. S. Government sought a rifle range during World War II, it took over the approximately 6 acres of marsh land remaining. The 1961 issue of the *Coast Pilot* mentions the fact that "Tiny Sharps Island is subject to rapid erosion." Very little remains of the island that geologists claim was once united with the present Tilghman Island.

Many Eastern Shore islands have suffered through erosion. A study made by J. F. Hunter for the Geological Survey of 1914 indicated that from 1848 to 1910 James Island had lost 385 acres of land or about one-half of its total area. Erosion since that time has taken another 150 acres or more. This island, situated 3 miles out from the mouth of the Little Choptank River, was once a prosperous watermen's community but now is not much larger than a golf course. From last reports it was inhabited by a dwindling herd of deer.

At one time James Island was linked with Taylors Island to the south. Now there is only a shallow tidal channel separating the two land masses. Residents of Taylors Island tried to stem the march of the tides on their homeland and had loads of granite from the upper Potomac River dumped along their more exposed shoreline. The waves washed over the rocks and they eventually sank out of sight. The shoreline continues to disappear into the Bay.

Tilghman Island is said to be losing from 10 to 12 feet of its western shoreline each year. Bulkheads and riprap have been used to help combat the erosion but the island grows smaller year by year.

Farms on the western border of Kent Island, near Love Point, have been reduced by 6 acres in 15 years; by 45 acres since first survey in 1803. A farm on Spaniard Point, where the Corsica River flows into the Chester River, lost 64 acres in 166 years, from 1771 to 1937; from 1937 to 1952 it lost another 12 acres.

The Western Shore of the Chesapeake has also been losing ground steadily. In Maryland the Bay sides of Anne Arundel, Calvert, and St. Marys Counties present a critical problem where from 3 to 12 feet of shoreline erodes each year. There is crumbling of the Calvert Cliffs due to wave action and heavy rains that loosen the dirt creating slides that carry trees and underbrush into the Bay.

The Potomac River, on its march to the Chesapeake, has carried with it a goodly amount of the Maryland and Virginia shoreline. The banks of Stratford and Wakefield, in Westmoreland County, Virginia, have been reduced a foot a year. The islands of St. George and Blackistone, off southern Maryland, have suffered considerably as their beaches and banks fall prey to the water's action. Blackistone has eroded to less than one-quarter of its size since the first Maryland settlers landed there in 1634. At that time it had an area of 400 acres; by 1896, it had eroded to about 90 acres. Since then, 30 more acres have been washed into the Potomac leaving bluffs 12 to 15 feet in height in some places.

The story is the same down along the Virginia shore. Gwynn's Island, at the mouth of the Piankatank River, composed of alluvial deposits of sand and clay accumulated by water currents, has also been cut away by those currents. About 1948, Cherry Point on the northern end of the island, reached out about one-third of the 2-mile distance across the Piankatank to Stingray Point. In a period of 8 years, approximately 4 acres of Cherry

Point disappeared and were stricken from the county tax records.

Lighthouses in exposed areas in the lower Bay have felt the effect of erosion. New Point Comfort lighthouse has lost most of its surrounding sandy point but still sends out its beam. Back River lighthouse was long abandoned before it finally collapsed in a hurricane in 1956. The point on which it stood had eroded and left it well offshore in the Bay and constant pounding of the waters upon its base eventually brought about its end.

Watts Island, one of a string of marshy islands separating Pocomoke Sound from Tangier Sound, was dominated by a white masonry lighthouse erected in 1833. The island had contributed its substance to the Chesapeake from time immemorial by creating shoals dangerous to boatmen. The lighthouse, on the other hand, was aiding the wary navigator for more than a century by helping him find his way up and down the Chesapeake. But the Bay eventually won its point and during a terrific storm in the late fall of 1944 waves were cast onto the island that swirled around and weakened the base of the lighthouse. Engineers were

Waters of Tangier Sound engulf Watts Island during a storm in the fall of 1944 and undermine the base of the 111-year-old lighthouse. A few weeks later it collapsed.
Photo: U. S. Coast Guard

sent to survey the damage and determine the possibility of salvaging the structure by the erection of a concrete wall around its base but before work could get under way, the tower collapsed. In December of that year a replacement for the lighthouse, an 18-inch diameter steel pipe light structure, was erected just off the remnants of the island. Since that time the size of the island itself has diminished considerably.

If the average annual land loss along the entire Chesapeake Bay shore were only one foot a year, it would represent 436 acres surrendered by Maryland and Virginia each year. No doubt it has been more—some good farm and timber land and the balance sand spits and scrub areas.

The soil thus removed fills in channels and im-

pairs or destroys feeding grounds for wildfowl, covers oyster beds, and destroys food for fish. Muddy waters over oyster beds do not permit sufficient light to penetrate to the oysters or to the microscopic organisms upon which they feed, and one of the Chesapeake's chief products succumbs.

Steps have been taken by governmental agencies and individuals to try to arrest this erosion. It has been found effective to bulldoze banks down and grade them level with the water's edge to allow the water to wash up over the shore rather than undermine it. Groins and jetties on an engineering principle retard the loss but they are expensive. Sea walls, pilings, cord grass, and the seeding of banks are also effective. But it is not likely that the encroachment of the Bay will cease.

The Chesapeake Bay gnaws away at the base of the Calvert Cliffs during a nor'easter, eroding the earth and exposing fossils. Photo: Author

Index

204

205